WORLD BALLET AND D

1993–1994

World Ballet and Dance 1993–1994

AN INTERNATIONAL YEARBOOK

Founder Editor
BENT SCHØNBERG

Associate Editors
JUDITH WOODS
CRISTINA SCHØNBERG

Consultant Editor
PETER BRINSON

Oxford   New York   Melbourne   Toronto
OXFORD UNIVERSITY PRESS
1994

Oxford University Press, Walton Street, Oxford OX2 6DP

Oxford New York
Athens Auckland Bangkok Bombay
Calcutta Cape Town Dar es Salaam Delhi
Florence Hong Kong Istanbul Karachi
Kuala Lumpur Madras Madrid Melbourne
Mexico City Nairobi Paris Singapore
Taipei Tokyo Toronto

and associated companies in
Berlin Ibadan

Oxford is a trade mark of Oxford University Press

Published in the United States
by Oxford University Press Inc., New York

British Library Cataloguing in Publication Data
Data available

Library of Congress Cataloging in Publication Data
Data available
ISBN 0–19–816427–0 (cloth)
ISBN 0–19–816428–9 (paperback)

1 3 5 7 9 10 8 6 4 2

Set by Hope Services (Abingdon) Ltd.
Printed in Great Britain
on acid-free paper by
Biddles Ltd
Guildford & King's Lynn

Contents

Illustrations

Drawings throughout by Cristina Schønberg

Feature Writers

Katharine Kanter, born in Quebec. BA (Slavic Studies) McGill University. BA (Law) Cambridge University. Dance columnist for several publications including *Ibykus* Magazine (Germany), *EIR* (USA).

Flemming Flindt, Danish dancer and choreographer. Principal dancer Royal Danish Ballet 1957. Principal at Festival Ballet, London, and *étoile* at Paris Opera. Artistic Director, Royal Danish Ballet 1966–78 and of Dallas Ballet 1981–8. Choreographed several ballets, *The Lesson, Triumph of the Death, The Overcoat, Caroline Mathilde, M, Salome*.

Robert Cohan, partner of Martha Graham and one of the most distinguished dancers in her Company. Co-directing it with her in 1966, Robert Cohan was invited to Britain in 1967 to help found, with the late Robin Howard, the London Contemporary Dance Theatre and School. Artistic director of both these immensely influential ventures until 1983, he remained artistic adviser while continuing also as a choreographer of international stature. He was artistic adviser to the Batsheva Dance Company, Israel, in 1980 and is recognized as one of the finest teachers of the Graham style of contemporary dance. Author of *The Dance Workshop*, 1986.

Frank Woods, MA (Architecture) Cambridge University. Partner of architectural practice, Austin-Smith Lord. Worked on the original designs for the Barbican Arts and Conference Centre (Architects: Chamberlin, Powell and Bon). Architect to the Sadlers Wells Theatre, London, for the replanning of the theatre and for the design of the Lilian Baylis Community Theatre at Sadlers Wells. Co-author of *Overlay Drafting*, a technical handbook published by The Architectural Press.

Stride for Dancers

BENT SCHØNBERG

We bring this year an extended coverage of the international dance and ballet world, feature articles on the dancer's environment—which as we have said before, needs radical improvement—wider photo coverage of companies and, for the first time, an index. We have also a new associate editor in Judith Woods and a consultant editor, Peter Brinson, who rejoins us after helping to edit our first issue.

We are delighted particularly that Oxford University Press has offered to publish us and provide a world-wide distribution network. One of the world's most influential publishers, they pressed us to continue beyond Volume 4 and have suggested many future improvements. With enormous regret this means we have parted with Dance Books and its gifted leader, David Leonard. Without his help none of the former yearbooks would have seen the light of day. He made real our notion of a yearbook. Therefore, we will, for obvious reasons, remain close to him and develop further the inspiration he gave us.

Next year we plan expansion to cover India, and more about South-east Asia and South America. Sadly South America is under-represented in this issue, because of last-minute illness. We plan also a review of the world's international dance organizations, as well as biographies of our distinguished contributors. This year and in the future, we will be published in hardback as well as paperback.

Improvements in the dancer's environment are crucial to the advancement of dancers and their art world-wide. By environment we mean not only the stages and spaces where they dance—strikingly introduced in this issue by the well-known London architect, Frank Woods—but also the choreography they are asked to dance, their training and life-styles. These needs are discussed by Katharine Kanter, Flemming Flindt, and Robert Cohan. Often their views are controversial and challenging. Good! We are convinced that the needs, status, and treatment of dancers deserve international discussion. The days of painters and poets living in garrets are over; the days of dancers living in poverty with inadequate support and poor working conditions should also be over. But are they? Responses and follow-up suggestions from our readers could help to develop our campaign for dancers, which may then be of help to them.

We have included also a section on dance development in Higher Education. This is a piece of kite-flying on our part because we believe that studying the performance of educationists is one of the most important ways not only to develop dancers and their audience, but also to initiate experiments, new ideas, and dance research. We plan to expand this important reportage to other countries in future issues.

Our aim, as our title implies, is constantly to bring into dialogue all aspects of dance world-wide. We welcome, therefore, the growth and development of international organizations in this field. The International Dance Council and the Dance Committee of the International Theatre Institute are long established, and we seek to work with them in whatever way we can. In May last year we were in Lisbon to discuss with representatives of many European countries the establishment of a European branch of the World Dance Alliance presently centred in Tokyo. In June we applauded a similar meeting in New York to establish a branch for the Americas. May the Alliance grow and grow, working in harmony with other dance bodies! Amongst these, of course, we count UNESCO, in many ways the largest of all centres of dance.

For this reason, our next issue will review the world's international network. Working in harmony, this network can strengthen dance everywhere and benefit immeasurably the artist's environment. For the moment our pleasant and grateful duty is to thank our correspondents throughout the world for responding so splendidly and quickly to the very short deadlines they were given. We are proud of them and hope they may be proud of us.

PART I

Dancers' Health and Environment

Bournonville and the Crisis in Classical Ballet Today

KATHARINE KANTER

The crisis which is gripping the classical ballet today is but one aspect of the crisis gripping Western society as a whole. We no longer believe in the dignity of man, which means that we no longer believe in life. Although, in the particular case of this art-form, the problem is so serious that ballet itself is at risk, ironically, there is hope that the pervasive and universal nature of the crisis may lead people not only to ask themselves the most fundamental questions, but to seek to solve them.

It is my considered belief that the old French or so-called 'Bournonville' school, based as it is on a completely different idea of man from what we now call the 'Anglo-Russian school', will restore to the ballet its dignity, its grandeur, and to the dancers, their freedom. As the theatre is a public institution, were this battle to be won, it would have a most stimulating and positive effect upon society as a whole.

I have been asked by Bent Schønberg to speak my mind freely, and as I am not employed by any clique or claque, I intend to do so. Over the last fifty years, the classical ballet has become increasingly ugly, and choreography, senseless. The more we have trodden upon the fundamental laws of physiology, the uglier we have become. There is an absolute correspondence between anti-physiological gestures and ugly ones, though, conversely, it is not true that a physiologically sound gesture is necessarily beautiful. Beauty is the intervention by man's free will, to go beyond what is merely necessary to live, to go beyond the boredom of 'hygiene', to express noble ideas. The classical ballet has the potential and the ability to become one of the greatest art-forms and to draw man towards the accord between the deepest thought and the boldest action, which is the essence of creativity.

In any art-form, you are dealing first and foremost with laws. This is blindingly obvious in the case of architecture when the 'beautiful' building collapses at your feet, but it should be just as obvious in the ballet. In the classical ballet, we are faced with the iron laws of physiology; that is our framework, those are our constraints. These laws will never change, unless we all become little Green Men from Mars, and even they will probably turn out to be built much like us. The mere fact that over the century, thanks to advances in medicine and nutrition, people have become considerably taller and better looking and with proportions that approximate in almost all cases to the so-called Golden Section, does not change that truth in any way, because the proportions and relations within the basic system have not changed.

At the outset, I would state my thesis: that virtually every innovation brought into the technique of classical ballet over the century has been worse than useless—dangerous, anti-physiological, and evil because harmful to man. First and foremost, I refer to the two related abuses of raising the leg in hyper-extension, and to dancing *en face* without *épaulement*; then the practice of dancing through an entire variation on *pointe* (as opposed to simply rising to the *pointe en pique* and then coming straight off it); the American practice of dancing with the raised heel, and the whole panoply of related disorders, such as the over-reached 'neo-classical' balances where the knee must necessarily hyper-extend.

Before going further, I can imagine readers jumping out of their skins and thinking: how dare she call matters of taste 'evil'? However, we are not dealing with abstractions on a piece of paper, but with real human beings, first and foremost the dancers, and then the public, who are on the receiving end of whatever horrors are being perpetrated. Even taking into account that he was writing before the development of the great jumps, Noverre tells us that a dancer should think about retiring at 'about age 45 or 50'; before the Second World War it was 40 or 45 years, and we are now hovering around the earlier end of the 30–35 mark, neither is it unusual today for people to retire in their late twenties. Ten years of study, for less than ten years of career. Is that not an evil? The question is, what is this evil? What are we doing to people so that they are physically worn out by 27 or 28 years of age.

To avoid a catalogue of laments, we should examine here only the most egregious of abuses. In the case of women, the one single example is the hyper-extension, those 'telephone calls' on stage where the leg is raised to the point where the foot presses smartly against the ear, or thereabouts. The hyper-extension has wrecked female dancing. This bizarre movement, straight out of the circus and which my American friends delicately call a 'crotch shot', is, as my colleague writes below, 'by definition, a pathological phenomenon'. It is farcical to talk about 'correct placement' when an abuse so central to the entire system is tolerated: in all cases, there is irreversible damage to the hip-joint. The head of the joint is consumed and the ilio-femoral ligaments, which will never recover their elasticity, stretched out.

I repeat that in all cases there is no individual, no matter how hyper-flexible, who can do this movement without, by the age of about 25 years of age at the latest, suffering to some degree irreversible harm. That is why it is absurd nowadays to tell a female dancer not to pick up the leg when you dance the so-called 'Romantic' ballets. Based as it is on the hyper-extension, her training has already damaged the body and she does not have the strength. There are, of course, some exceptionally strong individu-

Darcy Bussell of the Royal Ballet in *Tchaikovsky Pas de deux*, choreographed by George Balanchine.
PHOTO: LESLIE SPATT

als, but in general, the dancer has to pick up the leg because she cannot really control it at hip level, at 90 or 100 degrees.

Since at 90–100 degrees one cannot compensate by tilting the torso as a counter-balance in the opposite direction to the raised leg, the dancer attempting to hold the leg at hip level jiggles around like a container broken loose on a ship in heavy seas. That is why there is scarcely a female dancer in Europe today who can execute a lengthy adagio passage with any degree of stability and serenity. Lastly, try to perform a hyper-extended *développé*, and do the *épaulement* at the same time. It is impossible! The two systems are incompatible, and any step performed without *épaulement* is bad for the body.

This brings us to the *épaulement*, that technical and aesthetic feature at the heart of the French school, which masters such as Vestris took from the Contrapposto of Leonardo and Raphael; the Contrapposto is no stylistic gimmick, it is what conveys the movement of life. Note that here, *épaulement* refers only to what is practised in the old French school, only as taught by a great master such as Flemming Ryberg, professor at the Royal Theatre in Copenhagen, and not what the Vaganova school today calls *épaulement*.

As we had decided here to be sober in the extreme, and to avoid the crossing of swords on matters of taste, I would say only this on the aesthetic and moral role of the *épaulement*: precisely as you may observe it in Leonardo's *The Virgin of the Rocks*, the *épaulement*, by shedding light over the dancer's face, draws the eye of the spectator away from the body, and up towards the face and eyes of the dancer, the eyes, those pools of light which are, physiologically, part of the brain. If you begin, say, in *croisé devant*, and rotate slowly round in a full circle, you are going to end up in *effacé* after one full rotation; it is the infinitely varying degrees of light which are shed upon the face when this is done with the *épaulement* which draws the eye in, which sparks the interest ever fresh. Upon this elegant and simple principle of shading through circular action does the French school base itself— but it is also making a moral judgement by saying, look into the eyes, look into the mind.

It is extremely curious to compare the bodily attitude of a dancer practising the French school, to that in the Russian school. In the latter, the basic posture of staring fixedly ahead, with the flung-back shoulders, the raised chin, and the flaring nostrils, conveys a kind of superciliousness and arrogance. Whatever the individual's actual mental state may be, this attitude also bears a message: it shocks, it impresses the spectator, while thrusting him away. In the old French school, thanks to the *épaulement*, the head appears in three-quarter profile, its most noble aspect, the aspect whereby the dancer's individuality emerges most markedly. The body is closed, retained, in a quiet attitude of modesty and dignity, as though listening intently to a kind of inner music. Drawn in, the spectator 'strains his ear' to see.

Turning now to practical things: eliminate *épaulement*, and you not only get something which is flat, stale, and boring, namely ballet today, but you lay the ground for major injuries. The essence of the *épaulement* is the essence of the quality of all human movement, it is 'dissymetric'. Contrary to what everyone will tell you, children move, dance, and play with *épaulement* naturally. Then, if they wish to become professional dancers, we try to grind it out of them because we think they will become 'uncentred'; but those children are right! As Hans Brenaa once said, 'the *épaulement* is in every step', it moves to the left, and then to the right, and it is in that specific trajectory, in that specific kind of rotation, that the balance restores itself. 'Centring' does not mean artificially imposing upon the body a kind of static, petrified symmetry which does not exist in any living organism, because living organisms move. They should not be 'centred', not in that way.

At this juncture, I would draw the reader's attention to the following remarks on the *épaulement* by the French dancer Alexandre de la Caffinière, presently soloist at the Deutsche Oper Berlin, in his unpublished study, 'Why I Advocate a Return to the Old French School':

By definition, the hyper-extension is a pathological phenomenon . . . such torsion creates lines of stress in the back, the neck, the head; the effort cannot be hidden, and we move further and further away from these prerequisites of beauty, precision, and ease, which Bournonville cherished, and which are an integral part of the old French school. . . . It is the *épaulement* which expresses this sense of ease . . .

When a baby wants to move from a lying to a sitting position, he will never try to heave himself up vertically by the strength of his back, by hollowing his back. He cannot command his musculature, and therefore allows himself to be borne by the most elemental physical laws. The head, the heaviest part of the body, turns first to the side, which carrries the rest of the body along with it in a pivoting motion. From there, an elliptical movement, led always by the head, allows him to draw himself up; this is the least action principle, which lies at the basis of *épaulement* in classical dance.

All dancers should strive to master the *épaulement*; whenever it be countered by seeking, erroneously, to re-establish symmetry . . . there are brought to bear upon the skeleton noxious tensions which radiate through the entire body. In the type of rotation peculiar to the *épaulement*, only the cervical and dorsal vertebrae should be engaged, lest the lumbar vertebrae draw the hip-joint along with them. Whenever the *épaulement* is practised in this manner, i.e. precisely according to the aesthetic dictates of the Bournonville school, it is impossible to be sway-backed.

There, precisely there, in the question of the *épaulement* lies the link between art and science, and that is the crux of the whole debate. Taking another example, let us look at what have been, since the Second World War, those two archetypal sway-backed figures, arabesque and attitude, and which we now consider 'beautiful': the lowest degree at which they would ever be executed today would be 90 degrees. In Blasis's work, 1820 and 1830, he draws these figures at about 50 degrees; what is produced is an extremely graceful, sloping curve from the shoulder to the tip of the foot, a play of light and shadows so fascinating that in fact the low attitude is probably the most majestic, the most noble figure in the whole of ballet. Anatomically, this low arabesque, this low attitude, does not produce hyper-lordosis in the spine, because of the pelvic angle at which they are produced. As soon as the leg is picked up to around 90 degrees, there is an incipient hyper-lordosis, and just a little higher, depending on the individual's morphology, there begins the crushing of the *processus spinosi* and the usure of the head of the hip-joint. From an aesthetic standpoint, the right-angle attitude and arabesque are a vain attempt to reduce the human form, a mass of curves, to a figure of Euclidean plane geometry.

In the midst of all this, remember one thing, we are here to dance. It takes ten minutes, to use a figure of speech, to get into a hyper-extension, and ten minutes to creak out of it; meanwhile, we should have been out there dancing. We have lost the speed of thought, we have lost the fluency of the language in favour of producing effects. The same applies to hauling ourselves up and down on *pointe*, in those hideous, box-like armoured vehicles we now call *pointe* shoes, when on *demi-pointe* we could get on with dancing. Therefore, on all these grounds, using our reason, judging beauty by reason, we must decide to train our eye away from the excitement of these excesses.

Before people start crying that we are trying to take away their Petipa, their *Sleeping Beauty*, their *Giselle*, let us just recall that all of these so-called 'classic ballets' were actually danced with *épaulement* and according to the principles of the Old French School until a few decades ago!

If we really want to put a stop to injuries, we have to become serious about what we are teaching, we have to decide what we want. We cannot ask people to realign their entire skeleton five times a day to obey each faddish style. Even in such an apparently simple thing as the fifth position, the alignment of the skeleton with the *épaulement* is entirely different from that without. In the former case, the forward crossed leg will tend to lie almost flat rather than buckling at the knee, because the hip-joint is properly realigned and almost level; so striking is the difference that we are not, in point of fact, dealing with the same position.

In 1782, in his treatise on psycho-physical parallelism, known as 'Connection of the Two Natures of Man', the poet Schiller, who by profession was medical doctor to the armies, had the following to say:

The faculties of the body correspond to those of the mind, that is to say, that all great excitement of a certain mode of physical activity, just as, the equilibrium, the harmonic activity of spiritual forces, is in the most perfect agreement with the manner of being of the body. Furthermore, an indifference (nonchalance) of the soul weighs down the manner of being of the body, while its inactivity destroys it utterly. But, perfection being always associated to a pleasure, and imperfection to sorrow, one might summarise this law as follows: 'Spiritual pleasure is always accompanied by a material one, and spiritual sorrow, by a material pain' . . . Can one not see then, that that very constitution of the soul which can draw pleasure in each event, and resolve the disharmony of suffering through a perfect agreement with the universe, is also that which most greatly favours the functioning of the machine? Such a constitution is what we call Virtue.

Now, Schiller was neither a prude, nor a puritan, nor was he preaching abstinence from alcohol, nor any other legitimate pleasure. What he meant by virtue, is what the old Italians called *virtú*, and what the French call *science*. There is no such thing as morality without science, and art without science is not art, it is just an empty word, signifying vanity and folly.

A study has just appeared, according to which, at the time of writing, 20 per cent of all high-level professional dancers in Europe are afflicted by a severe, in some cases debilitating, injury, and most suffer, intermittently or chronically, from severe pain in major body parts. When I say injury, there is no doubt that certain types of minor injuries, notably to the knee, ankle, and foot, will be with us to the end of time, because they are mainly the outcome of a moment's fatigue or inattention. When I say pain, I do not mean minor muscular aches and tensions and so forth, which we will never be rid of, but the intense pain which is the warning sign of a developing pathology, of a serious accident. Today, in the 1990s, dancers do not retire because they are over 40 and just cannot hack the steps, but because they have been injured so often that they cannot take the pain any longer. But dancing is not a sport, it is not Greek wrestling or gladiatorial combat or whatever; we must get rid of the immoral idea that pain and severe injury are an occupational hazard, precisely because it is immoral.

What do we mean by 'a school'? We are talking about a system of thought. Its test is reality: the human body. Such a system must be sufficient unto itself or it is not a school, but a parasite dependent and adjunct upon something else. With what we now call the Anglo-Russian school, classical ballet has become a kind of hobby, which cannot be practised without the aid of an army of physiotherapists and orthopaedists, rushing after the dancers, picking up the pieces as they break off and shatter.

Against such pandemonium, the criteria of the French school are unambiguous, they are dictated by science; within a limited range of play, there is one, and only one physiological position for each figure within the placement specific to each single individual human being, as each single human body is completely different from every other, whereas, with the hyperextension, the 'higher' or 'highest' is a meaningless conceit, which abolishes any notion of proportions and relations. There are no more criteria, just as the 'broken-back' attitude, as it is now practised, is simply the attitude pushed as high as the anatomy appears to permit. To see what cannot necessarily be seen to the naked eye, without there being a process of reasoning, and to predict with surety what will happen though that cannot yet be seen, is the essence of science. The genius of the French school lies in the fact that, were its canons to be applied, the tidal wave of major injuries engulfing our theatres could be rolled back.

Yet, there is more. There is something else that we are doing to people that is making them, literally, sick. When we ask dancers to perform ugly, brutish movements counter to nature, movements which are harmful to the body, or to go out virtually naked or to imitate acts of copulation on stage, we are asking them to rape their own minds—not to speak of what is going on in the mind of the spectator, or better said, voyeur. That is one main reason why people are falling sick! They are soul sick! Much of the choreography we are seeing now adds only the *pointe* shoes to what they would otherwise be much better paid for at the Crazy Horse Saloon.

Now, we can reject these Facts, we can cry: 'I despise Reason. I prefer to worship taste. You can't roll the clock back,' etc. Well, everything you see about you, everything which makes it possible for you, as a discrete individual, to exist today, was created by mastering physical laws. To reject Reason in the ballet, is, from a philosophical standpoint, nothing more than proclaiming, 'I prefer Death to Life', and then rudely pushing away the pistol which someone so thoughtfully has procured for you.

'Movements counter to nature'
PHOTO: TANDY OF MUNICH

In ancient Greek, the word *tekhne* is a 'means', an instrument, a 'way or path' to something. To what? Well, if an art-form is judged by its adequacy to express ideas, everything in Technique must tend towards that end, and everything which does not, must be put aside. I repeat, dancing is not a sport. In the ballet, specifically, technique is the means to express musical and dramatic ideas. Everything which draws attention to the mechanics, everything which makes out of the body a mask, behind which the soul is hidden, as Noverre would say, everything which has an animal-like quality, all that must be put aside. The very art-form which is done by the body must be precisely that which frees itself from the chains of gross sensual impressions. Anyone who has seen a Bournonville class, or the remarkable 'stretto' passage from the end of the *pas de trois* in *Le Conservatoire*, the tumult, the profusion of ideas pressing at the gates, spilling out in the myriad steps until you feel your brain is almost bursting, knows exactly what I mean.

Let us look a little more closely at a typical Bournonville *enchaînement*, from the standpoint of our main argument, i.e. art and science as an indissoluble whole. Far longer than one of our present *enchaînements*, in terms of number of bars of music, a correspondingly far greater demand is put upon the dancer's memory, his power to concentrate, his ability to sustain the spectator's interest in a drawn-out musical idea. He must have an enquiring mind, or Bournonville's long, difficult adagios will put the spectator to sleep!

Look at the number of steps, the density of events in terms of steps, relative to the events in each musical phrase: where today, we would have, say, this hyper-extended *développé* lasting for an eternal number of beats, in the old French School you are in and out of any given step, and on to six new ideas in the same period of time. In the French school, dancing is a language, and an *enchaînement* is a poem, the steps are mere words. Words do not exist in and for themselves, you do not stand there and shout isolated words at people, unless you are ripe for the asylum. In any language, words are subordinated to an overall poetic concept, just as in a Rembrandt painting, the play of light and shade is defined by the idea. A person who shrieks out words develops pathological conditions of the vocal cords. A dancer who is forced to 'shriek out' isolated steps does not have a properly developed body. In particular, the deep muscle groups, and the foot musculature, which are greatly solicited by the varying size of the steps, by the countless tiny intermediary steps of the Bournonville school alternating with the great jumps, the *petite batterie*, the swishing of the 'conjunctions and articles' like the rustling of silk on the floor, these muscle groups, this higher level of neuro-muscular co-ordination, cannot develop in the modern Anglo-Russian school.

Returning to the vexed issue of the *pointes*: you do not need *pointe* work to make a good Bournonville *enchaînement* exciting. When the choreography is good you do not need it! The *pointes* are the exact equivalent of a third-register, or even fourth-register note in the human voice—as an extreme, to be used very sparingly, for a precise aesthetic or dramatic purpose only, a ray of moonlight through the casement, then vanishing. That is all. And that is all the human foot was designed for. *Fouettés* on *pointe* are ugly! Pirouettes on *pointe* do not, on the contrary, add anything to the fluent, carefree charm of a pirouette on the *demi-pointe*. All the hours female dancers spend on this nonsense, all these 'variation on *pointe*' classes, all this jumping around on *pointe*, it is all a complete, utter waste of time. What else must one add to the reams of paper written on the subject by the orthopaedists, who for once are absolutely unanimous; you may use the *pointes* for *piqués*, or for a *bourrée* here and there, but otherwise, STAY OFF THEM.

We have done away with all this 'tricky Bournonville stuff'! And in so doing, we have dug the grave of choreography, a Black Hole of Calcutta. Nothingness!

That Black Hole opens in the great academies. Let us look at what is taught there today: we teach them steps, we teach them what is mistakenly called 'technique', and then, so that we can call ourselves humanists, we also let them pass the baccalaureate or something like it. But the essence of dancing is between the steps, it comes from inner conviction of what is man, and choreography does not mean inventing some kinky new movement. Just as an old oak, putting out new leaves, new branches, and little acorns; once you prefigure in the mind the very shadow of a new musical and dramatic idea, you can always invent new steps.

This art-form was invented *ab nihilo* by the human mind. For it to go further, we must develop further the minds of our students. The complete blank expression which envelops the face of most students in the great academies, as soon as you talk to them about anything which does not have to do with ballet, proves that we are doing something wrong. Where will the new choreography, the great dramatic ideas come from, if we have taught them to care about nothing except mechanics and to see themselves only as cunning machines?

Here let me state how strongly opposed I am to the type of eugenic selection practised in the great academies today. Were our teaching methods any good, any normally constituted child with a keen mind and reasonably agreeable proportions should be able to become a classical dancer. But we are out there watching for the 'flash', the 'look', the kid with the tiny pin-head perched on filiform limbs, which happens to be the only morphology able to perform our current fad, the hyper-extension, and to make the most ludicrous choreography look 'chic'. In the short term, these cruel selection practices, aided by starvation diets, cleverly disguise the awful flaws in our teaching—but fear not, the injuries will explode a short decade or so later; you cannot fool the laws of nature for ever.

In the great academies today, Noverre is not on the curriculum, probably because people would ask awkward questions about their own training if they read him. We do not teach them to sing or to play instruments nor to read an orchestral score, because that would take valuable time from learning how to extend the leg or some other clownish prank. How can anyone be expected to choreograph anything beyond a touchy-feely act of self-indulgence if he cannot read a score, if he does not feel himself to be in direct mental contact with thinkers like Beethoven? If you do not learn these things before you are 18, you will probably never learn them—I know, I have been trying to learn how to read a score for the last decade. I can hear people out there in the bleachers bellowing the names of choreographers who could not, and cannot, but, as I have been asked here to write my own views, and not yours, my opinion of most twentieth-century choreography is probably unprintable. Only Balanchine could actually read music, which is probably the only reason that his choreography presents some vague, if not interest, at least curiosity value.

I see no point in being morbidly self-critical, when self-critical will be enough. With all its flaws, classical ballet training is, along with the training of classical musicians, virtually the only remaining area in the Western world where the explicit aim of the school is to create men of genius. In the Western world, ballet dancers are at present among the few individuals left who still believe in the life of the mind, who are tenacious, disciplined people, whose underlying motivation, no matter what the superficial varnish of ambition and vanity may be, is beauty and love. This is an intellectual élite, a strength to build upon, and one which can have positive effects upon the entire society—if we stop treating these people like animals.

If you want to know why there is no good choreography, and why there will be none until we change the present system, you have understood the problem. Were we to return to the old French school, a classical dancer could learn everything he needs to know about dancing in about three hours a day. The rest of the time he could spend thinking, a pastime, without which, nothing.

La Fille mal gardée

Passion, Indignation, and Aesthetic Art Nonsense

Comments on Katharine Kanter's article

FLEMMING FLINDT

Katharine Kanter's article is a hotchpotch with strong opinions, but I feel it lacks knowledge, especially concerning the issues around the Bournonville school. There is, however, passion and justified indignation about the way young dancers are misled, therefore forcing them physically to ruin their bodies.

First, some of the good news from Katharine. She thinks more attention should be paid to the French/Danish school and to the values found in the continued development of this classical ballet technique. As an 'old Danish guy' that sounds like good news to me; however, it is not that easy or simple. Historically there were always a handful of pedagogues within a decade who really knew about the Bournonville technique on a scientific level. And post-Bournonville, during the last hundred years, we have had pedagogues such as Hans Beck, Valborg Borchcenius, and, even later, in a bizarre, self-concocted way maybe, Karl Merrild. In the late 1920s and early 1930s, Elna J. Jensen and her husband, Leif Ornberg, possessed great knowledge about the Bournonville technique, the latter being a thoroughly wonderful teacher, as was the case with Toni Lander. Hans Brenaa was also important for the Danish Bournonville tradition and I will discuss him later in this commentary.

At different periods of time there were several other people with an instinct about this Bournonville technique. One who stands out particularly is Kirsten Ralov, a very intelligent dancer. She made an important contribution to the knowledge of Bournonville technique when she organized the six daily Bournonville classes in book form accompanied with sheet music. This brings me to Harald Lander. He was in charge of the Royal Danish Ballet for twenty years and continued to have great influence on French/Danish training when he later worked at the Paris Opera for more than a decade. Lander was the only one after Hans Beck to take a scientific look at, and subsequent approach to, the Bournonville heritage. He was a blessing for Danish dance tradition and later made a very important contribution in the development of classical ballet at the Paris Opera. Our Katharine Kanter can certainly find the true seeds to French/Danish development in Harald Lander's work.

Unfortunately, in Denmark at the end of the 1993/4 season, there are no great teachers to my knowledge and certainly none in the Bournonville technique. Hans Brenaa, a truly wonderful man, was an astute producer of the Bournonville repertory. He was also a very inspiring teacher, totally instinctive and with enormous theatrical flair. Mr Brenaa was in charge of the Bournonville tradition from approximately 1978 until his death in 1988. With no one to match his ideas and his intellectual and scientific reasoning about Bournonville, there has existed an obvious vacuum in the continuation of the master's school in Copenhagen.

Together with a lack of intellectual scholarly backbone in Danish Bournonville teaching, the Royal Danish Ballet has been strongly oriented towards Anglo-Canadian training which, in my opinion, has caused disastrous results as well as sickness and injury. I do not know whether this can be blamed on the Canadian system, but I do know that when I staged my ballet *Caroline Mathilde* in 1991, each day approximately 25–30 per cent of the dancers were out sick!

Before we address the question of injuries, Katharine has to know that the pedagogues have to be trained first before we can change the ballet world, at least if it has to come from Denmark. Perhaps it can happen in France, where we have seen some truly wonderful classical dancers from the Paris Opera and Claude Bessy's Académie Nationale de la Danse. Katharine's extensive and very precise observation of *épaulement* in dancing hits the nail on the head. I do not really think it needs any comment. I agree with her and can only say 'bravo'!

Heels Up Heels Down

In Bournonville dancing it is a must to put your heels down to the floor when executing steps. The so-called Balanchine way (with a raised heel all the time) is, in my opinion, not a school but a fashion. Maybe it happened simply because a dancer could not get his heels down to the floor. It was something that came out of the Balanchine empire later in his life, so I have my doubts whether he really believed in it.

When I worked with Balanchine at the Paris Opera in 1962 in three different ballets, he certainly never complained about my technique or that I put my heels down. I performed major roles in all three ballets, *The Four Temperaments*, *Symphony in C*, and *Scotch Symphony*. Whether or not heels on or off the floor is aesthetically beautiful is, of course, in the eye of the beholder, but it can give a dancer severe cramp in the calf muscle if he does not put them down. It also leaves important choreographic, musical accents in the wings.

Injury

There is no doubt that we have seen more injuries inflicted on dancers during the last twenty-five years than was ever previously observed and/or reported. I am not sure if these injuries are occurring because of strange technical demands or some sadistic tendencies in contemporary teaching. In either case, may I add that my childhood teacher, Karl Merrild, would have won the gold medal in any decade. By contrast, I see a lot of rather weak inconsistent training when dancers spend at least half of their daily class at the bar, approximately fifty-five minutes.

When Bournonville was training dancers, they spent a maximum of fifteen minutes at the bar, which is more than what is done now at a work-out studio before proceeding with the class. What we see in many ballet companies is an appalling lack of co-ordination between daily training and stage performing. Throughout Katharine's article there are many *enfants terribles*. One is the high extension which she amusingly refers to as the 'telephone call'. There is a training question about the use of the high extension, but I think that individual facility must be taken into consideration. When a dancer is born with the facility for high extension, it should be used, as it can be very exciting. In Bournonville's Biedermeier universe it is, of course, totally inappropriate. On the other hand, when this kind of high extension is forced on dancers it is extremely dangerous, which is also the case with a forced turn-out. Throughout my time in ballet I have seen far too many tragedies. I think especially of the unhappy men and women with ruined hips. I think, as of today, I know a dozen dancers walking badly with a plastic hip.

Another *enfant terrible* in Katharine's eyes is *pointe* work. Turning on *pointe* will not do you any good. This is what bulldozer Katharine is saying and to me it is right out of Ionesco. Of course dancing on the tips of your toes is not natural. The art-form of ballet is not natural but it can be very exciting. An example is the Georgian male dancers dancing on *pointe* and jumping on their knees. How exciting it is, but it is not good for their toes or knees. Being serious—I think *pointe* work used by Petipa is often absolutely brilliant. The end of the *pas de deux* in Act II of *Swan Lake* is a good example. It is poetic and breathtakingly beautiful. The prolonged series of *fouettés* is, of course, a circus stunt. They are not supposed to be pretty or beautiful, just plain stunning and exciting, which they can be on rare occasions with a dancer who can master that trick.

Professional Critics

When professional critics want to flaunt opinions about good or bad taste or choose between beautiful or ugly, we have to beware. There is, however, in Katharine's writing, a love of the understated and refined, which is rather disarming. It is but a limited point of view that she is expressing and often total wishful thinking. To dismiss all contemporary choreography is, to say the least, not very smart. There is an endless list of creative strengths, from Balanchine to Jiří Kylián and numerous others. Choreography today reflects an often tormented but exuberant world of beauty, energy, and, alas, violence. The clock is turning and many choreographers are facing a situation of violence around them that they cannot ignore. Here in the USA where I have my home, there is a hidden and undeclared civil war going on, especially in the major cities. Every morning a city can count its dead. Somewhere between eight and twelve victims is a normal sunrise. This tragedy and violence is being reflected in contemporary ballet, at least seen from this part of the world.

La Sylphide

Avoiding Injury

ROBERT COHAN

The environment of dancers—our theme for this issue—includes not only the spaces and stages on which they dance, described by Frank Woods, the techniques they use, questioned by Katharine Kanter, and the response by Flemming Flindt to Ms Kanter's article, but the dangers and stresses they face in the life of being a dancer. Five years ago, in our first issue, Robert Cohan, artistic adviser to London Contemporary Dance Theatre, wrote a perceptive piece about the working lives of dancers. It has been quoted often and referenced many times. Sadly the dangers and difficulties he describes remain as urgent for reform today as they did in 1989. For this reason and in response to letters from readers we reproduce below Robert Cohan's important article.   *Editor.*

The most common cause of injuries and strains is bad training. By bad training I do not mean careless training; I mean not sufficient training in the work to be done. If you know you are going to do a certain kind of choreography which involves a lot of jumping, more than your dancers have been doing for the last three or four months, it is insane to start rehearsal after rehearsal where everybody is jumping all the time, without having prepared for this in class. This applies to anything and everything.

If you are going to use the body in a different way you must prepare the dancers for it by exercises which will help to strengthen them and make them sensitive to that way of moving. Sometimes you can get around it by using your choreography period as a class to work on the movement, but of course that uses time and often you are very pressed for time. A good example was when Robert North choreographed *Troy Game*—many years ago now. We talked about it and my challenge to him was to create something where the men jumped for twenty minutes. We had very strong men at that time so I started adding jumps to the normal class material until the men were strong enough to do that choreography. This was before anything was choreographed.

That said, the other chief cause of injuries occurs in rehearsal and is related to what I have just said. It usually happens in rehearsal that a single movement is repeated many, many times, so that the tendons and the muscles of a particular joint become overstrained and do not function properly.

On the second and third days it gets worse. Frequently the choreographer uses the dancer over and over again, working hard trying to get the image he wants. So you get an injury at the beginning of a rehearsal period which will then persist. The choreographer should therefore be very sensitive to the state of training of his dancers and the way their bodies are at that moment, avoiding repetition as much as possible, since it is this repetition which does the damage.

If a video-recorder is used during rehearsal, there is no need to use dancers continually merely to gauge choreographic effects. By using it every third or fourth day, keeping a video machine in the corner of your studio, recording what you have done, it can be studied at home. A lot of choreographers say to their dancers 'OK, let's do it from the beginning!' Then, 'I need to see it again!' and 'I need to see it again!', when a recording would suffice. The ideal set-up is to have the video always there. Dancers can literally see what they are doing and will find it easier to do the material which is set, with less risk of injury.

When you have worked with one particular set of dancers initially, then go out on tour using a different set of dancers, that is when big problems start. *Troy Game* is a good case, because it really involves just jumping. When we are going out on tour with *Troy Game* I always specifically ask whoever is teaching to start some jumps a month or so beforehand. The dancers may be doing as many as 400 jumps in first, second, and fifth positions at the end of class so that they are really prepared and their muscle reaction becomes very fast and very strong. Jumping is a very specific skill you simply need to do well.

There is another problem on tour—dancers frequently get cold. Things are better than they were, but there is a constant problem of going through cold hallways and then on to the stage. Also the routine of being on tour sometimes itself causes injuries because the dancers get into a routine of doing a class, doing a bit of rehearsal, and then going outside to have something to eat. Then they come back and sit around. Maybe they are not dancing at 7.30 in the evening when the show starts. Maybe they are dancing later in the programme at 8.30 or 8.45 and are three or four weeks out on tour and are tired. So they do not warm up properly. They get on stage and they really try very hard to give a good performance and that frequently causes an injury. I believe that dancers at that point are responsible for themselves and I am responsible for seeing that they are responsible. You really can separate the good dancers, the well-disciplined ones, very easily. They *are* warmed up, they *are* prepared, and they do not get hurt. Others do get injured.

Yet, especially in a contemporary company, where dancers are frequently in every single dance in an evening, I do not see how they can avoid injury. They are going to get hurt at some point in a long tour or at some point in the year, if not in that tour, because they are dancing so much of the time. If it is complicated material then it is especially a problem for men, because they always injure their backs. The women generally strain their ankles, which is very hard to avoid. It is essential for the men to keep strengthening their backs. This means doing push-ups. In fact, we do push-ups for the men as part of class on tour, because if your arms are strong enough you

Anthony van Laast of the London Contemporary Dance Theatre in *Troy Game*, choreographed by Robert North.   PHOTO: ANTHONY CRICKMAY

can take an enormous amount of weight off your back. We tried using weights but the men did not like it, so we work on push-ups and on the body-training machine. Of course, our choreography uses very few straight arm-lifts, unlike classical ballet. It is very seldom that we lift a girl straight up into the air overhead. I use more contact lifts, where the body weight is shifted under the body, and if the arms are just that little stronger it makes all the difference in the world.

The floor! The quality of the floor of course is vital and can be another source of injury. We have our touring records so we know every floor where we have appeared. We know whether it is on steel or on wood or on concrete, and we carry a very dense quarter-inch or half-inch foam, which we put under the linoleum floor-covering that also accompanies us on tour. Even so, if the floor is really bad we are very careful. You can always land carefully from jumps, for instance. The fact is, though, that the demands of the kind of touring we have to do with a company of fifteen dancers for twenty-four weeks a year creates conditions which have, in the past, contributed to injuries. Dancers who are on stage all that time are bound to be hurt. It is unavoidable. It is not reasonable to expect so much of them. Compare the sort of situation which prevails in Britain with that in the United States. In the United States you would stay in what is considered here a four-star hotel. You do not have to worry about coming home after a performance to an unheated room. You do not have to worry about an unheated shared bathroom in digs somewhere—not that there are not some nice digs around. But there are others where you cannot get a hot bath at night because the landlady does not allow hot baths after 10 p.m. The touring allowance here is not enough for stays in the Holiday Inns, which are good, but not exceptional. In the United States it would be accepted that that is where you would stay. You would not tour unless you stayed there. In Europe there are a number of dancers who can return home every night, as in Holland. I just think that the facilities for touring here are below reasonable standards and the touring allowance does not recognize the problem.

In the theatres the situation has changed radically in the last ten years. Today, most theatres have good backstage facilities, but there are still a number of large theatres, including Sadler's Wells, where one has to go up two floors, in the cold, on concrete, to get to the shower. Raked stages, of course, are a problem. We do meet them sometimes, but then I insist that class be done on the stage and the teacher on the first day shows how to work on it. Not all dancers remember that you have a totally different assemblage of your weight and your centre of gravity. Literally, you have to press back against the floor.

Nowadays, to help our dancers, we often carpet the wings. We carry cheap black carpeting which we spread all over the exits from the stage as well as other off-stage areas, and the cross-over. This helps to keep the dancers warm and allows them to lie down flat out off-stage even during a performance, so they are not so tired. Also it makes a protective surface for the dancers, covers the cables, and even helps to prevent related accidents like rushing off stage and running into a stage weight or something similar.

In all this a choreographer has to bear in mind, all the time, not to demand too much of the dancers. Perhaps over the years I personally have borne it in mind too much, because if you are the artistic director of a company and the chief choreographer you have to keep your dancers in good condition for the whole year. I have seen choreographers come in who are only going to be with us for six weeks or so and they want us to do their dance. They do not want to know about so-and-so's bad knee or weak ankle. They are concerned only that their dance looks good; they are not really concerned about whether the dancers will be fit for the next six months. Experienced choreographers know the problem but because they are not going to stay with the company they choose to ignore it. A dancer can, of course, point out a danger, but this depends on the relationship between dancer and choreographer. The problem arises particularly with young choreographers who just do not know how quickly the body can be worn down through a rehearsal. They are insensitive to it. If they were dancing they would still be insensitive to it because they would be doing it with the kind of nervous energy and enthusiasm that is not realistic when put on a dancer. I think there is no doubt that the kind of dancing which has been done in the last five or ten years—extreme choreography—is making demands on the body for which the body is probably not prepared, any more than you are prepared, say, for swinging in trees!

This takes us back to training. You can train to do almost anything and the choreography your dancers dance can be a product of that training. At the same time you have to admit that the body is fallible and is going to wear out and is not going to work equally well for everything a choreographer demands. I do not think, though, that these demands are the cause of injury but rather the repetition of a movement over and over again. In the attempt to do something impossible an odd situation frequently arises. A good dancer, say, just cannot get a movement. In actual fact there is a block at that moment. The dancer will get it in three seconds, or one hour from now, or tomorrow. Some choreographers insist, and waste time insisting, that the dancers do the steps the way they want at once, RIGHT NOW! When you see choreographers demand such a thing you know they are not experienced or they are not sure of themselves. It is a very dangerous situation but it occurs. You have to learn to stop, let the dancers go and work on their own, let them come back with the step, or just change the mood in the studio and allow everybody to relax, because usually these situations become very tense.

This touches on the psychological issues in choreography. It does not have to be stressful on a dancer who is not achieving something. Wishing to please, however, can be. Some dancers want so desperately to do what you want and they throw themselves into it with such abandon that it becomes dangerous. They may get away with it for one or two rehearsals, but eventually they are going to injure themselves unless the choreographer is alert. One has to see very quickly that at a certain point the weight is not exactly right and you have to say, 'Be careful because you are almost off-balance and something's going to give,' or 'When you fall to the floor don't hit the point of the knee, make sure you slide off to the side.' A choreographer frequently has to say this to a dancer, or should be able to say it. One has to help the dancer to protect himself, because the dancer will, either in anger, in fear, or in sheer enthusiasm frequently go overboard. That is why he is dancing; he wants excitement, involvement, and easily goes too far.

Once again one comes back to training. If the training is really good and consistent and takes into account, not just making *a* dancer, but a dancer who can do specific choreographies, then one has no problems, or one reduces the problem enormously. I think that this is vital; absolutely vital. Frequently now there are so many different ideas of contemporary dance and so few teachers who can pull all those ideas together into a technique class that a lot of dancers are studying ballet. Then they go to a contemporary rehearsal of choreography and they get injured because it is not consistent training from the class into the repertory into the choreography with considerate coaching all the way through. I am not saying this will always happen, but there are certain movements you make which you know are dangerous. Choreographers know that, or they should. If they do not they are not choreographers! These movements may be very important to you as part of the dance but you have to keep them to a minimum and you have to treat them very carefully.

A good teacher, I think, has to take the responsibility that if a student gets injured in his or her class it is the fault of the teacher. The same thing is true of new choreography. If choreographers have this attitude then they will be more careful in rehearsal, especially if their body is different from the dancers' bodies—say a woman choreographing for a man, or vice versa, or a long back for short backs. A choreographer has to be able to pick up these differences early enough to avoid injury. It is hard to reconcile this with the image of the choreography you want because you are not concerned about injury when you go into rehearsal. You are concerned about your ideas and creating a dance which will express these ideas, but at some point you have to be concerned and care about the dancers. If you can do this you will reduce the injury danger to an acceptable degree. You will be doing your duty as a choreographer.

Space for Dance

FRANK WOODS

> Take any empty space and call it a bare stage. A man walks across this
> empty space whilst someone else is watching him, and this is all that is
> needed for an act of theatre to be engaged.
>
> Peter Brook, *The Empty Space*

This description of the act of theatre might well have been coined to
describe the opening of any ballet or dance—that moment of expectation
when, the house lights having been dimmed and the house curtain raised,
for the ordinary members of the audience all attention is engaged and
focused on the empty space; whether it is brightly or dimly lit, decorated or
bare, the focus and attention is rapt and total. Balanchine reported that
Stravinsky had said to him that 'Ballet is a performance. People watch! A
boy sits in the front row; he wants to look at the girl onstage. It should be
interesting.' At such a moment the magic of performance begins. There is
no distraction other than a silence that every performer or dancer knows so
well.

It is not necessarily the same experience for cultures outside the West
where the idea of a stage and an auditorium is not a prerequisite for performance. Bare earth is an equal substitute for the raised stage; tribal dance in
Africa or Aboriginal dance in Australia occurs in a clearing on the ground
and with the 'audience' on all four sides and without recourse to artificial
aids such as décor and lighting.

For many cultures it is difficult to separate the performer from the audience; both need each other. It is important to consider the spaces which
each requires as part and parcel of the same problem.

With the origin of dance as we know it in the West, deriving from the
Court presentations in the seventeenth century, we too often take for
granted that dance always focuses to the front. The word 'audience'
implies a hearing in front of an assembly as well as carrying the overtone of
a presentation before the head of state. Formal dance as an act of presentation has come to demand a certain kind of performance space, developing
in due course the need for a screen or proscenium to mask those performers not currently engaged in the presentation. The development, therefore,
of the proscenium arch is a fundamental part of classical ballet, exemplified
perhaps in its finest form in the eighteenth-century theatre at
Drottningholm in Sweden. It is, however, questionable whether classical
ballet would have developed in that way if the proscenium had not been
invented in the first place.

Dance is movement involving the body and is, by definition, three-dimensional; in this regard it has parallels with another kind of performance, namely the circus. The circus as we know it today is an arena surrounded on all sides by the audience, and the performance technique has been tuned to engage all of the audience all of the time. Experiments with theatre in the round have always stumbled on the problem of the performer's method of engagement which uses speech and eye contact. It has been said that Laurence Olivier once declared that initially he found it difficult to work effectively on the thrust stage in the theatre at Chichester because he could not maintain eye contact with all of the audience. Interestingly, this requirement for the performer also became part of the brief for the Royal Shakespeare Theatre at the Barbican in London where experiments with the actors' sight-lines from the point of command (approximately three metres back from the edge of the stage) led to a design of auditorium requiring that the arc of contact was of the order of 120 degrees.

The 'fronting' of classical ballet to the audience is a characteristic which became an essential requirement for the design of all spaces for dance for the last half-century, although it is changing now. The fact that dance can rarely fill a theatre for fifty-two weeks of the year has influenced those who commission new theatres. The need to fill the space with other performance modes involving speech and music has led to the need for some kind of complete or partial proscenium. Even the excellent new theatre in The Hague for the Nederlands Dans Theater is a wide fan form with a proscenium; however, the fan form is wider than would be comfortable for speech, which is a recognition of the differing needs of dance.

One of Peter Brook's experiments at the Bouffe du Nord in Paris for his production of *Carmen* explored the use of part of the auditorium as a performance space. Similarly, Trevor Nunn's production of *Cats* at the New Theatre in London exploits the potential of the stage revolve by mingling the dancers with the audience.

Although much has been written about the design of stages and auditoria, such material has tended to concentrate on the physical and geometrical characteristics of the spaces; because of the problems of sight-lines and audibility and of backstage requirements it is inevitable that designers should concentrate on the more easily definable problems rather than the less tangible aspects of performance space. A notable exception is Iain Mackintosh who, in his recent book *Architecture, Actor and Audience*, explores the relationship between performer and audience. Even so, he covers the full range of performance art and only deals in part with dance.

It is presumed that an audience is assembled for a specific purpose, almost certainly for entertainment, or possibly for instruction. Entertainment implies the expectation of pleasure or amusement, or at least a commitment to a few hours of concentration. This is not to say that comfort is an essential for the audience—very often the opposite is true. The trend in recent years, for example, to design auditoria with as near perfect sight-lines as possible has produced theatres which significantly lack any real presence. The aim of all designers is to give all the members of the audience an uninterrupted view of the stage. But the problem is that this produces an arrangement in which the assembled audience is ranged in rows in a steeply raked auditorium with no awareness of itself other than the not very stimulating sight of the backs of the heads of the people in front. It is a dilemma facing all designers that the more crowded and hence more uncomfortable the audience, the more likelihood there is that they will be more responsive during a performance.

In the original plans for the Royal Shakespeare Theatre at the Barbican Centre in London there was a proposal, not implemented, for the front rows of the stalls to be set aside for what in earlier times were called the 'groundlings'; these would be in the form of bench seats at low prices. The presence of such seating would have added considerable character to an already excellent auditorium. The ambience of the annual Promenade Concerts at the Albert Hall in London is due in no small measure to the presence of the promenaders who stand at the front immediately against the rostrum. No promenader would admit to being comfortable in the accepted sense of the word, but the whole audience would affirm that the presence of the promenaders adds to the pleasure of the audience in recognizing itself. This self-awareness is the key aspect of the design of the traditional horseshoe plan opera-house of the eighteenth century of which La Scala is a fine example.

Many dance lovers prefer to be seated in the dress circle because this gives a high viewpoint from which to perceive the form and pattern of the ballet composition. Conversely, many dance critics prefer to be seated in the stalls. The problem is that with a lower viewpoint good vision of the stage can only be achieved by tilting or raking the stage itself; this is obviously beneficial for a good view of the performance occurring at the back of the stage towards the cyclorama. One solution is to increase the seating rake, but this tends to produce an uncomfortably steep angle, which is unsettling for the audience.

The dilemma for dancers on a raked stage is less easily resolved. If the theatre design produces a raked stage then it is imperative that all dance rehearsal floors should have the same rake. If these are not available then it is important that, as Robert Cohan points out earlier in this book, class should be done on the stage. A straw poll of any group of dancers will produce a requirement for a flat floor, but this may be a counsel of perfection. Given that performance involves two fundamental components—the performer and the viewer—it is inevitable that compromises have to be made to satisfy both.

Critical factors which affect the dancer's performance hinge around the size of the auditorium. In many dance forms, though not necessarily in classical ballet, eye contact is paramount if the performer is to be in command of the audience. The great Danish character dancer and mime artist, Niels Bjørn Larsen, maintains that by making eye contact the dancer 'is nearly speaking to the audience'. The mime artist in dance must keep his face to the audience, not necessarily for him to be able to see the audience but principally because it is important that the audience can see the performer's eyes. For this reason the maximum arc which the character dancer can encompass is approximately a third of a circle—or one hundred and twenty degrees. The natural vertical movement of the head also predetermines the height at which meaningful communication is not possible. According to Bjørn Larsen, 'big and high theatres are difficult for the performer and well nigh impossible for mime'. He maintains that to be successful, the character dancer will generally focus his energy on performing to the balcony. However, not all dance involves facial expression; often it is posture and gesture which are equally important. In these instances the size of the auditorium is less critical and good communication is possible over larger distances. Obviously, in a large auditorium, it is necessary for the dancer to tune his performance to suit the scale of the space.

It is difficult to consider performance space for dance as a single subject since such spaces can vary so much. One would never envisage performing Wagner's *Götterdämmerung* in the local village hall, or a classical guitar recital in a large concert-hall seating two and a half thousand people. Yet architects and designers are often asked by their clients to design theatres capable of being used for such extremes. Acoustically, for concert-halls for example, this has led to quite complex briefs requiring expensive design solutions.

For music and its aural constraints this is an easier task than having to cope with the more difficult problems associated with dance and its requirements for good vision. Clearly there can be no perfect or ideal solution. Rarely can a dance company in any country justify filling a dance house for a full fifty-two weeks of the year. Sadlers Wells in London is not able to do this despite being located in a major city. The result is that dance has to share space with opera. From a performance space point of view, this is far from ideal since the stage requirements of opera frequently make demands on the architect and designer which are in conflict with the needs for dance—a simple stage floor without traps and without interruptions to the stage floor finish. Equally, the requirements of opera and classical ballet for an orchestra exacerbates the problem of maintaining a close contact between performer and audience across the chasm of the orchestra pit.

The only new theatre designed specifically for dance in recent years is the Dance Theatre in The Hague for the Nederlands Dans Theater by architect Rem Koolhas. The brief for the building was carefully considered and the building provides a full range of facilities for the resident dance

The auditorium and stage
at the Opéra, Lyons.
PHOTO: PAUL RAFTERY / ARCAID

company and visiting companies, in particular, gymnasia and physiotherapy rooms which are essential for the proper maintenance of a healthy dance company.

Other new theatres are the more usual combinations of performance spaces for opera and dance. Interesting examples which have most recently been opened are the newly converted and refurbished mid-eighteenth century opera-house in Lyons, France, by architect Jean Nouvel, and the newly designed opera-house in Helsinki in Finland by architects Hyvämäki-Karhunen-Parkinen, both of which clearly are concerned to ensure good sight-lines for the majority of the audience. At Lyons there is a very high auditorium with no less than six shallow tiers above the stalls level, producing a very high viewpoint for much of the audience; it will be interesting to learn the dancers' response to this and what sort of problems it presents, if any. There is a fine series of ballet rehearsal spaces and rooms at Lyons which, with the new work at the Royal Theatre at Copenhagen, the Dance Theatre at the Hague and the recently completed Roland Petit Ballet School in Marseilles, must set standards for future performance spaces yet to be designed.

Dance is an earthbound activity; much as they would like to, dancers cannot escape the law of gravity. It is interesting that so much writing about dance, be it criticism or history, refers time and again to dancers 'floating' or 'flying'—with the inference of weightlessness. In some cultures, such as Africa, India, aboriginal Australia, or Asia, dance has remained firmly rooted to the earth, and the illusory art of the interpretation of 'floating' is portrayed more by mime and manner. Even so, with or without the illusion of weightlessness, every dancer knows that gravity exerts its inevitable influence. Gravity is a severe taskmaster and to defy him is to risk injury.

Two of the greatest risks to the physical health of a dancer are the chore-

Auditorium of the Finnish
National Opera, Helsinki.
PHOTO: MAURITZ HELLSTRÖM

ographer and gravity. The third risk is, of course, the dancer who refuses to recognize the danger signals and who accordingly suffers injury. This is explicitly set out by Robert Cohan in the previous article on the health of the dancer. The dancer can only lose contact with the ground for a short moment and his or her contact at impact needs to be cushioned.

During the professional life of a dancer it is inevitable that he will be called upon to perform on all manner of unsuitable surfaces. It is not always possible to provide a sprung floor or to maintain it in good condition, particularly if the stage is being used for opera or drama where the demands of the stage designer will inevitably cause damage to the surface of the floor. Dancers who tour—a fact of life for most dancers—have to learn to live with whatever floor surface is available. The development of cushioned stage cloths which are portable can help in this respect, but these do not produce the best kind of surface on which to perform. Bearing in mind the fundamental importance of the floor quality to the dancer,

The ballet rehearsal room for the Opéra, at Lyons. PHOTO: PAUL RAFTERY / ARCAID

surprisingly little has been published about floor construction. Highly to be recommended is the book *A Handbook for Dance Floors* by Mark Foley in which he explains very fully the basic principles and construction solutions for a wide range of floors.

The ballet rehearsal room of the Roland Petit Dance School, Marseilles.

PHOTO: PAUL RAFTERY / ARCAID

Of all the physical aspects of the environment of dance that are fundamental to the dancer, the floor quality is by far the most important. Whilst there are innumerable ways of constructing the floor, the whole matter of the interpretation of floor quality is highly subjective; not all dancers like all floors, but equally all dancers know when they are faced with dancing on an unsuitable floor. The absence of resilience and floor springing are immediately recognized, but it is the degree of resilience and springing which is the subject of individual preference. There are two criteria to be fulfilled for a perfect solution. First, the area on which the dancer performs should be resilient or sprung so that there is a degree of 'give' from the floor as the dancer lands. Secondly, since the impact is taken on the foot, there is the need for local resilience at the point of impact. Each of these criteria require different technical solutions, but they are not mutually exclusive.

Although there are different ways of obtaining resilience in floor construction, they all are attempts at creating a springing in the floor structure which will 'give' on impact so that some of the dancer's downward energy is absorbed, and in so doing, the stresses on the dancer's body lessened. Essentially, all the varying constructions provide a floor plane which is supported on resilient mountings. The floor plane should be of timber planking or plywood or similar sheeting; this is supported on timber battens and these in turn are supported on either more timber battens or on rubber or plastic mounts. The spacing of the battens will obviously provide a 'springing' function and allow the floor plane to deflect. There are also a number of permutations of these methods of construction which allow the designer to tune the floor response. For example, the battens running in one direction can themselves be mounted on battens running in the other direction at right angles and in turn these battens can be mounted on yet a third layer of battens running in the opposite direction.

It is vitally important that the floor surface should be non-slip as well as resilient. The actual quality of the floor surface has been the subject of much experiment, ranging from finished but untreated floor planking, which requires considerable maintenance and upkeep, to the more recent development of plastic floor finishes, such as the one which was formerly known as the Marley floor and which is now usually replaced by various grades of Harlequin sheet. Other makes exist, for instance, the Pirouette, as used at the Royal Theatre in Copenhagen.

There are likely to be further developments in the application of newer construction techniques to sprung floors and their surfaces; sadly the usage of such floors for dance is not extensive enough to justify manufacturers investing heavily in this regard. However, dancers are likely to benefit as a result of manufacturers exploring and developing new methods of construction for sports-hall floors—a field of activity which is extensive enough to justify the necessary research and development.

Whether on or off the ground the dancer's environment is the air they breathe. Often, it is poor air quality which makes their work so much harder. Only a few years ago the Danish Royal Ballet suffered an interminably long period when their well-being and health suffered and for a while no one was able to pin-point the cause. This was very fully described, in Volume 1 (1989–90) of this yearbook, by Edgar Dahlin, in which he described the results of surveys carried out at the theatre at a time when the company suffered an extensive series of illnesses and health complaints shortly after the renovations to the building had been completed. Architects and engineers have, for a long time, been searching for a cure for what has come to be known as 'Sick Building Syndrome'. As a result of a considerable amount of effort and research, the cause of many of the problems has now been identified at the theatre. There is now a tendency throughout the world for heating and ventilating engineers, and architects, to be less and less dependent upon artificial or machine-driven methods of controlling the internal environment of buildings, and for more reliance to be placed on natural ventilation where this is feasible.

In the past, reliance has been placed on air-conditioning to provide environmental conditions that were perceived to be required. In many cases buildings could and should be designed to provide acceptable conditions by means of natural ventilation. Advantages gained from this approach include the subjective satisfaction gained by opening windows to obtain immediate control of air flow, thus avoiding the complexities of air-conditioning and thereby lowering energy consumption. However, it must be recognized that in certain environments, such as hot and humid climates as well as some urban environments, air-conditioning may be unavoidable.

The other spaces which dancers constantly use are rehearsal rooms and dressing-rooms. It is not enough for these spaces to be provided and planned for; to be of real value the air temperature and humidity levels must be properly controlled. These two factors are particularly critical for performers and athletes since they so impinge upon musculature and breathing. Damage can be done if they are not properly set and controlled. These areas do not exist in isolation. The linking spaces between them and with the stage should be considered with as much care as the main spaces. Cold and draughty corridors are the dancers' worst enemy.

In an ideal world it should not be necessary for dancers to have to perform in hot or stuffy conditions, but the presence of an audience, stage lighting, and the energy and humidity given off by physical exertion, inevitably increases the temperature of the space. As a result, here also there is the need for effective ventilation and air movement—no easy task when one considers the combined volumes of an auditorium, stage, and fly tower. Too fast an air-flow and both audience and performer suffer from the discomfort of draughts.

All dancers would agree with Olivier's complaint at the Old Vic in London that, whilst playing Othello in light clothing and sweating from the heat of the stage lighting and his own exertions, he suffered badly from the cold draught coming down from the fly tower. The problems of such draughts stem directly from the difficulty of trying to maintain the right air temperatures and humidity in the two differing spaces of the auditorium, one occupied by the audience, and the other, the stage, occupied by the performers. Interestingly, at the New London Theatre, in London, designed to a concept by Sean Kenny, one third of the audience seating shares the stage revolve. Here the air-conditioning was designed to be adjustable to accommodate the configuration of the seating to the stage; as a result the audience and the performers share the same air conditions, unlike those in a proscenium theatre. Similarly, at the Crucible Theatre in Sheffield, the facility of the thrust stage as well as a proscenium enables the performers to share the same conditions as the audience apart, of course, from the additional heat of the stage lighting. It is unavoidable that in matters of environmental control in space design, compromises have to be made, since the conditions needed by the energetic performer are, to a considerable extent, in conflict with those needed by the static audience.

All in all, it is too easy to be obsessive about space for dance and to be dissatisfied with anything but the best; in itself, this is laudable, but dancers and choreographers have to live in the real world and the perfect conditions and environment cannot always be guaranteed. From time to time they must be resolute and refuse to perform if the conditions are wholly wrong, as happened last year at the Palace Theatre in Manchester when the English National Ballet Company cancelled their performance of *The Nutcracker* because the temperature in the theatre was below the standard laid down as the minimum acceptable for performance. This does not happen that often but, notwithstanding the inevitable complaints from refusing to perform, the dance world must hold firm and not give way.

Apart from the stage lighting, care needs to be taken with the design of lighting in the backstage areas of a theatre. All too often this is ill considered and the resultant gloom does little to lift the spirits. Headaches and eyestrain are frequently brought on by flickering lighting and it is thought that stress induced by inadequate lighting may be one of the contributory factors of the sick building syndrome.

Times are changing; no longer is the producer's world limited to that of the theatre. Technology in film and television has moved on at an ever-increasing pace. Less than twenty years ago, John Percival stated in his book *Modern Ballet* that he could foresee that dancers and choreographers would need to understand and come to terms with the then emerging medium of television: 'considering how many more people can see ballet on film or television than on the stage, it seems astonishing that the problems translating it into the different media have met with little attention and even less success.'

This was written in 1969. In the ensuing years, there have been marked developments in this field and great steps have been taken by both choreographers and television producers to exploit the newly developing medium. Recent developments in multimedia, in CD-ROM, and in the next few months, particularly CD-I, will revolutionize entertainment, the performing arts, and publishing, but it will inevitably take time for the significance of the new ground rules to impact on dance. However, just as film did not spell the end of stage performance but rather enhanced it, so will the new dimensions of presentation signal a new phase in the development of dance to expand and enrich the traditional forms.

It is now possible to film a dance work from a number of fixed or mobile camera positions and record these in such a format as to allow the viewer to select which views he will see and in which sequence. In one sense this already happens in theatre productions where the spectator's eye can move about the scene at will, although it is the producer's task to control where the viewer looks at any given moment. What is now about to happen is that the viewer of recorded dance on CD-I will be able to select his viewing positions from a number predetermined by the producer. It will be interesting to observe the impact on choreographers' production techniques. For recorded performances the actual performance spaces will be the film or television studio or stage. Within these spaces the choreographer will need to rethink choreography 'in the round', and not necessarily from a single viewpoint. Recent productions by the distinguished television director Bob Lockyer, who specializes in ballet on television, emphasize this point; his recent production of performances specially choreographed by **DV8** and the **Shobana Jeyasingh Dance Company** on British television have demonstrated the considerable potential that is available in the medium.

As for the myriad factors which go to make the ideal performance conditions, there is so much more that needs to be considered which has not been touched upon here. For example, there has been no consideration given to the problems of, for instance, mirror alignment in rehearsal rooms or whether, as some would claim, mirrors are necessary at all. Nor has there been any discussion about the psychological aspects of colour in the environment both backstage and in rehearsal spaces.

The greatest luxury of all is space in which to dance. A large enough space with a flat surface, a good cushioned floor cloth, and a space for the audience are all that is needed for a performance to take place. Peter Brook was right—'take any empty space and call it a bare stage . . .'.

The Author is grateful to the following for their help and advice during the preparation of this article: ballet-master Niels Bjørn Larsen of the Royal Danish Ballet for his guidance and comments on the techniques of mime performance; Peter Goldfinger of Dale and Goldfinger for his advice on environmental control and air conditions based on his work at the Crucible Theatre in Sheffield and at the New London Theatre and the Old Vic Theatre in London.

Recommended Further Reading

Armstrong, L., and Morgan, R., *Space for Dance* (National Endowment for the Arts, Publishing Centre for Cultural Resources, New York, 1984).

Arnheim, D., *Dance Injuries* (Dance Books, London, 1986).

Foley, M., *A Handbook of Dance Floors* (Dance UK, London, 1992).

Forsyth, M., *Auditoria: Designing for the Performing Arts* (Mitchell Publishing, London, 1987).

Ham, R., *Theatre Planning* (Architectural Press, London, 1987).

Health and Safety Executive, *Sick Building Syndrome: A Review of Evidence on Causes and Solutions* (Health and Safety Contract Research Report No. 42, London, 1992).

Mackintosh, I., *Architecture, Actor and Audience* (Routledge, London, 1993).

PART II

The Dancing World

Africa

ADRIENNE SICHEL

Cultural linkage and exchange were two vital initiatives in Southern African dance. They have triggered off a process with exciting regional and international ramifications.

The divisive term 'black dance' comes seriously into question in culturally diverse Southern African countries such as Botswana, Malawi, Zimbabwe, Mozambique, and South Africa, where the transition from traditional dancing grounds to the proscenium stage has been in progress for the past decade. Due to the cultural boycott, which cut South Africa off from the world and most of Africa, these developments happened in isolation—till the watershed year of 1993. At the annual Dance Umbrella and later at the Market Theatre and Natal Playhouse, **Tumbuka**, Zimbabwe's fledgling first contemporary dance company, conquered sophisticated audiences in Johannesburg and Durban. In September, Senegalese master teacher and African dance virtuoso Germaine Acogny mesmerized Johannesburg and Soweto.

In South Africa, even during the vice grip of apartheid, there has been a concerted effort in certain progressive quarters not to marginalize any dance form. The heated debates of the 1980s about ethnocentric versus eurocentric dance—the banishment of Western classical ballet and contemporary dance techniques in favour of new techniques suited to the African physique—have been partially resolved by action and ongoing questioning. The exploration and creation of new aesthetics continues while constantly blurring or annihilating the definitions and segregations implicit in labels like 'black', 'African', or 'eurocentric' dance.

The emergence of fusions of techniques, rhythms, and traditions exploded on to the formal South African dance stage in Johannesburg five years ago at the inaugural Dance Umbrella, a national platform for all South African choreographers—urban and rural, mainstream and grass roots, cities and townships. Fusion, which originated in the mid 1970s, has had its detractors and its opportunists, but gradually choreographers have applied thought process and integrity to creating various truly syncretic forms. It is not unusual to see Graham technique layered with gumboot dynamics, *pantsula* (township jive) moves, and Zulu *indlamu* (traditional dance) kicks performed to foot rattle stamps and percussion twinned with 'foreign' music as familiar as Ravel's *Bolero*. Or flamenco dancers stamping their way through the people's national anthem 'iAfrica' by Nkosi Sikelel. Or classical ballet steps and phrases synthesized with Bharatha Natyam vocabulary, African and Western contractions plus Zulu stamps and

Eric Lehana and company, Moving into Dance, in *Paths of Sound*, choreographed by Sylvia Glasser.   PHOTO: MOTLHALEFI MAHLABE

weaves. Or a skilled mingling of Swazi, Venda, Shangaan, Zulu, Sotho, and West African motifs and rhythms performed by trained dancers who are no strangers to Graham, Cunningham, or Humphrey.

The dawn of a new government after 27 April 1994, and a new cultural dispensation, will sorely test all South African artists and perhaps jeopardize the existence of the thirty-year-old state-funded classical ballet companies run by arts councils in Pretoria and Cape Town. Whatever the outcome the dance community cannot be accused of being inactive or silent. In March 1993, the former director of NAPAC Dance Company, Garry Trinder, hosted a national dance forum in Durban at which a healthy cross-section of the country's educationists, dancers, and choreographers were enriched by Peter Brinson's address on 'Dance Power'. This provided an international perspective to a developing dance culture ravaged by the cultural boycott and insularity.

In Johannesburg in April the Dance Alliance presented a discussion paper outlining a new dance policy for South Africa at the African National Congress's historic Department of Arts and Culture conference. The paper, presented by Dr Fred Hagemann of the University of the Witwatersrand, focused on 'the crises of identity faced by a multi-cultural society and the relationship of dance to its own communities and beyond; funding: the hegemonic grip by the state-funded arts councils, and regional and national organisation'. A lobby, heavily fuelled by the Johannesburg-based politically non-aligned Dance Alliance, has linked up with the National Arts Coalition which will present a new government with guide-lines for a comprehensive arts policy.

The Coalition, a representative and inclusive yet politically independent body, started out in Johannesburg in December 1992 as the National Arts Plenary which transformed into the National Arts Initiative. The NAI held a watershed conference in Durban in December 1993. The NAI dance working group was led by Professor Gary Gordon of Grahamstown University. In Durban former Rhodes University Lecturer and choreographer Lulu Khumalo, newly resident in Johannesburg/Soweto, was elected the Coalition's national representative for dance, joining the representative council which, apart from dance, will serve arts education, art in a community context, arts funding, film, literature, music, theatre, and visual art.

The most significant artistic and culturally momentous development in the past year, as the opening paragraph of this report suggested, emanated from Harare in Zimbabwe. It all began in November 1992 when the Tumbuka Dance Company, taken from the Shona word meaning 'to flower or bloom', was founded under the artistic direction of Britain's Neville Campbell, former artistic director of the Phoenix Dance Company. Tumbuka echoes many of the dilemmas and difficulties experienced all over Africa and specifically South Africa. Within months Campbell produced over a dozen challenging works on a dazzling, predominantly male company of trainee dancers. Five of the eight potently athletic performers are graduates of the National Ballet of Zimbabwe's educational outreach Dance Foundation Course which from 1990 trained twenty-one men and women from the high density areas of Harare townships. Drawn from street dance troupes, community theatre groups, and high-school drop-outs, these dancers parallel the plights and aspirations of millions of South Africans, a small number of whom are gradually being trained in visionary projects. Yet Tumbuka receives no government funding and its director, choreographer, and teacher, Campbell, is caught in the middle of bitter opposition from the die-hard traditionalists, the central government, and the national arts council who see no place for contemporary (i.e Western) theatre dance. One hopes this scenario does not develop in South Africa—despite existing safeguards.

Meanwhile, over in war-scarred Mozambique the **Companhia Nacional de Canto e Danca**, founded in 1975 and gaining professional status and backing by the Ministry of Culture in 1983, has made tremendous progress in finding creative solutions to the problems of transition from authentic forms drawn from the provinces, and moving them into a theatrical setting without alienating the traditionalists.

The Mozambicans, under the direction of David Abilio Mondlane, have toured extensively internationally, are heavily involved in a voter education programme for the 1994 elections, and may make their South African début at a major arts festival in July 1994. In May 1993 the twenty Maputo-based dancers and four musicians forged an important link when they shared a Harare stage with Tumbuka in Zimbabwe, and performed at the five Mozambican refugee camps on the eastern borders. Mozambican dancers have subsequently trained with Tumbuka and soon the exchange may include South Africa.

Africa has its own artistic hazards—notably the curio syndrome which trivializes ritual and cultural expression for international currency—and still untapped riches. As new generations of choreographer and dancer in the southern zone are exposed for the first time to highly evolved Western modern dance training, they are developing their individual brand of new dance infused with a distinctive cultural ethos and organic multicultural-ism. Make way world!

Australia

JILL SYKES

At a time when there have been significant changes in the leadership of Australia's smaller dance groups, the enthusiasm of the federal arts funding body, the Australia Council, for individual and project grants, has resulted in some new entrants and diverse presentations on the Australian dance scene. Quite where it will take the art-form, if anywhere, remains to be seen: there is little opportunity for ensemble development over such short rehearsal periods and often no chance of follow-up productions to build on what was achieved as a starting-point. In the short term, however, it adds to the breadth and richness of dance in this country, encouraging independent artists to test their ideas on an audience and even providing a springboard for a few small companies to emerge.

One of these has been the **Australian Choreographic Ensemble**, better known as ACE, a long-held dream of Paul Mercurio, a former member of the Sydney Dance Company and star of the film *Strictly Ballroom*. He launched ACE in Sydney in 1992 with a handful of interesting dancers and his first full evening work, *Contact*, offered some promising and accessible dance-theatre concepts despite signs of an overlong gestation period.

Living up to its title and aims of providing an outlet for a variety of choreographers, ACE combined the efforts of four creative artists, Paul Mercurio, Stephen Page, Carolyn Hammer, and Jan Pinkerton for its most interesting work of 1993, *Imprint*. Even so, the workshop basis tethered the presentation in a way that suggested it might take years at this rate for the level of choreographic sophistication to equal the quality of the dancing. Will ACE get that chance?

On the other side of the continent, in Perth, the **Chrissie Parrott Dance Company** (formerly Collective) is battling for greater continuity whilst producing some lively and eclectic programmes. *Life, Love and Beauty* was one of these: an evanescent exploration of its titular themes through seductively graceful movement and striking imagery. It shared the contrasting double bill with her savage, theatrical attack on television as a killer of creativity, *Sabotage—The Box*.

It is an inescapable fact of Australian life that too few of this vast country's performing artists are seen nation-wide. Chrissie Parrott's company reached Sydney in 1993 only as a major element of a cabaret collaboration with singer Robyn Archer, *See Ya Next Century*, for the Sydney Festival.

Similarly, the **Meryl Tankard Australian Dance Theatre** (retitled to include her name since she took over as artistic director at the beginning of 1993) toured interstate from its Adelaide base as a pivotal part of the Australian Opera's bold new production of *Orpheus and Eurydice*, which was directed by Stefan Lazaridis with a significant contribution from Tankard. Her Dance of the Furies is a vivid evocation of rage, with the performers leaping and clinging to a giant revolving wall. In what she called a 'year of dancing dangerously', Tankard had her dancers swinging from ropes in the company's major new production, *Furioso*. In her first venture for a larger group with an even mix of male and female performers, she had notable success in extending the physicality of her bold and vigorous choreographic ideas but they have yet to reach their full potential.

Dance Canberra, which was formed to fill that city's vacant dance residency after Tankard's departure, has established a contrasting, far more cerebral style under the artistic direction of Sue Healey. Her first work for the new company, *Utter Heart*, was subtle and restrained yet rich in the choreographic expression of emotions.

Meanwhile, the previous artistic director of the Australian Dance Theatre has formed a touring group bearing his name, **Leigh Warren and Dancers**, after a defiantly impressive farewell programme with ADT, which included, for the first time by an Australian company, a presentation of a William Forsythe ballet, *Enemy in the Figure*. On its début tour, the new group depended on established works, including Warren's striking version of Petrushka.

The **One Extra Company** has produced some interesting and individual works under the direction of Graeme Watson since 1992, notably those which have involved older dancers. *Cats Step Softly*, inspired by the poetry and life of Jack Kerouac, featured Patrick Harding-Irmer and Watson himself in a memorable piece of dance theatre: hard-shelled with a vulnerably sensitive centre. *Blossoms and Wrinkles* brought together two generations of performers, with the senior dancers—Mary Duchesne, Chrissie Koltai, Harding-Irmer, and Watson—tending to steal the show.

But it was not only the changes of director which pumped adrenalin into Australian dance. Russell Dumas, for example, created in 1993 what is arguably his best work for **Dance Exchange**, which he founded with Nanette Hassall in 1976. In *Surround*, Dumas ambushed his audience by decentralizing his dancers in a low-key but concentrated blend of dance, imagery, and content.

Dance North, based in Townsville under Cheryl Stock's continuing direction, not only built on its repertory of works balanced between local and universal themes, but developed its links with Vietnam in a remarkable project. The whole company presented joint performances with the Hanoi Ballet, and took part in a month-long residency to work with company members and students in creating a collaborative piece.

The **West Australian Ballet** celebrated its fortieth anniversary in 1993, with its founder, Kira Bousloff, a vivacious focus of the celebrations, and a new *Hamlet* by their artistic director, Barry Moreland, a substantial indication of the company's performing strengths. As is the way with dance companies throughout the world, however, he had to postpone a multiple bill with commissioned works to make way for a revenue-raising *Nutcracker* at the end of the year.

With **Queensland Ballet's** characteristic mix of old and new in themes and choreography, and under the pragmatic guidance of their artistic director, Harold Collins, they ranged from a much-praised staging of *Giselle* by Garth Welch to a new three-act version of *The Tempest*. This had a commissioned score by Carl Vine and choreography by Jacqui Carroll, who combined excerpts from Shakespeare's text with her dance realization of spirits and humans.

At the **Sydney Dance Company**, Graeme Murphy carried forward his determined push to involve musicians in performance by creating a full-length work around the percussion group, Synergy. *Synergy with Synergy* was the highlight of the SDC's programme for 1992. In 1993 Murphy drew most interestingly on his earlier, quirkier sculptural style to develop a stream of atmospheric cameos in *The Protecting Veil*, a title drawn from its accompanying music by John Tavener.

The **Australian Ballet** has maintained its level of technical excellence to such a standard that stylistic expectations are raised to meet it—and frustratingly not always realized. After a burst of creativity in 1992—Graeme Murphy's new *Nutcracker* was described in the previous issue of this publication, and Gideon Obarzanek's less spectacular but promising short work,

Sand Siren, was premièred at the end of the year—the company settled back into established repertory for 1993.

Don Quixote was an improvement on its last revival (despite the stodgy new set for the town square) but it has never equalled the vitality of its early stagings by Rudolf Nureyev. A Balanchine addition, *Symphony in C*, while technically accomplished, lacked the style that makes this ballet a masterwork. It was that sort of year: so near and yet so far for much of the time.

Finally, though, came a full evening of ballets by Jiří Kylián: *Sinfonietta*, *Nuages* (both new to the company), *Symphony in D*, and *Forgotten Land*. The dancers seized on their expressive possibilities and performed them with fervour as well as finesse, completing the 1993 schedule with an artistic success which counteracted the public airing of company discontent about the directorial style of Maina Gielgud, artistic director for the past eleven years. After being accused of favouritism, maternalism, and a lack of respect for the senior dancers, Gielgud resolved publicly to take a more formal approach to running the company, leaving more of the detail to ballet staff while maintaining her overall commitment and involvement in upholding its standards.

Sian Stokes and Adam Marchant of the Australian Ballet in *Forgotten Land*.

In the Company of Angels, performed by Danceworks.   PHOTO: DAVID B. SIMMONDS

Around the nation, there seems to be no slackening of dance activity. There has been consolidation in the area of Aboriginal and Torres Strait Islander dance by **Bangarra Dance Theatre** and the **Aboriginal Islander Dance Theatre**. Asian influences have continued to make an impact, with Chandrabhanu's **Bharatam Dance Company** entering the mainstream arena at the 1993 Melbourne International Festival, butoh dance in the out-back with Tess de Quincey's *Square of Infinity* on the dried bed of Lake Mungo, and Malaysian-born Chinese dancer Chin Kham Yoke bringing Japanese traditions to her arresting *Naratic Visions*—just to give three examples. **Tasdance, Danceworks, Outlet Dance, Expressions, 2 Dance Plus,** and **Dark Swan** are outstanding amongst the habitually underfunded but inventive and energetic groups which have continued to make a contribution to the art-form and to audience appreciation of it.

As in any country, there are stylistic divisions and attitudes which tend to split the dance community and prevent its members acting as a unified lobby for greater financial support from governments. Yet there can be closer ties, as the inaugural Green Mill Dance Project illustrated in January 1993. Held in Melbourne and with dance activist and educator Dr Peter Brinson as the keynote speaker, it brought together an unprecedented range of dance practitioners and non-performing contributors over twelve days of creative sessions, forums, classes, and performances. The pivotal organizer, Shirley McKechnie, chairperson of Ausdance, the Australian Dance Council, referred to it as a kind of 'creative broth'. A year later, the second such event took place and plans are under way for the third in 1995. Its development could affect the shape of dance in Australia.

Austria

EDITH M. WOLF PEREZ

Although Elena Tchernichova did not prove a lucky hand during her directorship of the **Ballet of the Vienna Staatsoper**, she left the ballet with an artistic success. In the second year of her directorship she choreographed *Giselle* as an alpine fairy-tale in black and white with sets by Ingulf Bruun, costumes by Clarisse Praun-Maylunas. Not only did the soloists of the performance, Brigitte Stadler and Vladimir Malakhov, earn the much-deserved enthusiasm of the audience but so did the *corps de ballet*. Despite the many conflicts she had with the director of the Staatsoper, the union, and the dancers, Elena Tchernichova had achieved what she had set out to do in the first place: to improve the technical standard of dancing in the company.

Thus when Anne Woolliams took up the artistic direction of the ballet this autumn she had a company with remarkable soloists and a well-prepared *corps de ballet*. Her repertory policy is orientated towards modern works, and she started her first season with a busy schedule of premières. Her connections with Stuttgart were acknowledged through guest performances by Richard Cragun and Birgit Keil in *Enas*, a choreography which Marcia Haydée had created for the two former soloists of the Stuttgart Ballet. Last season Renato Zernatto, choreographer (and maybe soon director) of the Stuttgart Ballet, had staged the short ballet *Voyage* for the first soloist of the ballet of the Vienna Staatsoper, Vladimir Malakhov. It was premièred in October in Vienna. In the spring two more short pieces will be premièred: *The Wonderful Mandarin* to the choreography of Uwe Scholz and *Empty Spaces* by Renato Zanella.

In November the opening of *Manon*, the full-length ballet of this season, was very well received by press and audience alike. Restaged in its original choreography by Kenneth MacMillan (1974), the ballet received new sets and costumes by Peter Farmer, who chose brown-grey tones as the principal colours. It was a clever choice on the part of the new director, because the choreography is a show-case for a number of soloists who gave splendid performances on the opening night.

Svetlana Kuznetsova as Manon played all the shadows of the role—playful, hedonistic, innocent, and seductive. Vladimir Malakhov is very convincing as the naïve lover Des Grieux as well as in his transformation from an innocent student to a thief and murderer. The *pas de deux* between them are a sheer joy to watch. Tamás Solymosi is a new soloist in the ballet; as Lescaut he left an excellent impression, as did Jan Stripling as Monsieur G. M. and Maurizio Gianetti as beggar-king. The scenes for the *corps de ballet* were loosely rehearsed—or have the dancers again lost the discipline so much admired in *Giselle*?

Another success story comes from Innsbruck, where Eva-Maria Lerchenberg-Thöny has firmly established her new **Tanztheater Company**. The majority of her choreographies are reflections on social and political issues, which the company is able to deliver with emotional intensity. Their impact, however, is never achieved by bold expressionism but by repetition and increase of speed and attack. Quite in contrast to her habitual style of choosing tragic themes for her choreographies, Lerchenberg-Thöny's latest première also showed her humorous side. In *Bahnhof* she explored comic encounters at a railway station. In their ongoing attempt to win new audiences for dance the company went to the station in Innsbruck to perform the *Bahnhof* piece there—much to the enjoyment of the travellers, it seems. The second part of the double bill however, showed again the political consciousness of the choreographer: *Rosa Winter* told the story of a Romany woman who survived the concentration camp in the Second World War.

Tanztheater in *Rosa Winter*, choreographed by Eva-Maria Lerchenberg-Thöny.

Canada

MICHAEL CRABB

The celebration in November 1993 of **Toronto Dance Theatre**'s twenty-fifth anniversary could not have come at a better time for Canadian dance. With the economy still in the grip of a severe recession with its concomitant reductions in arts funding and corporate sponsorship, the dance community needed something to cheer about.

Toronto Dance Theatre (TDT) is effectively Canada's only mainstream modern-dance troupe. Although it is a long time since its co-founders—

David Earle, Patricia Beatty, and Peter Randazzo—worked in an overtly Grahamesque style, their respect for Martha Graham's movement principles and humanistic approach to the art have remained.

When it was launched, TDT and its school soon became a rallying point for those seeking an alternative to Canada's established ballet companies. As Karen Kain, Canada's pre-eminent ballerina, recalls: 'It was a revelation. The movement was so organic, so rooted in real human feelings.' It played a key role in stimulating a modern dance movement in Canada yet, ironically, by the early 1980s the company was being openly derided by a younger and more individualistic generation of avant-garde choreographers as old-fashioned. TDT continued, against all post-modern logic, to insist that dance could and should be beautiful. It thus reached the unenviable position of being seen by the new dance revolutionaries as 'establishment'. Fortunately, despite chronic financial problems, TDT stuck to its guns and continued to present dance that was expressive, often dramatic, and rooted in a discernible technique. The company also nurtured a new choreographer within its midst, Christopher House, who will succeed Earle as artistic director in June 1994.

The success of TDT's two-week twenty-fifth anniversary home-town season—a range of works spanning the company's entire creative history— was a vindication of the company's dogged refusal to grasp at passing dance fads. Critics noted, not without some surprise, how well the older works, many unseen for years, held up. The company then moved on to New York where its six-performance run at the Joyce Theatre was sold out even before opening night.

Yet, while TDT has retaken the high ground of Canadian modern dance, the peripheral scene of smaller troupes and multitudinous independent dancer-choreographers remains a fertile and important territory for the discovery of new ideas and forms of dance expression. Some of the most interesting of these are slowly emerging from the multicultural ferment which is so central to the character of Canada's urban communities. It is a ferment from which many art-dance choreographers have remained oddly aloof, bolstered in their monopoly of what meagre public resources have existed by government-funding policies, which for many years cavalierly dismissed from eligibility Spanish, Indian classical, Ukrainian, African, or any other expression that could be categorized as 'ethnic' dance.

Now, however, the grip of a once confidently dominant white, anglo-culture, with its own culturally derived notions of what constitutes 'art', is rapidly loosening, and over the past few years we have been seeing not only recognition of different cultural traditions but interesting cross-overs between these and more conventionally acknowledged forms.

Perhaps because of its very obvious formal complexities and rich tradition, Indian classical dance has enjoyed a respected position within the broader dance community here. Now such exponents as Menaka Thakkar,

Sean Marye and Coralee McLaren of the Toronto Dance Theatre in *Artemis Madrigals*, choreographed by Christopher House.   PHOTO: CYLLA VAN TIEDMANN

Lata Pada, and Deepti Gupta are experimenting with their own traditions, combining different regional styles and also integrating them with Western modern dance compositional forms and vocabulary.

Pada and Gupta's *Panchabhoota*, for example, explored the expressive possibilities of combining Bharat Natyam and Kathak styles. Thakkar in her latest work, *Shapes and Rhythms*, dressed her eleven dancers in simple costumes that allowed a much broader range of movement and, while retaining many gestural elements of Indian dance, set her company moving in elaborate complex stage patterns, to an original score by Ron Allen, that mixed Western and South Asian rhythms.

Canadian dancers and choreographers of African heritage are also starting to gain recognition for their exploration of new expressive forms. Montreal-based Zab Maboungou has conducted extensive research into a variety of African dance traditions. In her latest solo work, *Reverdanse*, Maboungou stripped away the showy, super-energized image of African dance made popular by various folkloric troupes and offered an intimate dance dialogue between herself and the evocative rhythms generated by her two drummers. Maboungou achieved what many early American modern dance pioneers had sought in exploring what they called 'exotic' forms, reaching a point where music and movement appear to connect in an elemental celebration of life.

You could hardly look for a more striking contrast of dance traditions than to fly west to Canada's prairies where in October 1993 the **Royal Winnipeg Ballet** added a new staging of *The Sleeping Beauty* to its growing repertory of full-length classics. The ballet's artistic director, John Meehan, had hoped to present a new production of *Don Quixote* in 1992 but the costs involved became the flashpoint for a smouldering back-office tussle between Meehan and the RWB's general manager, William Riske. In the end, Riske left, to be replaced by the respected American arts administrator, Jeffrey Bentley. Meehan, however, still did not get his Cervantes. It was one of a number of factors, personal and professional, which eventually led Meehan to resign, but not before he had found another way of putting a big stamp on the repertory.

The Sleeping Beauty—with sets and costumes hired from Salt Lake City's **Ballet West** for a fraction of the cost of a new production—was, as Meehan described it, his 'parting gift'. With a bit of judicious editing to bring the production in at two and a half hours, Meehan and his associate in the project, Georgina Parkinson, settled for a very straightforward dramatic treatment focusing attention on very expressive dancing from the twenty-seven-member troupe, augmented by students from the RWB's professional school.

Meehan left Winnipeg on 31 October 1993 and his successor, William Whitener, started work the next day. The choice of Whitener took many people by surprise. He had just completed a season as director of Montreal's **Les Ballets Jazz** and as a dancer was best remembered in Canada for his years with Twyla Tharp. Whitener, however, had been a protégé of Robert Joffrey and begun his career dancing everything from Balanchine and Ashton to Ailey and Sokolow. Whitener's wide-ranging experience and the excellent reputation he had quickly

The Royal Winnipeg Ballet performing *Angels in the Architecture*, choreographed by Mark Godden.   PHOTO: PAUL MARTENS

established in Montreal no doubt convinced the RWB that he was the best choice.

Whitener says he will continue to promote the work of the Ballet's resident choreographer, Mark Godden, who during the 1992–3 season also created a work for Montreal's **Les Grands Ballets Canadiens**, and will continue to programme a mixture of classic and contemporary works. Among Whitener's plans is a restaging of Ashton's *Façade* to be supervised by Alexander Grant who, sadly, although a Canadian citizen, has hardly worked here since his unhappy departure from the **National Ballet** a decade ago.

Whitener's honeymoon in Winnipeg, however, could be brief and brutal. The RWB is almost $450,000 in debt and has to bolster box-office revenues without incurring heavy production costs. It will take all Whitener's patience and ingenuity to accomplish this.

The RWB has always prided itself on its flexibility, in being able to go from *The Sleeping Beauty* on big city stages to compact, mixed bills suitable for smaller communities. It may begin to find some competition for that

Cherice Barton of the Alberta Ballet in John Butler's *Carmina Burana*.   PHOTO: DAVID COOPER

section of the touring market from the **Alberta Ballet**, based in Calgary. The eighteen-dancer troupe, miraculously free of debt, has just begun to perform with live orchestra and under its director, Ali Pourfarrokh, has developed a distinctive style that shows particularly well in neo-classical and cross-over ballet-modern works.

The Toronto-based **National Ballet of Canada**, although still saddled with a hefty debt, has continued to weather tough economic times remarkably well, notably presenting new works by John Neumeier (*Now and Then* set to Ravel's *Piano Concerto in G Major*, February 1992) and James Kudelka (Bela Bartok's *The Miraculous Mandarin*, May 1993). Neumeier, with the company's senior ballerina, Karen Kain, as his muse, offered an abstracted yet intensely humane ballet about loss and the passage of time. Kudelka, the National Ballet's artist-in-residence, took an unusual and controversial approach to *The Miraculous Mandarin*, turning it into a portrait of a dysfunctional family in which the mother, Kain again in the first case, procures her son as a sexual plaything for perverted visitors.

The National Ballet has not added any new evening-length productions to its repertory since *The Taming of the Shrew* in 1992 but in November 1993 it did restage Erik Bruhn's version of *La Sylphide* with more elaborate sets and costumes by Desmond Heeley, borrowed from American Ballet Theater. It has also received private funding to redesign completely Cranko's *Romeo and Juliet* and is planning, after thirty seasons, to replace the company founder, Celia Franca's, staging of *The Nutcracker* with a new version, probably to be produced by Kudelka.

China

OU JIAN-PING

In the cultural life of China, particularly of Beijing where twenty song-and-dance companies have been located for the past forty years, theatre dance has always been a very popular phenomenon, even a symbol of cultural elegance. The best example was the stimulating scene in the spring of 1993 when over 12,000 beautiful boys and girls vied with each other in the audition for 120 places at the Associate School of the Beijing Dance Academy. The sad tears of those eliminated and the financial sacrifices which parents of these young would-be dancers were prepared to make (the cost would be Y60,000 when the average monthly salary of an ordinary Chinese parent is no more than Y300), showed how much theatre dance is regarded as a glorious art by the Chinese people.

At the Beijing Dance Academy (BDA), the first Modern Dance Major was established in September 1993 under the Choreography Department, based on experiences gathered from its one-semester Modern Dance

Experimental Workshop in 1991. The faculty members include Zhang Shou-he, a graduate from the Choreography Department of BDA and a Modern Dance Major from the Dance School at the Hong Kong Academy for Performing Arts; Wang Mei, a graduate from the Folk Dance Department of BDA and Guangdong Modern Dance Company's early training programme; and this writer, one of the first MAs in Dance in China and a twice participant in the Dance Critics Conference and the Improvization and Choreography courses at the American Dance Festival in 1988 and 1993. Dr George Jackson, the well-known American dance critic and historian, was the first foreign expert invited to lecture to the twenty regular students, enrolled from all over China after a strict audition and a series of entrance examinations in cultural courses. Thus, the first fledgling modern dance company can be expected to emerge from Beijing, a metropolitan city in northern China as well as the political and cultural capital of China. Following in the footsteps of its established elder brother in southern China, the Guangdong Modern Dance Company, it will raise the status of modern dance in China from regional to national level. Already, the geographical advantage of Beijing is evident; in November 1993 the students had a splendid opportunity to revive the training system of the 'Father of Chinese New Dance', Mr Wu Xiao-bang, and to record it on video.

Once more, recent seasons on the Chinese dance stage proved very busy. The biggest event, which took place between 25 November and 5 December 1992, was the First All-China Dance Drama Festival in Shenyang. This is an important heavy-industry city in northern China, where companies from all over the country presented thirteen full-length dance dramas. Dance drama as a form was created some forty years ago in the mode of Russian classical ballet and with some influence from Chinese traditional operatic dance. Gradually it has taken on more of Chinese and contemporary characteristics, not only in its literary themes but also in its movement vocabularies, and the ontological entity of dance, treating the fundamental reasons why dance could and should exist and endure. Among the thirteen dance dramas presented at this festival, all were Chinese, and five were contemporary: *A Village Girl Named Jujube Flower* from Dalian, *Echo in the Polar Region* from Liaoning, *The Fifth Daughter* from Jiangsu, and *A Memorial Ceremony for the Red Wintersweet* from Chengdu. An interesting question arises amid the transient glamour of this festival: how is it that this most expensive and thus often short-lived form of dance drama survives when, over the past hundred years, the Western classical ballet has had to meet the challenge of survival and the Chinese Traditional Opera is also experiencing its most serious crisis in recent years?

Contrary to this heavy and expensive form of dance drama, another light and less costly dance form, Fable Dance, was born in a tiny coal-mining town in North China named Gujiao City. The eight fable dances on the stage were all quite familiar to the audience, so we could sit down quietly, thinking attentively how well the dance was used to retell the fables, and at the same time associating them with the situations around us. The first piece, *Three Monks*, was a very clever and significant appetizer, in which we saw three comic monks, living in a far-from-water-source temple, competing to see who was lazier, and who would be reckless enough to steal the sacrificial water for the Bodhisattva on their sacred altar. The creators' intention was obvious when placing this work at the very beginning of the whole evening programme; the present 'everyone has the same meal' employment system in mainland China should cease to exist as soon as possible.

The Chinese army dance has always projected its dazzling charm over the past forty years, not only through its well-trained male dancers, but also through its brightly shining female dancers. In the past seasons, two well-known female dancing stars, Liu Min and Shen Pei-yi, from the Song and Dance Ensemble of the General Political Department of the People's Liberation Army, presented two separate dance concerts in the spring of 1993, each launching a different aesthetic attack upon the audience.

Liu is the only dancer to win three all-China dance championships, and has been famous for her strong technique and ability to create heroic characters. Moreover, several representative works were created for her in the 1980s, a time of drastic changes following the end of the Cultural Revolution. One of these, choreographed by Jiang Hua-xuan, a prominent army choreographer, was danced at this concert and must be mentioned. Jiang's *Zhao Jun Goes Beyond the Great Wall* is based on a theme which has been popular in traditional Chinese opera since the thirteenth century. Based on a historical legend, it depicts the homesickness and resentment against an incompetent regime felt by a princess of the Han Dynasty (206 BC–AD 220), who was forced to marry a Mongolian king in order to put a stop to border wars. By emphasizing Liu's tall stature and heroic presence, the choreographer bravely changed his heroine's originally bitter attitude towards her marriage into a totally positive willingness to marry a foreign prince for the noble purpose of peace. Liu used a huge, billowing cloak and a traditional rippling step called 'Floating on the Water Surface' to symbolize the long distance she resolutely covered, whilst her flying-to-the-sky, long white sleeves, and her off-balance, whirlwind spins effectively evoked the tears of her homesickness. Nevertheless, the biggest challenge for Liu at this concert was the only contemporary piece, *Purple Colour*, innovatively choreographed by an unknown young choreographer named Yang Wei. Having no narrative underpinnings, which placed greater emphasis on musicality and movement design, it thus seemed very fresh and striking to the audience.

In contrast to Liu, Shen Pei-yi both danced and choreographed. Well known for her delicate nuances and excellence in creating tragic characters,

Liu Min in *Zhao Jun Goes
Beyond the Great Wall*,
choreographed by Jiang
Hua-xuan

she, consciously or not, gave stage life to all the typically oriental images of
beautiful women in a strictly traditional sense; beautiful in face, sick in
body, weak in momentum, and sentimental in soul, which always arouses
so much sympathy and aesthetic feeling among the audience. *My Bed, My
Coffin*, a solo choreographed by Liu Ying, another outstanding army choreographer, proved the best piece to demonstrate her capacity for depicting
tragedy, whilst an ensemble led by herself, *Emotional Up and Down*, was her
maiden work as a choreographer.

Ideally, dance should be something beyond politics; but in fact, politics
sometimes does promote dance. As the international cold war was ended,
the relationship between Mainland China and Taiwan and Hong Kong
became closer and closer. It so happened that during the past seasons, all
the three modern dance personalities—Henry Yu, the only Chinese who
once danced with Martha Graham and taught as her assistant, Liu Feng-
shueh, a descendent from the root of German Modern Dance and with a
Ph.D. from the Laban Centre, and Lin Hwai-min, another Graham inspired
Chinese and the founder of the first Taiwan-based modern dance company,
Cloud Gate Dance Theatre—came to dance in Beijing and other big cities
in Mainland China. Each came with their own companies, each displaying
his or her unique background, individual understanding, and respective
contribution to the development of Chinese Modern Dance. Roughly
speaking, Yu's dances were more movement-oriented and Graham-based,
thus fairly stimulating on the stage; Liu's works seemed more of a conscious combination of both Chinese traditional movements and the

German Modern Dance concept of three-dimensional space, in this way quite dazzling to our visual senses. Liu's representative dance theatre *Legacy*, created in 1978 and popular in Mainland China for the past ten years through videos, struck us as more experimental in its natural but well-selected movements and its symbolic associations, therefore minimalist in form but provocative in content.

In September 1992 the Hong Kong Contemporary Dance Company made a very successful visit to Dalian, Shenyang, Beijing, and Tianjin with two well-mixed programmes. They included: *When I Need You, Long Sleeves, Young Sky*, and *Wanderings In The Cosmos* by Willy Tsao, its founder-director and resident choreographer. *Exits and Entrances* by Helen Lai, another Hong Kong-based choreographer, and *Soirée* by the American choreographer, John Mead. The seamless blending of Chinese and Western concepts and vocabularies in Tsao's dances and Mead's purely American energy and momentum produced a beautiful and comfortable contrast. On another level, these two male choreographers' bold and unconstrained spirits illuminated the female sensitivity and insight of Lai's work in a pleasant way.

Continuing with these peaceful international visits, the Chinese audience were fortunate enough to witness the high-quality performances by the Korea Contemporary Dance Company, the Israeli Kibbutz Contemporary Dance Company and Vietnam's Traditional Music, Dance and Song Theatre; each becoming it's nation's first cultural ambassador since their Governments set up formal or normal diplomatic relations with China.

In the summer of 1994, China will be honoured to hold the Beijing International Dance Event, which includes an International Festival for Dance Academies and an International Dance Conference. An efficient organizing committee has been established and all the preparations are progressing smoothly. Lu Yi-sheng, Chairman of Beijing Dance Academy, has been appointed Executive Chairman of the Festival while Zi Hua-yun, Director of the Beijing-located Dance Research Institute, has been appointed Director of the Conference, and I, Ou Jian-ping, the Conference's Secretary-General.

Cuba

JANE KING

Hard currency—a foreign tour to finance a new work—that is what every Cuban company dreams of, works for. Salaries and premises are guaranteed still, but without that hard currency there is not a shoe, not a pair of tights, a metre of cloth, a cassette, a light bulb, paper for publicity, petrol for transport—until, in 1993, Pablo Milanese, Cuba's great revolutionary singer, with fees from his many successful foreign tours, established a fund to support artistic enterprises at home.

One of the first to avail himself of the fund, the dancer and choreographer Narciso Medina, has set up his own dance centre, the Estudio-Academia de la Danza Narciso Medina. It occupies two rooms and the patio of a shabby but gracious old house in Vedado, Havana. A dancer distinguished for his talent and his fine physique, Medina is an idealist who seeks to involve in his project all young people with a taste for dance theatre. Already he has enrolled more than 200 students who are taught in small groups by himself and members of his company from morning to evening throughout the week. The enthusiasm which this project has engendered was evident at the launching of Medina's new work, *Como el Ave Fénix*, at the Mella Theatre in November 1993. A flamboyant, sprawling mixture of magic realism, social comment, folklore, and philosophy, starring Medina himself, and performed by a mixed cast of professionals and students of Medina's own Gestos Transitorios method, the work attracted a youthful audience whose response was positive and vocal.

Marianela Boán's work for her well-established company, **Danza Abierta**, is small-scale, intellectual, and tightly structured. An actress as well as a dancer, she is mistress of speech and mime, and her two most recent pieces, both solos, have strong dramatic impact. *Gaviota* (loosely inspired by *Jonathan Livingstone Seagull*) and *Fast Food* deliver a serious message with the voice and gesture of a skilled comedienne. *Gaviota* is a thirty-minute danced monologue, witty in word and movement. *Fast Food* makes a satirical, tragi-comic comment, in four minutes, and to Beethoven, on the survival diet of Cubans during the harshest year of the 'special period'.

Retazos, founded in 1987 by the Ecuadorian dancer and choreographer, Isabel Bustos, now inhabits a small community centre in a side street close to Havana's giant Teatro Nacional. Classes, in which poetry predominates, take place on a floor tiled in marble, and there is a small stage. Bustos's lyrical piece, *Ah que tu escapes*, inspired by a poem of Lezama Lima, was performed by her attractive young company, as in a dream, to an exquisite sound collage, in the large Mella Theatre. But the problems involved during this difficult period in working in theatres resulted in a decision to become a 'chamber group', and to use their rehearsal space for their next production, Bustos's enigmatic dance drama, *La Casa de Maria*. Like Boán, Bustos claims that her work is more akin to drama than to dance, and she seeks, with the use of everyday gesture, to 'interpret universal problems'. Retazos too is a company which attracts a discriminating audience, and does not disappoint. Latin-American critics speak approvingly of the 'neo-expressionism of the Caribbean' in Retazos's work.

Lesme Grenot, an exciting young dancer with both ballet and contemporary experience, created two popular pieces for Laura Alonso's New Choreographers programmes before forming his own group, of four dancers and a graphic designer, **Fuera de Balance**, in 1993. *Unidos* is a *pas de deux*, originally for two men, now for a man and a woman, in which heart and mind are locked in a struggle to remain in accord. In Grenot's own solo, *Un Cuerpo, un Salto*, a man, like a broken bird, strives heroically to fly. In all their work Grenot and his company display the innovative technical and serious philosophical concerns of Cuba's young experimental artists, creating bravely with minimal resources.

Shortage of petrol and of vehicles in good repair have made touring within Cuba virtually impossible, but happily the Thirtieth Anniversary Festival of the Conjunto Folklorico Nacional in May 1993 brought **Danza Libre** to Havana: a fourteen-hour coach journey from Guantanamo in temperatures of over 30°C. This company, just four years old, and formerly known as **Conjunto de Danzas de Guantánamo**, is the only company in Cuba to include both folk and contemporary works in its repertory. On their first visit to the capital the Guantanameros astonished the Habañeros with the ferocity of their *Rebellion*, the skill and the gaiety of their *Chancletas*, performed in the open air, and the elegance and originality of the contemporary works they showed in the theatres. The greatest surprise of all was to find on the programmes—a rare luxury these days (paper is almost unobtainable)—the name of the great Ramiro Guerra, Cuba's first contemporary dancer, pupil of Martha Graham, and creator in 1959 of Cuba's first **Modern Dance Company** (today the **Danza Contemporanea Nacional**). It was Danza Libre's director, Elfrida Mahler, a colleague of Ramiro's in Danza Moderna's early days, who finally persuaded him to leave his academic studies in Havana and take a plane to provincial Guantánamo, to work with her dancers on a revival of his *Suite Yoruba* (1960), a classic of Cuban choreography—modern dance based on a Yoruba folklore theme.

Out of this visit came a new Ramiro Guerra work, a hilarious satire on the current social scene which reduces audiences everywhere to helpless laughter. *Tiempo de Quimera* grew out of the choreographer's improvisation workshops with Danza Libre, whose dancers, he says, reminded him of the youthful eagerness of those with whom he started to create in 1959.

1993 was Ramiro's year. A biography, *Ramiro Guerra y la Danza en Cuba*, published in Ecuador, provided, largely in interview form, outlines of his career, his works, his theories, his methods, and the rich research to be found in his writings on dance and the theatre, from antiquity to William Forsythe. The author, Fidel Pajares, worked with his subject as pupil, dancer, and finally biographer. Guerra's own book, *De la Teoría de la Danza*, to be published in Venezuela in 1994—the paper shortage again!—contains a collection of essays ending with *Del Posmodernismo en la Danza*. Ramiro Guerra is a dance scholar and practitioner of universal significance. Publishers and translators from the Spanish, please note.

This year it is necessary to give space to those experimental companies of whom little is known outside Latin America, even Cuba itself. For them, in this deprived period, survival seems sometimes little short of miraculous. Next year there are still others who must be given more attention: Lorna Burdsall, another of Ramiro's Danza Moderna pioneers, and her group, **Asi Somos**; Rosario Cárdenas and **Danza Combinatoria**, abstract and elegant; Laura Alonso, director of the ever-expanding **Pro Danza Centre**, home of the **Joven Guardia**. Laura has won her long battle for a bigger, better building to house her multifarious activities. She has moved them all to a magnificent, crumbling mansion in Marianao, some distance from the city centre, and is appealing for donations—for pots of white paint, obtainable only with dollars! The Joven Guardia is now directed by Laura's son, Iván Monreal, who choreographs both for his own company and for the **National Ballet**, where his grandmother, the *prima ballerina assoluta*, Alicia Alonso, dances roles which he creates for her.

The forty-fifth anniversary of Alonso's first performance of *Giselle* was celebrated in November last year with a week of performances in Havana's Gran Teatro, and commemorative performances in theatres throughout the island. The National Ballet have been frequent visitors to Spain since their appearance in Madrid in 1992 at the 500th Anniversary Celebrations. Alicia Alonso, director of the **Cuban Ballet** and now also Professor of Ballet at the seventy-seven-year-old Complutence University, is often in Madrid, giving master classes and organizing the Alicia Alonso degree courses. These started in October 1993, and are taught by Cuban professors and other invited specialists. Many leading Cuban choreographers and teachers are working abroad, and this, combined with the ever-increasing difficulties of obtaining materials for shoes and costumes, has resulted in very little new work being produced at home. In compensation, however, there has been a welcome development in the promotion of a number of younger members of the company to leading roles. Fortunately there are still impressive, gold-medal-winning students graduating from the national school to fill the places of some of the brilliant young dancers at present under contract to major companies abroad.

The National Ballet and the **Conjunto Folklórico**, both with studios close to Havana's sea wall, suffered severely when the April floods created havoc in their classrooms, workshops, and wardrobes. Fortunately the water reached no further than the entrance to the Mella Theatre, where the Folklórico were making preparations for their Thirtieth Anniversary Festival, postponed from 1992. In May, twenty-three dance groups, six theatre companies, and eleven music groups performed, over ten days, in Havana's theatres and sunlit open spaces. The Folklórico themselves presented four new pieces, lively, colourful, and musical as always, before setting off for a triumphal six-week tour of Japan, sponsored by the cultural association, Min On, who sent them back to Cuba with a brochure of magnificent photographs and a warm invitation to return in 1994.

Another great folklore group, **Cutumba**, from Santiago de Cuba, is a favourite visitor in Spain where they tour regularly for three months at a time. At home this year they were not so fortunate. Transport difficulties prevented them from reaching Havana for the Folklore Festival in May, and in November, their eagerly awaited visit to Guantánamo's first-ever dance festival was frustrated by three days of torrential rain, followed by death-dealing floods which cut off all vital services and communications in the Oriente area.

It was not Cuba's happiest year. The weather was cruel. Frustration and hunger were everywhere. But inside every Cuban there is a dancer, and creativity survives. In Cuba they say it too: 'la necesidad es la madre de las invenciones.' Tights, make-up, shoes, cassettes, and much else are still needed. Cuban embassies will always help to send things. It is not politics but a matter of dancers helping dancers.

Editor's Note

Jane King regrets not being able to comment on **Ballet de Camagüey** because of transport difficulties whilst in Cuba last year. As some recompense, we include a photograph of one of their recent productions.

The Ballet de Camagüey of Cuba in *Vivaldiana*, choreographed by José Antonio Chávez.

Denmark

The Royal Danish Ballet

BENT SCHØNBERG

After all the hard work and achievement with the Bournonville Festival, the Royal Theatre aimed high again in the following season which was dedicated to Balanchine. Its impudence was rewarded. The **Royal Ballet** managed to shift from the domestic style of the last century to the extremely different manner of the Russian-American genius. Much of the honour goes, of course, to the guests, Suzanne Farrell and the sisters Colleen and Patricia Neary, who were responsible for many of the productions. However, there was also another important and positive factor—the presence of a handful of young and gifted girls in a multitude never experienced before. The fact that the company creates good male dancers has been known for many, many decades, but a cornucopia of highly talented female dancers, the answer to Mr B's prayers, is something never seen before at this national theatre.

Patricia Neary was responsible for *Serenade*—directed by the master himself in 1957—an inspiring and elegantly cool version without the superfluous sentiments which often have marred this work. Both the speed and the discipline came as near to perfection as the choreographer could have wished.

Ms Neary supervised the excellent *Apollon Musagète*—still danced under this title—in the long version which Balanchine made for the company back in 1931. Nikolaj Hübbe had developed from the uncertain figure he gave some years ago to a majestic, commanding god. Christina Olsson, the company's most recently appointed principal dancer, was a lovely Calliope, Silja Schandorff a moving Terpsichore, and Rose Gad again impressed with her dramatic expression and marvellous technique. Later, Kenneth Greve showed wonderful lines and Caroline Cavallo was an intriguing Polyhymnia.

The *Tchaikovsky Pas de deux* will be remembered for the continually developing Olsson with her glittering pirouettes but she was not too well partnered by Greve who, however, shone with well-executed *grandes jetées*.

Theme and Variations showed the newly returned Aage Thordal Christensen's outstanding musical sense and his fine partnership with Rose Gad, who at the première was less sure in this demanding role but later mastered it. She also sparkled in *Tchaikovsky Piano Concerto No. 2*—the old Ballet Imperial—where she and Thordal suited each other in a lively, dynamic way. Claire Still was elegant and inspiring in front of the company which mastered Balanchine in this satisfying ballet.

Suzanne Farrell, for whom Mr B made *Tzigane* when she returned to his company in 1975 after some seasons in Europe, succeeded in conveying the choreographer's intentions to the company's leading lady, Heidi Ryom. She was more than able to fill the stage alone in that gruelling and long opening scene with her perfectly executed, intricate steps and commanding personality. When Lloyd Riggins appeared they were fascinating in their flirtatious rapture.

It goes without saying that, for a Balanchine festival, *The Sleep Walker* (known also as *La Somnambule* and *Night Shadow*) was a must. Maybe we of the older generations have seen it too often; thirty or forty years ago you could not spit for ladies carrying candles on the international ballet circuit—but today there is no excitement or drama left to tickle the spectator.

By all means, the dancers did what they could. Arne Villumsen, who lent his statuesque body and fascinating personality to the Baron, was just as dramatic as Lis Jeppesen was moving and lovely as the lady in the nightgown. Tommy Frishøi was too young for the nobleman, Silja Schandorff was supremely beautiful. Mette-Ida Kirk was shrewd and calculating as the cocotte and Caroline Cavallo, who took over later, was dangerous, and flaming with jealousy. Riggins was a moving romantic poet, whereas Possokhov was more down to earth.

Anna Lærkesen, the theatre's former *prima ballerina assoluta*, is an outstanding choreographic talent and her first six ballets have all been received with enthusiasm by audiences as well as critics. But for reasons I have never been able to understand, they are very, very seldom danced. Now she has made a new work, *Kindertotenlieder* to Gustav Mahler's music and Friederich Ruckert's songs. Inevitably it will be compared to Tudor's *Dark Elegies*, especially because she, like Tudor, does not tell a story but just shows the feelings.

Two women and two men defend Lærkesen's impressive step language. Lis Jeppesen, who can show stronger sentiment than anyone in that company, is heart-rending in her sorrow, but in a delightfully executed *pas de deux* with Peter Bo Bendixen in the fourth song, you feel the tragedy disappears a little. Olsson had difficulties in inflicting the loss upon us, whereas the young Yuri Possokhov, imported from the Bolshoi, showed highly evolved technique which was overshadowed by his burning and contagious sense of tragedy. The ballet was danced to the piano version; I wish we could see it one day with the full orchestra. Now we are wishing too. . . when will the theatre let Lærkesen make a full-length ballet? She, and all we others as well, deserve it.

During the season, the world's leading character dancer, Niels Bjørn Larsen, former artistic director of the company, celebrated his eightieth birthday. He appeared in one of his ingenious roles, Dr Coppelius, and thereby gained entrance in the *Guinness Book of Records* as the world's oldest active dancer. His TV interviews, which were sent to all European stations, the foreign critics world-wide who flocked to Copenhagen, and a grateful audience, all payed homage to this outstanding artist.

Harald Lander's *Etudes* was directed by Josette Amiel, the former lovely *danseuse étoile* from the Paris Opéra. She is an intelligent, commanding teacher, who has the gift of getting the best out of a dancer, and this version, like the others she does so successfully around the world, is precise and clever. Yet I cannot but wonder why the greatest Danish ballet in this century has to be reborn with the help of a foreign midwife, although it must be admitted that Mlle Amiel's pedagogic talents and respect for this outstanding ballet were impressive. But it was, and is, the Paris version. Why in Terpsichore's name could not we have the Copenhagen one?

Olsson was conspicuously nervous in the beginning but soon shone in that role to which she seems predestined, the *prima ballerina*. Later, Schandorff was surprisingly strong with a marked attack and a flawless execution. Riggins and Greve had more authority than Kobborg and Thordal, though both showed promise of development.

Lise la Cour made her fourth children's ballet again from one of Hans Christian Andersen's fairy-tales. This time it was the tragic *Little Mermaid*. The music was by la Cour's favourite composer, Bent Fabricious Bjerre, who made a special theme for each of the main characters. The world-

Johann Kobborg, Christina Olsson, and Lloyd Riggins of the Royal Danish Ballet in *Etudes*, choreographed by Harald Lander.

famous multi-artist, Bjørn Wiinblad, was responsible for the setting inspired by Andersen's own silhouettes and with the use of his own strong colours and round curves.

This was la Cour's fourth ballet by and for children and it was by far her best one. Wisely she declined to use Disney's sugary ending but instead used the terrible horror story just as the old fairy story-teller himself told it. However, the youthful audience did not seem to mind, and the clever kids on stage, all from the Royal Theatre's school, seemed to like it just as much. These children's ballets seem to have grown into an institution and, hopefully, they will continue.

Helgi Tomasson and Jens Jacob Worsaae made *The Sleeping Beauty* some seasons ago in San Francisco. It was, however, only an introduction to the work the Royal Theatre performed as the last mammoth initiative of Frank Andersen's reign. With more than 250 costumes and overwhelming décor, it was the greatest production the company has staged in its two hundred years or more of history.

Worsaae let the action take place in Russia in the fifteenth century. The opening was in a Byzantine court of the tsars with heavy, warm red and gold colours, icons, furs, and also onion domes which gleamed through the enormous window in the backdrop. The second act, historically correct by the way, and set in the new Russia which came into existence 116 years later, had refined costumes and golden rococo staircases—all the elegance imported from the courts of Louis XIV to Louis XVI.

The success was at the same high level. The audience shrieked and swooned, performances were sold out for the rest of the season, all the young dancers were given chances or had breakthroughs, and the critics raved over the work.

Rose Gad, the theatre's wilful technical ballerina, shone as Aurora and was a worthy opponent to Yuri Possokhov's elegant prince. Silja Schandorff was an even greater hit. Her beauty, her lines, and her confidence showed her as an international ballerina in her own right, and in Kenneth Greve, she was partnered by a prince just as elegant and with technical skills to match hers. As a result, the ballet reached the fairy-tale optimum intended. But if I understand my colleagues right, it was Caroline Cavallo with her fascinating charisma who turned out to be the belle of the immortal story. Her unblemished career took a new step forward when as the princess she was as enchanting as the audience was enchanted by her performance, with the Rose Adagio especially breathtaking. With Lloyd Riggins, that rare thing an intellectual dancer, as her partner, they made an elegant and triumphant romantic couple.

After having been the artistic director of the Royal Ballet for almost ten years, and having been responsible for not a few successes, Frank Andersen's contract was not renewed. As new leader of the company, Peter Schaufuss from the ballet of Deutsche Oper Berlin was appointed as from

Silja Schandorff and Kenneth Greve of the Royal Danish Ballet in *Tornerose*.
PHOTO: DAVID AMZALLAG

August 1994. He was followed by another former principal dancer from the Danish company, Johnny Eliasen, who is to be deputy artistic director together with Lise la Cour, who will continue in this job.

Schaufuss's first action was to fire the leader of the school, Anne Marie Vessel Schlüter, wife of the former Danish Prime Minister, because he wanted to take over that role himself. It was always the responsibility of the artistic director to be head of that department and only Andersen had changed it. It is with the school that the whole future of the Royal, and more or less, Danish Ballet lies. Let them for better or worse change Bournonville's works, the atmosphere, the intentions. Schaufuss has already made two remarkable productions of the old master's inheritance and one not so convincing. But should the next ones be bad even, no catastrophe waits in the wings for the company so long as all Lander's and Brenaa's versions exist on video.

The school will be further strengthened by Schaufuss's success in luring Vivi Flindt back from Dallas to her old theatre which, to the regret of all, she left in 1978. In the future Flindt, together with the artistic director and Eliasen—also a highly regarded pedagogue—will lead the dancers principally in accordance with the teachings of Bournonville, Vaganova, and Volkova.

As long as the old Bournonville school is preserved and lovingly taught, the generations to come in that company will continue to be world class. And so much bigger may the expectations for the future be, as the theatre, under the hyper-dynamic new chief, Michael Christiansen—former permanent under-secretary at the Ministry of Defence—sees its artists score success after success.

Modern Dance

PETER THYGESEN

During the past years, dance life in Denmark outside the Royal Theatre has become strangled by public goodwill and lack of money. From many sides appreciative comments are made of achievements in the alternative dance world throughout the last two decades. Reality shows us a constant and unfair battle with far too small budgets and many too few new productions. This young dance life is exhausted already but still active despite the conditions. As once said by a prominent commentator, modern dance has not really had the chance to show what it is capable of.

It was first and foremost a group of young, foreign dancers and choreographers who, fifteen to twenty years ago, created a Danish dance life outside the Royal Danish Ballet. Many of these pioneers are still working, but for many years they had to live with a striking lack of official support, though their activities, to a very high degree, changed the conception of dance in the Scandinavian countries. Today, conditions for the relatively small companies have improved a bit, but none of them can afford to engage dancers and choreographers on a full-time basis. As a result, many dancers still have to support themselves through extra jobs such as waitresses in bars and doormen in cinemas.

During the last year, important members of the dance community have asked politicians several times to make up their minds: do they want an active and sparkling Danish dance world at all? If not, the ten to twelve small companies will have to go on limping and performing towards economic and artistic disaster. If the latter is what the politicians intend, the dancers might just as well get the message now.

Modern dance in Denmark is annually supported by the government with approximately 1.3 million dollars. The new Secretary of Cultural Affairs, Jytte Hilden, could not promise the dance community better conditions immediately after she took office in January 1993. She did, however, acknowledge the special difficulties facing companies. The theatre law will be revised within the next year, when many dancers hope that the art of dance will get a better and more suitable position in the cultural landscape.

In the late summer of 1993 a new eminent dance stage opened in

Suzie Davies and Esa Alanne of Uppercut Danseteater in *Birds and Stones*.

Copenhagen, an event which marks a big step forward. The stage is open to Danish and foreign groups and companies who can perform at a very low rate. Since opening, the house has been full of activities. The same can be said for **Dansens Hus**—the House of Dancing, also in Copenhagen. After some reconstruction, Dansens Hus has fine training facilities, and with a newly established dance school for twenty young dancers.

The most prominent and promising company is still **Nyt Dansk Danseteater**, but other groups have also done some good work. Just to name them indicates the growth of modern dance in Denmark: **Corona, Dance Lab, Marie Brolin Tani Danseteater, Micado, Palle Granhoej Danseteater, New Now Dancers, Katryn Ricketts Dance Co., Teater Tango** and **Uppercut Danseteater**. If Danish modern dance has not yet really had the chance to show what it can do, it is, nevertheless, extremely promising.

Estonia

HEILI EINASTO

The dance scene in Estonia has become considerably more diverse since 1991. Besides the two state companies—**Estonia** and **Vanemuine**—there are two independent companies with an emphasis on modern dance. The first, **Dance Thetre Nordstar**, was formed in 1991 by Saima Kranig, former ballerina of the Estonian Theatre, and secondly, **Fine 5**, grouped around the choreographer René Nõmmik, was founded in 1993.

Besides repertory companies, there have been one-off projects such as *Empalov*—a combination of singing by the Estonian Chamber Choir, dancing by Marika Blossfeldt, and live painting by Epp-Maria Kokamägi. The idea was conceived by Bonnie Sue Stein from GOH Productions (New York) together with Marika Blossfeldt, and it expressed various faces of woman, her mental journey from childhood to motherhood. Major events were performances by Jacob's Pillow **Men Dancers** with the Ted Shawn Legacy programme—the first time American modern dance has been seen live in Estonia—and seminars of jazz and modern dance, organized by the Centre of Dance Information in Estonia.

Mai Murdmaa, one of the pillars of Estonian ballet since the 1960s, won the Award of the Director of the Year (which includes drama and opera as well), for *Crime and Punishment*, based on Dostoyevsky's novel and with music by Arvo Pärt—a selection of his works—which demonstrates clearly her striving for modern ballet even though it has a classical ground. Her following works: *Don Juan Play*, where the purely neo-classical interludes of Don Juan's consciousness (music by Stockhausen) is combined with early nineteenth-century stylization and quotes from *Giselle* (music by Gluck), and her choreographies of Orff's *Carmina Burana* and *Catulli Carmina*, have been less successful, but the mastery still works.

Mare Tommingas in Tartu has her own studio and her recent works, of which *Romeo and Juliet* is the most important, have had the advantage of her students dancing in the *corps* while the solo parts are danced by Vanemuine dancers. She too, is on the look-out for her own style, with an inclination towards the modern.

In classical ballet, the major events were: *Fairy Tale in Pictures*, Kennet Oberly's restoration of the Auguste Bournonville ballet from 1871, and *Esmeralda*, choreographed by Ülo Vilimaa in Vanemuine. Vilimaa is another noteworthy choreographer in Estonia, his career beginning in the 1960s.

France

ANNA PAKES

French dance, both classical and contemporary, has become a paragon and model for dance in other industrialized countries. The Paris Opéra Ballet, under its director Patrick Dupond, has re-established the standards achieved in the early years of Nureyev's directorship but built on these standards. He has reshaped the repertory to embrace some of today's most challengingly innovative choreographers. Fifteen new ballets have been added to the repertory since Dupond succeeded Nureyev in 1990. They include work by Neumeier, William Forsythe, and, especially in terms of his iconoclasm, the Swede, Mats Ek.

'We've brought a whole new audience to the Palais Garnier,' says Dupond, quoted by the *Guardian*'s Paris correspondent, Paul Webster. 'Annual attendance has jumped by as much as a fifth. The programme is now about fifty-fifty classic and modern.'

This capacity for development and success, seemingly unaffected by change of government in 1993, is matched by France's modern dancers. Developing their own very French concept of 'modern' rather than borrowing from Martha Graham or other influences, these dancers and their companies are now exporting their ideas through seasons and tours outside France, to The Place Theatre,

London, for example. They are attracting dancers from other countries to study French techniques and choreography.

Against this background, and with our correspondent in France unable at the last moment to meet our deadline, we invited Anna Pakes, a British student who studied for two years at the Centre National de Danse Contemporaine, to describe her experience. How different is study at Angers from comparable dance study in the UK, say, or other countries developing modern-dance forms? What does it feel like to be in such a French environment with free classes and a small salary? Should other dance students from the European Community seek the same opportunity? Anna offers a few answers. *Editor.*

The residency of Michael Clark, Stephen Petronio, and Company at the Centre National de Danse Contemporaine during the summer of 1991 caused something of a stir in the Centre's home town of Angers. Mingling with fur-coated, poodle-carrying middle-aged women, the two choreographers, one with no hair, the other sporting a miniskirt, would shop in the local market-hall, much to the bemusement of the stall-holders. Judging from the reports in the local press, such incidents would simply confirm the townspeople's general suspicion of Anglo-Saxon eccentricity. But then they were perhaps used to this sort of thing in Angers. Used to the presence of the small but often highly visible (and sometimes bizarre) contingent of contemporary dance artists in their midst.

The Centre National de Danse Contemporaine (CNDC) is a unique European institution, combining all the advantages of a 'Centre National Chorégraphique' with a quality school which provides professional training to contemporary dancers of all nationalities. The school itself has its own peculiarity. During my own time there as a student (1990–2), not only was all tuition free, but any EEC national was also entitled to a salary, albeit minimal, from the local French government authority. The French 'formation professionelle' scheme is designed to allow individuals the opportunity to develop and extend their professional skills with state subsidy. Arriving from Britain, where even the most recognized professions cannot benefit from such a provision, I was astounded that the arts, and more particularly dance, could command such resources.

The fact that I was the CNDC's first British student is surely an indication of the ignorance which prevails in the UK regarding dance opportunities abroad. Perhaps the insular mentality of the British still dominates even the most mobile of professions. When I speak of my CNDC background, the most common English reaction is for the listener to wonder at my daring, or rather oddity, in choosing to go abroad to pursue my dance career—'it must have been very difficult' or 'but weren't all the classes in French?' So much for dance's status as universal language.

In reality, training in France was no more difficult than training anywhere else. My own decision to choose France was governed at least in part by a desire also to expand my knowledge of French language and

Centre Chorégraphique National de Nantes in *Émigrants*.   PHOTO: LAURENT PHILIPPE

culture. And I suppose that the difficulties one faces in coming to terms with a largely alien culture are comparable with those that arise when appropriating a new physical language and its baggage. You have to be able to make a fool of yourself and laugh about it later—a useful skill in any kind of performance training, as well as off-stage generally.

Ultimately, we were four foreign students in a group of fifteen; by the end of our second year, being already sufficiently well versed in the relevant French terminology, we were all studying anatomy, history of dance, and music theory without encountering significant problems. The bias of the course as a whole, however, was practical and creative: the first year consisted mainly of technique classes and choreographic workshops, as well as voice and music training and some performance work. During the second year, we functioned as a performance group, working on two main pieces which were then toured throughout France and elsewhere. There was time and the opportunity in such a context to become aware of cultural difference: and the presence of two Spaniards, one Andorran, and myself seemed to enrich rather than hinder the creative work in progress.

I had to look to the professional performances, however, to see the real particularities of the French contemporary style. Steeped as it is in a strong tradition of avant-garde theatre, it is unsurprising that this style should be more self-consciously theatrical than its Anglo-American counterpart. Hence the emphasis in much current French work upon the complete stage image, and the fondness for the trappings of set, costume, and lighting design. The artificial, and often surreal nature of the scenic medium tends to be highlighted to a much greater extent, and the dancer consequently tends to function more as just another part of the whole scenic apparatus. A case in point is the work of Philippe Decouflé. His stage shows are more like his 1992 Winter Olympics extravaganza than one might think possible on a smaller scale.

Often the French dancer appears somehow detached from the movement he or she is performing. It is as if the intellectual self is watching the action of the body with a sense of curiosity, conscious of its theatrical effect. In comparison, British contemporary dance, more clearly marked as it is by American influence, seemed to me to bear evidence of a greater investment in the movement itself and its human implications, be this through high-powered and all-encompassing physical intensity or the apparently unselfconscious gesture of release technique. Where the British style begs a kinaesthetic response from its audience, French dance seems to call for a more general aesthetic appreciation. Even in dance, the French today seem more image-conscious.

During some of the performances I saw, this heightened sense of the theatrical often spilled over into a kind of melodramatic pretension which, I used to like to think, was antithetical to the ironic Anglo-Saxon mentality. Perhaps that was just my excuse for remaining unmoved when the rest of the audience were enraptured. Yet in my other capacity as student-choreographer, the general penchant of the French artists of the time served me well. What I might have thought twice about doing in Britain, for fear of being laughed off stage or dismissed as incomprehensible, suddenly became possible from the other side of the Channel. Where I chose to be funny, my *ironie britannique*, like Michael Clark's miniskirt, was greeted with a genial indulgence. When I sought depth, exploring some obscure personal obsession through a combination of movement and dramatic English text, the audience's puzzled gaze tended to resolve itself into appreciation. Maybe I had struck a chord. More likely they did not like to write off something they hardly felt they understood. In any case, I got away with murder.

None the less, the generally encouraging attitude of the French establishment towards artistic experiment is something which, in this country, we can only envy. And the French public too has learnt to welcome innovation. Also to their credit, French audiences seem to delight in being slightly bewildered by what passes before them. They require only partial explanation, if indeed they need to 'understand' dance theatre literally at all. Moreover, what I might interpret as shameless melodrama could equally well be seen to be freedom of expression. A dancer's detachment from the movement can only go so far before it becomes the reserve for which the British are so notorious. The French emphasis upon complete theatrical involvement, while retaining a sort of intellectual perspective, was revealed not only in performance but also in training. In technique class, I was often criticized for appearing too detached, too reserved, and seeming to with-hold both energy and enthusiasm. On one occasion, I remember travelling across the floor with what I thought at the time was confidence, until I heard the visiting teacher (British, actually) screaming '*Move*, Anna! don't be so bloody *English*' from the other side of the studio.

In contrast, it is common to hear teachers and choreographers remark upon the typical arrogance of French dancers. I suppose this is what sports commentators like to call 'gallic flair'. The nose-in-the-air glamour of French dance professionalism can be daunting. Useful, though, in the audi-tion situation, where reserve is certainly no asset. With so many European dancers migrating to Paris as word spreads of the comparative health of the French dance scene, hundreds turn up to seek a diminishing number of jobs. At least 350 hopefuls, for example, auditioned for **Compagnie Michele Anne de Mey** in Paris during the spring of 1992; the same selection process was to occur in London, Barcelona, and Brussels; and the choreo-grapher was seeking a maximum of eight dancers. Even during training, competitiveness between dancers was startling; and this increases when the secure environment of school is withdrawn.

My CNDC group's visit to the American Dance Festival in July 1991 was, in many ways, a trial encounter with the wider professional dance world we were soon to enter. Suddenly, everything took place on a much bigger scale and, after the initial shock, a whole range of exciting possibilities opened up.

I have to say that it gave me some satisfaction to watch my French friends struggle initially with a sense of displacement similar to my own during that first year of training. Most of the difficulties posed by cultural difference were soon overcome, however, as the spirit of collaboration once again took hold.

The episode also served to reinforce our group identity, and confirm our mutual interests and desires. And by now, I was very much a part of the 'French' group. As we sat watching performances by some of the major American companies (Paul Taylor, Pilobolus, Bill T. Jones, among others), I too would sometimes long to return to what had, by now, come to seem familiar. I would feel nostalgic (as I do now I am back in Britain) for the sheer finesse of the style I had sometimes criticized, for the theatrical flair which, after all, did seem so essentially Gallic.

Germany

HORST KOEGLER

Alive, to quote the last word of the German report in Volume 4 of *World Ballet and Dance*, still describes the German ballet scene at the time when 1993 is gradually giving way to 1994. However, there are alarming signs that things are no longer developing as smoothly as we have been accustomed to expect. It is not so much the companies which are threatened by the severe budget cuts announced for the future. Smaller cities like Kassel, Ulm, Bochum, and even Bremen may well have to reduce their dance activities, if they are not already planning to disband their companies altogether (like Bochum).

Berlin still maintains its three ballet companies at its three opera-houses, but there are discussions whether two will not be enough—and especially so since artistic results have been rather meagre recently. At the **Ballet der Deutschen Oper Berlin**, Peter Schaufuss left during the middle of the season to take up his new job in Copenhagen. He realized his big project of staging the three Tchaikovsky classics as a trilogy, with connecting psychological links between Siegfried, Florimund, and Drosselmeier plus the composer himself, but his dramaturgy did not really convince and what he added choreographically to the heritage of Messrs Petipa and Ivanov looked dreadfully uninspired. Ray Barra, formerly of the **Stuttgarter Ballett** and more recently free-wheeling ballet-master, has been engaged as temporary artistic director, while the General Manager of the house desperately tries to lure Marcia Haydée to Berlin when her Stuttgart contract runs out in 1995. Madame has shown some interest, all the more so since her recent Stuttgart activities have come under heavy critical fire, but what she really wants to become seems to be a kind of super manager of all the three Berlin companies, preferably in addition to her jobs in Santiago de Chile and Stuttgart. At the **Ballett der Staatsoper Unter den Linden** Michael Denard is now fully installed as artistic director of the ballet company, which definitely ranks first among Berlin's three, due to its splendidly trained ensemble of soloists and *corps de ballet*, most of them coming from the former East Berlin State School of Ballet, still headed by Martin Puttke. However the *éminence grise* who is really in control seems to be Maurice Béjart. His contribution to the repertory so far has been the revival of *Transfigured Night* and *Miraculous Mandarin* from his Lausanne stock, while Roland Petit has staged a full-length piece, inspired by paintings of Otto Dix. Its acid socio-critical comments on the excrescences of the Weimar Republic are watered down by Petit into chic Revue tableaux seasoned with Folies Bergère glamour. At the **Tanztheater der Komischen Oper**, Doris

Laine has followed her invitation to Flemming Flindt to stage his *Three Musketeers* with her even less successful invitation to Arila Siegert to create a full-length ballet on *Circe and Ulysses*, with a specially commissioned score from Gerald Humel, the American composer who wrote the music for her *Othello and Desdemona* ballet. It would not be surprising though, if the new General Manager of the Comic Opera appoints a new artistic director for his ballet company. As he comes from Cologne, his candidate may be Jochen Ulrich of the Cologne Dance Forum who, anyway, has been invited for a revival of his Cologne *Coppélia* production, which is based upon the original E. T. A. Hoffmann story rather than on the libretto by Messrs Nuitter and Saint-Léon.

In the former German Democratic Republic, Leipzig has made some progress under Uwe Scholz's hardly inspired but busybody leadership. His two last premières offered a double bill of Beethoven's *Seventh Symphony* and Berlioz's *Symphonie fantastique* and a triple bill of Stravinsky pieces to much local acclaim but of little interest beyond the city's walls. At the **Staatsoper Dresden** all choreographic hope is based upon Stephan Thoss, a local boy who is working at his first big production, Prokofiev's *Romeo and Juliet*, while Vladimir Derevianko has been appointed artistic director—without any choreographic ambitions whatsoever—as from 1994/5.

In what was formerly West Germany, Hamburg, Düsseldorf, Stuttgart, and Munich still head the list of major companies, while Frankfurt under William Forsythe has strengthened its reputation as the foremost laboratory to explore what ballet in the twenty-first century may look like.

In Hamburg, John Neumeier has reigned now for twenty years and he has built up a company and repertory of solid strength. Reason enough to celebrate the anniversary with a super gala, for which all the companies with which he has collaborated over the years sent some of their best dancers—including Natalia Makarova, Carla Fracci, Karen Kain, and Marcia Haydée. Neumeier's latest creation was a completely rethought *Cinderella Story*, which assumed almost Shakespearean dimensions. At present he is working on a Ravel multi-bill, built around his *Now and Then*, recently created for the Canadian National Ballet, to be followed at the end of the season with his Henze *Ondine*.

In Düsseldorf, Heinz Spoerli goes from strength to strength and the progress of his company is truly amazing. His *Goldberg Variations* have become a real box-office hit, and, if his recent *Firebird* does not count among his *chefs-d'œuvres*, the two supplementary pieces of the triple-bill programme easily make up for its deficiencies. They are Hans van Manen's unusually poetic *Visions fugitives* and that black diamond of a ballet, Stravinsky's *Violin Concerto* by Balanchine, meticulously staged by Karin von Aroldingen and Bart Cook, and danced by the company with crystalline precision. Announced for spring 1994 is Spoerli's *Midsummer Night's Dream*.

In Stuttgart things have gone astray recently—due mainly to Marcia Haydée's escalating absences while running her second company in Santiago de Chile, where she has recently staged *Firebird* and *Coppélia*. Standards have deteriorated somewhat and there have been two major flops in quick succession: the import of Béjart's banal *Magic Flute* (a flop already at its Brussels première back in 1981) and *Mata Hari*, a full-length vehicle specially created for Haydée, who wanders through it like a zombie in search of a choreographer. At the moment the company looks desperately leaderless, for though Egon Madsen is listed as deputy director he seems to exercise little authority. Renato Zanella, until last season a *corps de ballet* dancer with choreographic ambitions, has been appointed resident choreographer, and he certainly has created some short, abstract pieces of arresting individuality, but he has utterly failed to meet the challenges of a full company work with concrete historic characters. The company has still an impressive reserve of talented young dancers, but they are blocked on their way up by the gang of over-age soloists who have to be employed because they cannot be given notice. Meanwhile Madame seems to have

Marcia Haydée and Benito Marcelino of the Stuttgarter Ballett in Renato Zanella's *Mata Hari*.

PHOTO: GUNDEL KILIAN

Alma Muntegna and Gregor Seyffert of the Tanztheater der Komischen Oper Berlin in *Circe and Odysseus*, choreographed by Arila Siegert.   PHOTO: ARWID LAGENPUSCH

become somewhat tired of Stuttgart—after all she has been living there now for more than thirty years, which may be quite a strain for somebody coming from South America. Therefore she cultivates her Chilean pastures and seems to listen attentively to the siren sounds which are reaching her from Berlin.

Finally Munich. There the **Bayerisches Staatsballett** under the inspired leadership of Konstanze Vernon has made great strides over the last two years, culminating in a visiting season at Lincoln Center which went much better than anybody had dared to hope. Recent distinct successes included Ray Barra's conventional but eminently professional staging of *Don Quixote* and the Neumeier *Midsummer Night's Dream*, which both proved ideal show-cases for the company's splendid array of talented youngsters. Munich's main problem is the lack of a really creative resident choreographer. So Vernon has no alternative but to invite people from abroad—her last imports were van Manen with *Lieder ohne Worte*, Angelin Preljocaj with *Larmes blanches*, and Ohad Naharin with *Passomezzo* and *Innostress*. Announced for its next première is an American programme with choreographies by Lucinda Childs, Karole Armitage, and Twyla Tharp. At

Munich's second opera-house, the Theater am Gaertnerplatz, Guenther Pick has staged a revue on *Lola Montez*.

Meanwhile William Forsythe in Frankfurt, and with his Frankfurt troupe at his second base in Paris, explores the paths which may lead towards the future. All his ballets are works in progress, and it is to be hoped that his recent *Quintet* will be just the start of a greater project—it is an unusually quiet and even intimate piece with obviously some autobiographical connotations. He has now built up in Frankfurt a distinctly cultish flock of followers, very young, rather freakish and very off-off, but I have the suspicion that their genuine love for dance is rather low-key, and that they are customers of 'the scene' rather than true theatre fans.

Interesting things are also happening to and by people in other cities: in Cologne, where Jochen Ulrich has come forward with a full-length *Peer Gynt*, in Ulm, Joachim Schloemer moves next season to Weimar, Saarbruecken, Birgit Scherzer—another candidate to take over the **Tanztheater der Komischen Oper Berlin**, and Freiburg, Pavel Mikulastik... but then one could continue for quite some time. Winner of the German Dance Award 1993 was Hans van Manen and of the 1994 award, Maurice Béjart.

Hungary

LIVIA FUCHS

Dance life in Hungary has been characterized by two main tendencies. The ballet and folk-dance companies—still striving on state subsidy—dare not take artistic risks, whereas independent groups have been formed which lack a stable financial background, and essay various tried and untried ways. Thus real artistic effervescence is confined to these latter troupes.

In the autumn of 1992 György Szakály took over the directorship of the **Hungarian National Ballet**. Besides the revival of Ashton's always successful *La Fille mal gardée* the company gave only two premières, both performed brilliantly. The choreographer of the full-length *All That Dance* and the Bartók double bill, Antal Fodor, has not produced anything for nine years. This long silence might have helped him to renew his creativity; it did not, however. All the three ballets show that Fodor is trying to score successes by unsystematically reusing other artists'—namely Kylián,

Bausch, Fosse's—already successful ideas, the result of which is absolute unoriginality in his works.

At the **Pécs Ballet**, István Herczog attempted to recapture the interest of a rejective audience by composing two shorter pieces to music by Pink Floyd, who are still quite popular here, mainly among young people. He followed this with *Coppélia*, which was—knowing the ingenious choreography by Harangozó—rather a bold endeavour. But Herczog was able to stage the familiar story in a dense and witty manner, and he found a Coppélius—namely Pál Solymos—who can be compared to the memory of Harangozó.

The **Györ Ballet** has had difficulties in finding its new identity, the reason for which is partly the absence of a good resident choreographer and partly the absence of good dancers. The company could not manage to produce anything of value because the two one-acts by Ottó Demcsák and Libor Vačulik lack real choreographic talent. Only the *Dire Sisters* by Barbara Bombicz—a founding member of the company—can be described as a harmonious and homogeneous work. To refresh the repertory the company has invited two foreign artists. They put on *Entre dos Aquas*, a well-known piece by Robert North, and *Miniatures* also by him, then *Firebird*, a male duet by Hungarian-born Ferenc Barbay, who, apart from this, came up with an original piece as well.

The director of the most flourishing company, Zoltán Imre, became discontented with the hopeless financial situation, and left **Szeged Ballet**. However, he presented his audience with a grand season. They gave three premières, and it was not only Tamáz Juronics—who by the way, took over the company—but also Éva Molnár, who has never before worked with a professional company, to whom Imre gave the opportunity to compose. For the Franz Kafka memorial evening Yvette Bozsik produced a grotesque, gesturesque-based one-act. Her other new work, the *Williks*, inspired by *Giselle*, is also a theatrical and suggestive vision. Imre himself made only one choreography, a *Dream of Kafka*, in which he summarized everything dance theatre had meant for him in the past decade. He also invited Roberto Galvan, whose dynamic *Concerto for Bandoneon and Orchestra* was performed with tempestuous vigour by the pre-eminent company. The new director also invited Galvan. Thus was born *Requiem*, commemorating the victims of AIDS through the lyrical language of dance.

Both premières of the **Veszprém Dance Workshop** were composed by Katalin Lórinc. Her first full-length work, *Once Upon A Time . . . And Once Again* was based on Marqúez's *A Hundred Years of Solitude*. Lórinc's one-act, *Salome*, was inspired by the exceptionally gifted and suggestive Andrea Ladányi, who depicts the queer, all-penetrating nature of desire with dramatic energy and density.

The independent companies, whose existence lasts from one production to another, premièred various pieces of high quality. The **Bozsik Company** is a new group, but their leader, Yvette Bozsik—who left the **Collective of Natural Disaster**—is the most experienced choreographer and performer of experimental dance. As soon as it was ready, they set out on an international tour with their one-act, *The Soirée*. Bozsik also produced a duet, which she performed together with Robin Blackledge, in order to show the possibilities provided by the unswaying yet still eloquent body.

The **Sarbo Company**, formed by four danseuses, still only imitate their role model, the Belgian Rosas. *Wall to Wall*, the work which they performed on international Caravan programme, appeared to be an excellent start.

The main characteristic of the **Artus Company** is its ability to renew itself with every production. In their new piece, *The Song of the Pearl*, prose, puppetry, oratorio, contact dance, and acrobatics all have a share.

TranzDanz, too, provides a complexity of theatrical elements, although placing more emphasis on dance. *Temporary Title*, which was awarded a prize at the Bagnolet Competition and combines folklore and jazz improvisation with post-modern texts, was expanded into a one-hour work by Péter Gerzson Kovács, thus giving it its final form. Apart from these, they put on *Astral Years*, a new production which utilizes painting as well as the magic powers of words, picture, movements, sound, and colours.

Artus Company in *The Song of the Pearl*, choreographed by Goda.
PHOTO: BEATRICE ROSSI

The homecoming of Andrea Ladányi—a former soloist of Györ Ballet and the star of Jorma Uotinen's company—reanimated the world of independents. She put on a very powerful performance with Benny Bell where they pressed against each other as true representatives of two different cultures.

The number of independents also increased. The company **Art of Dance**, formed by dancers coming from various theatres, aim mainly at popularizing jazz dance. **Budapest Ballet** is another new independent company. They select their repertory exclusively from works by foreign choreographers (such as Raza Hammadi, Joe Alegado, Rami Beér, Bruce Taylor) and most of their excellent dancers come from Szeged Ballet.

The First Hungarian Contemporary Dance Festival can be regarded as a closure of a ten-year-long 'struggling, heroic age', where all contemporary trends from the semi-professional recital by Ákos Hargitai to the France-based Sofa Trio were represented. The Second Festival in 1993 proves that despite the circumstances, not only the old companies survive but new ones, for example **DekaDance**, are formed, and new choreographers, Ildikó Mándy and Eszter Gál, start out, as well. Their future, at least artistically, seems sure.

Israel

GIORA MANOR

In 1964 Israel's leading dance company, **Batsheva**, was founded by Baroness Batsheva de Rothschild—hence the company's name. The company is celebrating its thirtieth birthday with a whole series of festive performances, commencing in November 1993 and going on for the whole of 1994. With Ohad Naharin at the helm, it is now enjoying the popularity it had in its early years. The works it performs are very up to date, sometimes even 'trendy', often to live music by pop groups appealing to young audiences, so Batsheva has very good reasons to celebrate.

Batsheva's first decade was dominated by Martha Graham and her works. But since 1973 the performing rights of the Graham masterpieces were withdrawn thanks to a new policy of the Graham Foundation in New York, which until now has refused to license any company save Graham's own to perform the late choreographer's works.

So it came as a surprise that **Bat-Dor**, de Rothschild's second company, founded in 1967, has now been granted the performing rights of the Graham canon in Israel, free of charge. This is a gesture both commemorating de Rothschild's substantial help to Graham back in the 1940s as well as helping the company to overcome the difficulties it found itself in after a fire gutted the building on one of the main streets of Tel-Aviv, where the company's studios and theatre are housed. It remains to be seen how Bat-Dor, many of whose dancers are ballet-trained immigrants from Russia and Israelis who have had no experience with Graham technique, are going to cope with this bonanza.

The **Kibbutz Contemporary Dance Company** has continued to perform works by its house choreographer Rami Be'er, among these, full-length dances such as *Black Angels* (to commemorate the 500th anniversary of the expulsion of the Jews from Spain, exactly in the year Columbus discovered the New World) and *Naked City*, a portrait of a modern megalopolis. The Kibbutz Company was the first Israeli dance company to be invited to perform in Beijing during the summer of 1993.

Two government-appointed committees have published their reports. These may or may not change some of the basic conditions in which Israel's dance companies are struggling to make ends meet. If the proposals pertaining to the financing of four permanent companies and several 'seasonal' ones are going to be adopted and implemented, this will improve the situation fundamentally. Experimental work is also to enjoy increased funding, if and when the suggestions of the committee are implemented.

A new company, run by Liat Dror and Nir Ben-Gal, has established itself as a possible new permanent outfit, adding another variant of innovative dance theatre to the Israeli dance scene. This company has already extensively performed not only at home, but all over Europe as well. Thanks to the recommendations of the committee, it is also a candidate for a substantial governmental subsidy.

Another committee had the unenviable task of deciding what to do about the ailing **Inbal Dance Theatre**, Israel's most senior and special company, which served for more than forty years as the vehicle for performing the *œuvres* of its founder and choreographer, Sara Levi-Tanai. She is in her eighties, and was unceremoniously ousted from her position about two years ago. Since then Inbal has ceased to perform her works and has not found as yet any new *raison d'être*. The committee proposed a complete replacement of the company's artistic and administrative management and recommended new ways to preserve and present Levi-Tanai's works, while continuing to use folklore traditions in modern choreography.

Other companies, such as the **Israel Ballet** and Moshe Efrati's **Kol Demama**, have been presenting new works and performing at home and on tours abroad, mainly in Europe.

The most positive development has been a whole new wave of young

Figs, choreographed by Liat Dror and Nir Ben-Gal.   PHOTO:VARDI CAHANNA

choreographers, who were given the chance to show their works at government-sponsored show-case performances, held mainly at the Suzanne Dellal Centre for Dance and Theatre in Tel Aviv. Some of these promising choreographers, such as Noa Wertheim and Adi Sha'al, Inbal Pinto, Tamar Borer, Nimrod Fried and Tomer Shar'abi with Maya Stern, have shown remarkable originality in their works. A few were also invited to perform abroad: Tamar Borer at the Montpellier Festival in France and Noa Wertheim with Adi Sha'al in London, under the framework of the Dance Umbrella Festival.

Altogether, international co-operation has been much in evidence; Batsheva having 'French seasons' in which works by leading choreographers, such as the late Dominique Bagouet, Joseph Nadj (who also taught a course for young choreographers), Angelin Preljocaj, and others were presented. There were also well-attended seminars and screenings of video dance in co-operation with the British Council and The Place in London.

The Karmiel Dance Festival held each summer for the past six years has again attracted more than a hundred thousand visitors and participants. One of the most interesting features of the 1993 festival—apart from pre-mières by most of the leading artistic dance companies—were jazz impro-visation performances by some of the leading young dancers, which took place after midnight in Karmiel's town park.

The Israeli dance scene in all its aspects is lively, a new young generation of artists emerging while at the same time, many of the established dancers and choreographers continue working. Whether the newly signed peace treaties with the Palestinians will have a beneficial influence on the arts in Israel is still to be seen. At least there is hope.

Italy

FREDA PITT

With the recession biting hard, seasons were curtailed, there were fewer new productions, fewer expensive visitors, and some summer festivals were cancelled, most notably the one at Nervi. Taormina Arte again omitted dance in favour of Wagner, and the Panatenee Pompeiane and Festival delle Ville Vesuviane also turned their backs on what had been a staple ingredi-ent of their programmes.

However, despite the undoubted difficulties, those few theatres, manage-ments, and organizations with a sincere interest in dance forged ahead. The palm must go to the Teatro Valli in Reggio Emilia, which—even if occa-sionally over-susceptible to fashion in its choices—continued to present a variety of visiting companies as well as **Aterballetto**, the Cosi-Stefanuscu group, and the company from the Teatro Nuovo in Turin, with much-admired Luciana Savignano. William Forsythe earned fewer plaudits than usual when, in February 1993, the announced Frankfurt Ballet triple bill was replaced by his confusing *Alienaction*. Also in February, the **Rudra Béjart Lausanne** company (which opened at the Fenice in Venice and also appeared at Modena and at the Teatro Verdi in Florence, as well as the Valli) was praised more for Sylvie Guillem and Koen Onzia's contributions than for the cinema-linked content.

Instead of the customary biennial autumn festival, the Valli opened a series of performances spread over several months, with the Paris Opéra Ballet in three masterpieces from the Diaghilev repertory: *Prodigal Son*, *L'Après-midi d'un faune*, and *Petrushka*. This was an important occasion not only because of the rarity of this great company's visits but also because remakes are the order of the day in Italy, the original choreography often remaining almost unknown. There is, indeed, no guarantee that the closing programme of reworkings by Angelin Preljocaj, *Parade*, *Le Spectre de la rose*, and *Les Noces*, previously aired in Rome during the wide-ranging RomaEuropa summer festival, will not be received with even greater enthusiasm, particularly as in the last thirty years, at least, Nijinska's *Les Noces* has been given only once in Italy.

During this same Valli season, Maguy Marin's company gave the world première in November 1993 of her *Waterzooi*, a largely spoken pendant to *Cortex*, which was presented at the 1992 Spoleto Festival. In early 1994, Amedeo Amodio's Aterballetto—now battling for survival—performed a triple bill of works by Balanchine, Petit, and Kylián.

Another town that seems to be aiming at occupying the high ground, with different methods, is Turin. The Regio opera-house dismissed its small, under-employed resident ballet company in 1992, so it depends on guests now for the annual ballet in its winter opera season. In May the Deutsche Oper Ballet brought Peter Schaufuss's production of *Giselle*, with himself and Alessandra Ferri, and a gathering of scholars and critics talked about the ballet. Two different groups of Italian and foreign speakers were assembled in September to discuss on the one hand 'The Dance and Italy' and on the other, as part of the Monteverdi celebrations, 'The Art of the Dance at the Time of Claudio Monteverdi', i.e. sixteenth–seventeenth centuries. Turin also boasts a specialized library, Centro Documentazione Danza, where a wide range of books, periodicals, and videos can be consulted by the general public. Turin possesses two active small classical companies, as well as contemporary ones such as **Sutki**.

In July, **TorinoDanza** moved from its previous unsatisfactory park setting, where the weather frequently played havoc with performances, to the more august, more central, and more comfortable one of the Teatro Regio. The Ballets de Monte-Carlo, which has now appeared at both venues, must have appreciated the difference, groups such as La La La Human Steps perhaps less so. The Royal Ballet, the only company to have live accompaniment, made its Turin début, opening the festival with MacMillan's *Mayerling*, which neither audience nor critics took to their hearts, although some of the dancers were admired. *Swan Lake* was, predictably, more enthusiastically received—the Regio audience is on the whole rather conservative in its tastes. Before Turin, the company had given *Swan Lake* in the lovely outdoor summer home of the Massimo opera-house in Palermo.

Other theatres are active for dance in the Sicilian capital. For example, in May the Incontrazione Festival presented 'Four from London', with the Siobhan Davies Dance Company, the Volcano Theatre Company of Swansea, Shared Experience, and the V-Tol Dance Company.

After the departure of Elisabetta Terabust, who has replaced Giuseppe Carbone as director of the ballet at La Scala, Milan, the **Rome Opera Ballet** virtually fell to pieces. She had wrought great improvements both in the company and at the school, whose 1992 annual show at the Teatro Brancaccio, including a piece by the then ballet-master Derek Deane and Matz Skoog's staging of Act III of *Napoli*, testified to the progress made. The opera house management cancelled the remaining ballet programmes, replacing them with Mario Pistoni's much-revived *La Strada*, then with an intolerably long series of performances of Lorca Massine's *Zorba the Greek*, which they had the affrontery to present for the third consecutive year at the Baths of Caracalla.

As a result, there was only one classical offering of serious interest in Rome the whole year, when the Accademia Filarmonica Romana brought a group of thirty Kirov dancers led by Julia Makhalina and Alexander Kirkov to the Teatro Olimpico in a programme of excerpts. The couple who gained most plaudits, Margarita Kullik and Vladimir Kim, later appeared in a different repertory with an interesting mixed Russian group at the Teatro Carcano in Milan in July. In two *pas de deux* with Andrey Tikhorminov, Valeria Zoi demonstrated exceptional delicacy and expressiveness as well as virtuosity. The same theatre presented Twyla Tharp's company, opening its European tour, in early October.

Rudolf Nureyev's death resulted in a number of 'homages', of varying worth. Some performances acquired a 'homage to Nureyev' label with a minimum of justification, a plaque in his memory was affixed outside the Rome Opera House, and two biographies were published, one a gossipy and hurried affair by a Turin journalist, the other a much better produced and more serious book by the Milan music and dance critic Mario Pasi.

The **Scala Ballet** had performed Nureyev's productions of *The Sleeping Beauty* (made for them in 1966), *Swan Lake*, and *The Nutcracker* in his lifetime, with his participation. They were all revived in 1993, with Maximiliano Guerra, in evidence all over Italy during the year, as guest hero in the former two. Anita Magyari and Isabel Seabra remain the two resident principals. Followed by guest Viviana Durante, Seabra made her début as Aurora in October. She needs to settle into the role but will be able to do so in early 1994.

In March, Carla Fracci had a huge success as Tatiana in John Cranko's *Onegin*, her best role for years. Rex Harrington appeared in the title-role.

Fracci is also due to appear in the opening opera of the new season, Spontini's *La Vestale*, in which the twenty-minute ballet will have choreography by Amodio.

Carla Fracci and Rex Harrington of La Scala, Milan, in *Onegin*.   PHOTO: LELLI & MASOTTI

The **Balletto di Toscana** toured energetically, a frequent choice being Fabrizio Monteverde's stark semi-contemporary version of *Romeo and Juliet*. A former Aterballetto dancer, Mauro Bigonzetti set up with some success as a choreographer, his works going into several repertories including that of the Tuscan company. Another youngish choreographer to earn respect was Luciano Cannito, director of the **Balletto di Napoli**, who was awarded a prize by the Gino Tani Cultural Foundation in Rome in November, when Alessandra Ferri received the dancer's prize. Cannito's *Marco Polo* is being performed also by the company of the San Carlo in Naples, directed by Roberto Fascilla. Evgeny Polyakov's company at the Teatro Comunale in Florence replaced the announced homage to Balanchine with one in favour of Tchaikovsky when the general director of the opera-house, Massimo Bogianckino, decided to sue the Balanchine Trust for allegedly excessive charges.

In Castiglioncello, the summer festival paid homage to Maurice Béjart with a variety of pieces, including one by the festival's director, Micha van Hoecke, previously a Béjart collaborator. He was less well employed as choreographer of the Scala's *Le Baiser de la fée*, with Ferri, Julio Bocca, and Oriella Dorella, earlier in the year. Riccardo Muti made a magnificent job of the Stravinsky score, but he has no understanding of the choreographic art.

The Perm State Opera Ballet took *Swan Lake* to the Teatro Smeraldo in Milan in March and *The Sleeping Beauty* to open-air venues including Venice, Lugo di Ravenna, and Tagliacozzo in August. The female *corps de ballet* made the strongest impression.

A number of small contemporary groups appeared in small off-centre theatres, sometimes with small audiences, in Rome from September to November, the best dancers at the Teatro del Vascello being those of Joseph Fontano's company. Expressing dissatisfaction with conditions in the capital, Fontano is reported to be moving to Turin. One sympathizes.

Japan

KENJI USUI

The overall characteristic of the past year in the Japanese ballet scene has been the influx of visiting foreign companies. Early in 1993, the Maly Theatre Ballet of St Petersburg—a group led by Nina Ananiashvili and Maya Plisetskaya—the Roland Petit Company, the Ballet of Lyon Opéra, the Pina Bausch Group, Faroukh Ruzimatov and his friends, the Royal Danish Ballet, and Ballet Philippines all performed in Tokyo and other major Japanese cities. Of all these the best was the visit by the Royal Danish Ballet; *Napoli* by Bournonville is always well received in Japan. In a country where the history of ballet is almost entirely neglected, it is important to show the audience how ballet looked in the first half of the nineteenth century.

Apart from visiting foreign groups, there has been a very busy schedule for Japanese companies. For instance, in January 1993 alone, we had full-length performances of *Swan Lake* by two major companies in Tokyo— **Tokyo Ballet** and **Matsuyama Ballet**, *Don Quixote* by **Tani Ballet**, and *Fountain of Bakhchisarai* staged in both Tokyo and Nagoya. Therefore, I will report on only the most important performances of the past season.

In the autumn of 1992, the first Opera and Ballet Theatre opened in Nagoya, the third biggest city in Japan. To commemorate the opening of the theatre, the city, together with the Tokai TV Company and the local prefecture, held the first international Ballet and Modern Dance Competition in January. The judges of the ballet section were headed by

Hiroshi Shimada, the President of the Japanese Ballet Association. Also included on the panel were Vladimir Vasiliev of Russia, André-Philippe Hersin of France, Thalia Mara from the USA, and from Japan, Yoko Morishito and myself. The Modern Dance panel of judges included Boris Eifman of Russia and Bruce Marks and Yuriko from the USA. The Gold Medal winner of the junior section was Tan Yuan Yuan from Shanghai; in the Classical Ballet and Modern Dance sections, the Gold Medallists were Mie Conquempot from Switzerland and Pascal Montrouge, France. Apart from the prize-winners, there were very promising performances by Joseph Dolinsky of Slovakia and Jaime Vargas.

In February 1993, the Japan Ballet Association staged Konstantin Sergeyev's version of *Swan Lake*. The Association covers almost all of the ballet teachers and dancers country-wide, therefore the performers for this occasion were chosen from the cream of Japan's dancers. We sincerely hope that a project such as this will lead to the formation of a national company. This version, first staged in 1991 by Mary Ann Holmes and approved by the choreographer, was led with great success by Ludmilla Vasilieva and Vladimir Malakhov. Among the Japanese cast, Morihiro Iwata, who danced the part of the Jester, was most impressive with his clear-cut movements and soaring jumps; he is a Japanese member of the Russian State Ballet in Moscow and received the Gold Medal in the Seventh Moscow International Ballet Competition in September.

On 1 May, there was a ceremony and performance to commemorate the one hundredth anniversary of the birth of Michio Ito, who died in Tokyo in 1961. Ito developed his own special plastic movement from a combination of the Dalcroze System and Japanese traditional stage art. He made his début at the Coliseum Theatre in London in 1915, and later was a popular performer and teacher in the United States.

In late July, the **Noriko Kobayashi Ballet Theatre** revived Dame Ninette de Valois's *Checkmate*. Such a project is always welcome in Japan because we can trace the path of national ballet in England—the path we may follow in the future when the Japanese ballet world realizes the necessity of establishing our own National Ballet.

Also in July, Maurice Béjart choreographed a new full-length ballet called *M* for the Tokyo Ballet, premièred on 31 July. *M*, means basically the author Yuko Mishima, to whom Béjart pays special devotion; but *M* can be Magic, Mer, Mort, or Mythology as well, according to the choreographer's whim. Béjart says that he analysed Mishima from the realistic, supernatural, and poetic point of view. The music was commissioned from Toshiro Mayuzumi, who is also a great admirer of Mishima. The ballet was a great success and critics and audience alike admired the work. One review read as follows:

Béjart's stage was full of symbolism. Mishima gave to his last work the title *The Fertile Sea* as a paradox, but this ballet can be called *The Symbolic Sea* without paradox. Masks, Mirrors and uniforms are seen on the stage, but all of them are surrounded by the ocean. . . . On the stage, Mishima's works are shown but only as the reflection of Béjart's former dances. The two are one and the same. . . . Béjart saw himself in Mishima. . . . (extract from review by Masashi Miura in *Mainiche-Shinburn*)

There was another international ballet competition in Tokyo in August. It was called the Asian Pacific Ballet Competition but Turkey, Vietnam, and the Asian part of the former Soviet Republics were omitted. The Korean participants showed excellent results and the First Prize in the Senior division was awarded to the male dancer, Kim Yon Gul.

André Prokovsky's *Three Musketeers* was premièred in Tokyo on 22 October by the **Asami Maki Ballet Company**. The leading part of D'Artagnan was danced by Ilgis Galimoulline from Russia, but all other parts were danced by local dancers. The ballet was received enthusiastically because of the choreographer's skill in telling the story clearly through well-conceived dances.

Among the modern dance performances, *Decameron*, choreographed by

Tokyo Ballet in *M*, choreographed by K. Hasegawa.

Tatsuo Mochizuki to the music of Eiji Furusawa, is worth a mention. It was staged on 27 June in Tokyo and was very popular with the audiences. Mochizuki studied both ballet and modern dance in New York and danced there for some years. He is well known in Japan as a creator of very original movement.

Mexico

CLAIRE DE ROBILANT

Mexico has one of the liveliest dance scenes in Latin America, a scene which at the same time can be rather confusing; it presents almost too much of the same. The Mexican writer and historian, César Delgado Martinez, who has provided the background to this information, needed four issues of the daily paper *Excelsior*, in tightly written articles, to sum up the manifold events of 1993 in different venues in this beautiful country.

The many festivals which take place every year in Mexico, in 1993 seemed to be dedicated almost entirely to Contemporary Dance. One of the events which took place in the town of Mexicali in April 1993 was the First Binational Meeting of Contemporary Dance (1 Encuentro Binacional De Danza Contemporanea), organized by the Autonomous University of Lower California supported by the National Fund for Culture and Arts. This seems to have been a highly successful event of twelve performances, with an average attendance of about 300 spectators. Such success is important, because despite enormous efforts and many groups and companies, Contemporary Dance in Mexico does not have a large following. In Mexico City itself, for example, it is difficult to attract that size of audience.

In January 1993, the CENIDI-Danza, José Limón, the Mexican dance archive, celebrated its tenth anniversary. It was founded in 1983 by Patricia Aulestia de Alba, a former dancer from Ecuador, educated in Chile. Now it has been taken over by the very professional dance researcher and writer Lin Durán whose principal objectives, and very necessary ones too, are to establish a closer relationship between research and dance education. She pointed out in a speech that 'there are good and bad researchers but the principal problem is that there is no centre where serious applicants for research can be prepared'. I wish Lin Durán, a very knowledgeable professional, the very best for her dedicated work and programme.

The annual celebration of the International Day of Dance, held on 29 April 1993, saw performances of various ballet and dance groups and companies. New videos were shown on Mexican dance activities and a photographic exhibition by Rafael Rodrigues called *Mexican Dancers* was opened. In the evening, in Mexico City's beautiful and impressive art deco operahouse, el Palacio de Bellas Artes, the annual homage took place to *A life in dance* organized by CENIDI-Danza, José Limón, with performances by **Ballet Independiente** and the classical **Compañia Nacional de Danza**. Having been the recipient a few years ago of such an honour, I can say truly that this is a very moving occasion. It was one of the highlights in my often chequered professional teaching and dance researcher's life. Another memory I cherish is that Mexico has the most eager audience for anything to do with dance and its history. I hope therefore that Lin Durán, as head of the Dance Archive, and her close collaborators, will achieve finally their goal to develop dance education. Mexico is an extraordinarily fruitful soil in which to sow.

From César Delgado Martinez's excellent and lengthy report, it emerges that the Theatre and Dance Departments of the UNAM (Universidad Autónoma Metropolitana, Mexico City) has had a rather 'grey year', the result of some not unusual interior bureaucratic petty squabbles. Theatre was favoured, leaving dance at a secondary, lower level, an extraordinary attitude in Mexico's most prestigious educational establishment.

In July, another festival took place, called *Mercates* (Mercado de las Artes de Vº.Gran Festival Ciudad de México—Market of the Vth Great Festival in Mexico City). Not only local dance groups performed here, but also groups from other Latin American countries. This opened the doors for several Mexican groups to be invited abroad: **el Ballet Teatro des Espacio** went to Guatemala, for example, and also to the closing ceremony of the VIII Iberoamerican Festival in Cadiz, Spain. There are future possibilities to perform in Canada and the USA.

There was yet another festival in July in Mexico City called *Multiarte Escénico INBA 93* (INBA meaning Instituto Nacional de Bellas Artes) with foreign groups from different countries. This showed very clearly the road now being taken by theatre arts at the beginning of the twenty-first century. It emerged also that Contemporary Dance has been nourished in recent years by other artistic disciplines and movement techniques, which do not belong precisely to dance.

Some stir, and unhappiness, was caused by the cancellation of the annual season of Contemporary Dance at the main venue in Mexico City, the Palacio de Bellas Artes (INBA). The artistic director of the company Ballet Teatro des Espacio, Gladiola Orósco and Michel Descomby, in their frustration said that this had not happened before in twenty years, that continuity was synonymous with development, and that no explanation for this cancellation had been given. They are hoping, together with Guillermina

Bravo, Mexico's foremost Contemporary Dance pioneer and artistic director of **Ballet Nacional de México**, that during the next 365 days, the lost
time can be regained.

A curious event took place during the XIII National and IV International
Contemporary Dance Festival at the Teatro de la Paz in San Luis de Potosi
in August 1993. Ballet Nacional de México, under its director and choreographer Guillermina Bravo, attracted such a large audience that they broke
down the door and occupied the 1,500 seats of the Teatro de la Paz, while
others stood in the aisles. This is not unusual for rock concerts, but it seldom, if ever, happens at a dance performance. The programme included a
work by Guillermina Bravo, *El Ilamado* (*The Call*) 1983, and dance works by
Jaime Blanc and Federico Castro. Isaacs McCabled and Dancers came from
the USA. From Mexico City, besides the Ballet Teatro del Espacio, came as
always, the **Ballet Independiente**, whose founder is Raul Flores Canelo.

During this festival, several prizes were given, in particular to the historian and journalist Luis Bruno Ruiz, to Oscar Flores Martinez, critic and
writer of *El Universal*, to Alejandro Roque of *Heraldo de San Luis*, and an
important prize to choreographer Serafin Aponte for *El Universo visto por el
ojo de una cerradura* (*The universe as seen through the keyhole*), danced by the
Barro Rojo group. It was a prize received with great applause.

Much more could be written about the Mexican dance year 1993. I have
shortened and condensed what happened because it is appropriate to add a
word about the history of dance and ballet in Latin America as a whole.
The history of ballet in Latin America is the great absentee in the general
and universal history of ballet so far researched. While undertaking the
vast research to correct this imbalance, it was strange for me to realize that
this history is much older than that of ballet in Australia, which begins in
1834. It goes back in Mexico particularly to about 1783. From then on pio-
neering companies brought ballets based on works by Noverre and
D'Egville, to mention only two famous names. This vast research now covers nine Latin American countries and is the result of a labour of nineteen
years, mostly on a shoe-string or no shoe-string at all, at times threatened
almost to extinction. There is a golden thread, however, extending through
that history in the nineteenth century from Europe to the Americas, via
Australia and back. This has kept the research going. It is not yet complete.
Much more needs to be done.

What has come to light also is the fact, long forgotten, that many British
dancers and companies particularly after the Second World War made their
way successfully to Latin America. Dame Alicia Markova, for example, has
been several times since 1947 and it was not always easy. It is a history
almost in itself. Two years ago, Buenos Aires became the Iberian capital of
culture and through the British Council organized a festival in which the
Rambert Dance Company participated. In 1993 the English National Ballet
made yet another trip to Brazil and Argentina. The general public outside

Latin America is hardly aware of such contacts. Critics, writers, and historians rarely mention the subject. For them South America remains isolated in dance.

This archive collection, together with other dance subjects, nearly was lost to the United Kingdom for which it was intended in the first place. The great New York Public Library for the Performing Arts wanted it badly. Maybe that would have been the right place for it because of the number of Spanish-speaking researchers now available there. Happily, the British Theatre Museum has recently taken over, and the big collection remains in the United Kingdom. In a few months' time it will be ready for research, and will begin to be integrated properly with other subjects. It will be, for example, the only archive in the UK where one can find almost every single programme of the 1913 and 1917 South American tours by the Diaghilev Ballets Russes, plus reviews, cuttings, and so on. There is much, much more. There is, in fact, the history of classical ballet in Latin America.

The Netherlands

EVA VAN SCHAIK

According to the latest annual reports of ten structurally subsidized companies, dance certainly is a flowering art in Holland—their statistics can only be read in that way. Since 1986 the number of performances by the **Dutch National Ballet**, the **Nederlands Dans Theater**, **Folkloristic Dance Theatre**, **Djazzex**, **Scapino Ballet**, **Introdans**, **Dansgroep Krisztina de Chatel**, **Rotterdamse Dansgroep**, and **Reflex** has increased by 55 per cent. According to other statistics given by the research office Motivaction, the Dutch audience for dance showed a similar growth, 40 per cent in the last season alone. Meanwhile the amount of Dutch dance performances abroad showed an increase of 57 per cent within five years. The quantitive prosperity of this sector in the performing arts is also registered by the Dutch *Dance Yearbook* of 1992/3: within one season more than 250 new dance creations were presented by 121 Dutch dance companies, while 75 companies from abroad were presented to the Dutch public. These calculations speak for themselves.

But what happened to the art itself during these five flowering years? At the Dutch National Ballet, the new artistic director, Wayne Eagling, continued the artistic policy of Rudi van Dantzig, generally known as the 'three pillars' system. In practice this means a combination of the good old classics, *Sleeping Beauty, Swan Lake, Giselle,* the good new classics, and more risky experiments by younger talents within the company. In 1993 the Dutch National proudly presented Martha Graham's *Diversion of Angels* (1948) next to Ashton's *Scènes de ballet,* Nijinska's *Les Noces,* Fokine's *Petrushka,* several Balanchine ballets, and last but not least the complete *Artifact* (four acts) by William Forsythe. For the third pillar, Laurie Booth, Ashley Page, Ted Brandsen, Luis Damas, Krystof Pastor, and Wayne Eagling showed their choreographic ambitions. As could be predicted, not all these creations were warmly received. After his successful début on the Dutch stage with *Ruins of Time,* a melancholy mix in remembrance of Nureyev's roles in works by MacMillan, Van Dantzig, and Béjart, Eagling's *Frankenstein* was regarded a downright disaster and a financial waste. For the 1993/4 season, ballets by Glen Tetley, Léonide Massine, Toer van Schayk, and Wayne Eagling himself will be programmed, while the full-length *Artifact* of Forsythe gave the company a new zeal and impetus last September and October. At the Holland Festival in June 1994 the National Ballet dancers will also present new works by four young choreographers: Bruno Barat, Pieter de Ruiter, Paul Selwyn Norton, and Itzik Galili.

At The Hague, the Nederlands Dans Theater—divided into the main company, the juniors, and the seniors—witnessed a very strong season, with new and older works by Jiří Kylián, Hans van Manen, Paul Lightfoot, Paolo Ribiero, Susanne Linke, Mats Ek, Ohad Naharin, Itzik Galili, and William Forsythe. Most interesting was their choreographic workshop this year, which showed a real abundance of fresh talent. The latest creations by Kylián once more displayed his genius: he sublimated his curiosity in the unknown whereabouts of dance by the depiction of a wandering and wondering dancing soul; his dancers are haunted across civilization by those intimate but nevertheless strange forces which we call time, space, and the marks of memory. Van Manen contributed with *Shorthand, Six Stravinsky Pieces,* and *Fantasia on Chorales of Bach,* by which he showed his preference for undulating, quivering hips and arms with a Spanish-flavoured idiom.

Although the Netherlands Dans Theater 3 company was started in 1991 as a one-off experiment, the success of the dancers aged 40 and over was so overwhelming that this senior division has rooted itself firmly on NDT grounds, with Sabine Kupferberg and Gerard Lemaître as its nucleus. Last season they were assisted by Martine van Hamel, Niklas Ek, and Gary Christ in new creations for them by Ohad Naharin, Martha Clarke, Jiří Kylián, Christopher Bruce, Carolyn Carlson, and Hans van Manen.

At the **Scapino Ballet** in Rotterdam a big change took place, with the unexpected departure of artistic leader Nils Christe, whose function was taken over by Ed Wubbe. This Dutch choreographer represents a new spirit: he wants to get rid of the traditional triple-bill system with two intervals for a cup of coffee. His visiting-card was clearly marked by his stormy *Kathleen*, immediately nicknamed the West Side Story of the nineties, as it showed the hard uncompromising world of youngsters, searching for a glimpse of love and finding no spark of tenderness in a grey world of bunkers.

A policy of consolidation was followed by most smaller, subsidized companies. At the Rotterdamse Dansgroep, Kathy Gosschalk (artistic leader since 1975) reinforced the repertory with beautiful choreography by Ton Simons, called *The Idea of Order*, while at Introdans, new works by Paoluzzi, Lustig, Dietrich, and Wisman were presented. In the north of Holland the company Reflex strived for the integration of dance with other arts.

Introdans in Graham Lustig's *Transit*.   PHOTO: HANS GERRITSEN

Of all Dutch dance companies the Folkloristic Dance Theatre and Djazzex showed the highest level of growing popularity. The first ensemble, established in Amsterdam, followed the old dance traces of European folklore. The second ensemble, established in The Hague, enjoyed its tenth anniversary with great success and public approval.

Meanwhile, the sector hardest stricken by financial restrictions, the so-called modern dance, had difficulty in surviving. In refusing an offered platform to combine their forces by co-productions and to reduce their scattered, inefficient overhead costs, they sealed their own fate. The only modern dance company that survived the financial problem was

Dansgroep Krisztina de Chatel. The Dutch-Hungarian representative of reduction by minimal dance in combination with movement-bounding sculptures prolonged her leading position with *Paletta* and *Concave*. In *Paletta* she put her female dancers in huge perspex tubes, leaving her male dancers to the open space. In *Concave* she reversed their roles, by putting three male dancers in enormous circular constellations and leaving the universe around them to three star-like females.

Meanwhile new studios, centres, and working places are founded for the guidance of new talents who search for a way of their own. Amongst these clubs and houses, the Dansers Studio under the guidance of Beppie Blankert and Danswerkplaats under Ger Jager probably will be the most fruitful in Amsterdam. The start of the 1993/4 season, however, witnessed the definite end of Foundation Dance Production and the Concern.

In this survey the last place is saved for soloist performer-dance artist Truus Bronkhorst, the recipient of the Dutch Sonia Gaskell prize 1993. Bronkhorst can still be seen as one of the wildest exotic flowers in the Dutch dance bouquet. In her production *Blood*, she needed only one drop of red ink for her impressive statement about bloodshed on the world-wide scale of today.

In the second and third week of October 1993 the Holland Dance Festival took place in different-sized theatres in The Hague. Director Marc Jonkers (also responsible for the dance programmes of the Holland Festival) is firmly interested in the way—how and why tradition is formed in and by contemporary dance. He adjusted his programme to the 'Re' of Reconstruction, Reinterpretation, and Renovation in dance, with respect to the past, present, and possible future of today's stage dance. The highly interesting Reconstruction part was given to six Dutch choreographers and their reconstruction of works from the period 1975–88; the Reinterpretation part of well-known, ever-returning themes was represented by the latest Commedia production by Carolyn Carlson, *Perpetuum on Strauss Walzer* by Ohad Naharin and *Forgotten Land* by Jiří Kylián (1982); and the Renovation was to be seen in the newest uncompromising works of Mehmet Sander and Terence O'Connor.

The death of Rudolf Nureyev shook the Dutch dance community to the roots. In several productions his fate was remembered and visualized as a symbolic symptom of the doom of the new age.

Ten months after the burial of Rudolf Nureyev in Paris, his friend Rudi van Dantzig published a book about their remarkable friendship, which started in 1968. *Nureyev: The Track of a Comet*, is a very unconventional, honest effort to depict the man who once saved the National Ballet by being a welcome but very difficult guest. It depicts an unknown Nureyev, and his direct and indirect importance for the Dutch ballet during the 1970s and 1980s. It also depicts the former artistic leader of the Dutch National Ballet as his counterweight. In the two Rudis *extrêmes se touchent*. With respect to the general trend to retrospection of the last thirty years of ballet and dance this book surely is a historical document of great value.

New Zealand

JENNIFER SHENNAN

The year 1993 has seen a heartening turnaround in fortunes for the **Royal New Zealand Ballet**. Their plea to be funded, not via the Arts Council, but directly by government, on a parallel footing with the National Symphony Orchestra, continues to go unheeded, and a crisis in financial and administrative affairs in late 1992 almost brought the Company to a halt. There is plenty of precedent in this Company's history for fighting back, however, and a successful though demanding tour of the USA brought dollars as well as critical recognition of Killar's *Dark Waves* and Parmenter's *Tantra*. Back in New Zealand, strict budget and programme pruning resulted in two quality programmes, *Giselle/Sarabande* and *Petrushka/Pineapple Poll* which both had sell-out national tours. The dancers opted for a salary cut in favour of year-long contracts being maintained, and a new public fund-raising campaign. The Dancers' Appeal has been launched, thus averting a crisis for the mean time.

The RNZB's small company, **Jon Trimmer and Friends**, toured to smaller centres with *Coppélia* excerpts and a striking new work, *World News*, by Eric Languet. There have been well-attended open rehearsals, and a show-case of new works choreographed by the Company's dancers including several collaborations with the New Zealand School of Dance.

The casting of Douglas Wright, the country's foremost contemporary dancer/choreographer, in the title-role of *Petrushka* proved an inspired one. Russell Kerr's production was memorable and many spoke of Wright's uncanny evocation of Nijinsky's creation of the role over eighty years ago. Wright also had phenomenal success with a national tour of his new work, *Forever*. Of epic proportions, and involving film collaboration, *Forever* was a study of the boundaries between encounter and friendship, gender, passion, aggression, life, and the after-life. There are plans to tour the work to Europe in 1994, following the revival of Wright's earlier work, *How on Earth*, in the International Arts Festival, Wellington, in March. Wright also choreographed a striking piece, *Elegy*, for a controversial television

Jon Trimmer, Sonya Behrnes, and Kim Broad of the Royal New Zealand Ballet in *Dark Waves*, choreographed by Ashley Killar.

dance/film project which was screened nationally. *Elegy* subsequently won an award at the Frankfurt Dance on Screen Festival. Another film in the same project was by Michael Parmenter who also had extremely successful seasons of his new choreography *The Dark Forest*. A Kafka-inspired study of the private fears and hopes of siblings, the work had an impressive set design by Andrew Thomas and used music by Anthony Watson.

Other project-based dance artists include Paul Jenden, whose design ideas always supplement his choreography in an impressive fusion; a reworked *Dancing the Gay Fandango*, which had a male cast alternating with female, will attend the next Adelaide Festival. Susan Jordan choreographed several programmes, prominently *Bone of Contention*, to mark the centenary of Women's Suffrage in New Zealand. Ann Dewey choreographed and danced in *33⅓ rpm*, in a Wellington season which proved highly popular. **Footnote Dance Company** continued with their national education programme, and also presented a season in which *Mary, Mary*, choreographed by Shona McCullagh, was an unexpected sensation.

The new director at the New Zealand School of Dance is Rochelle Zide-Booth, formerly of the Joffrey Company, Nederlands Dans Theater, and

Adelphi University, New York. The Graduation season of NZSD included *Les Sylphides*, a modern-dress version of *The Shakers*, and *Albatross*, a new work by Nicholas Carroll.

An exhibition, *A Family in Dance*, based on the Tomlinson and Lowe manuscripts and a wider collection of rare dance books was at the National Library for four months, November 1993 to March 1994.

Taiao, the Maori contemporary dance group under Steven Bradshaw's direction, has consolidated repertory and will appear at the biennial International Festival of the Arts in March 1994, as also will the formidable traditional group, **Te Roopu Manutaki**, under its leader, Pita Sharples.

International visitors will include William Forsythe's Frankfurt Ballet, Rosas from Belgium, and the Australian Dance Theatre led by Meryl Tankard. The RNZB will present, for the first time, an all-Balanchine programme, and they, with all New Zealand dance followers, will hope for a repeat of all the successes of 1993 but none of its near disasters.

Kia ora tatou Kia kaha. Good health, bright courage, fierce pride and high morale to dancers and choreographers in all countries and languages . . . to those who write books about them, and to those indispensable audiences who are the *sine qua non* of it all.

Norway

HANS-CHRISTIAN ARENT

Dance in Norway has always enjoyed close contacts with British dancers and choreographers. It is, therefore, not so surprising that a former Royal Ballet dancer, Michael Corder, should be the one who introduced the Norwegian audience to a highly successful production of *Romeo and Juliet* to Prokofiev's music and Nadine Baylis's marvellous costumes and design. The leads were performed by two young British-trained dancers, Katherine Olsen and Richard Suttie, who were justly promoted to principal status the same season. The choreography showed in many ways Corder's familiarity with the Royal Ballet repertory, but without being a mere copy. The ballet was a hit, both with the audience and the critics, and it will also be shown on Norwegian state television during the next Christmas season.

However, Christmas 1992 offered, as usual, the inevitable *Nutcracker*. It was a proud ballet director who during the opening performance could announce that the company had now officially been granted the title of the

Norwegian National Ballet, a title that for many years had been its internationally recognized name instead of the Oslo Opera Ballet.

During the few years that Danish Dinna Bjørn has been the company's ballet director, the change has been quite remarkable. She has transformed the company from a rather lacklustre one to a company with plenty of spunk and with many talents among its young dancers.

The year 1992 ended with a well-publicized row between Kjersti Alveberg, the choreographer of last season's *Volven*, and the Lillehammer Winter Olympics, which led to the resignation of both Alveberg and the arts committee leader. Responsible for the choreography both at the opening and the concluding ceremonies in February 1994 were Dans Design's artistic directors, Anne Grethe Eriksen and Leif Hernes, who are at the head of Norway's post-modern dance movement.

Oslo's Black Box Theatre—why an English name for a Norwegian theatre I have never fully comprehended, if it is not to signal the Anglo-Norse dance connection—is the main stage for presenting modern dance in Norway and a centre for the so-called 'free groups'. In June 1992 a number of Norwegian male choreographers and dancers presented a week of dance named quite aptly *Men Dancing*, followed later that autumn by Dans Design's *Temple Sleep*, a multimedia performance which included an English text based on an Ibsen play, and with a somewhat confusing action. **Collage**, our oldest modern dance company, which has managed to survive for the last fifteen years, presented Kristin Gjems's *Et Cetera*, which the company also took to Norway's other state-supported dance theatre in Bergen, Danseteateret. This is the home of **Nye Carte Blanche**, with its rather nonconformist repertory and with Fredrik Rütter as artistic director. The company had asked Anerz Døving, one of our most versatile young choreographers, to produce with the help of Bergen Philharmonics an interesting piece of dance to Mozart's *Requiem* called *Omnis Caro*, later presented in a more condensed version during the Bergen International Festival. Nye Carte Blanche has also toured extensively on the west coast with both new and old ballets.

The Bergen Festival was also host to Ballett der Deutscher Oper with Béjart's *Ring um der Ring*, a rather lengthy work, but fairly well received.

The year 1993 opened with much publicity as the Year of Dance, and under royal patronage. The Norwegian dance community was offered a rare chance to come out in strength, backed financially by the Ministry of Culture. The lasting impression, however, was that of too much of the same. Somewhat more originality in choice of subject and form, as well as some self-restraint, would have been welcomed.

The long-awaited report on the arts, issued by the Ministry for once, promoted the status of dance in Norway, this time not only with words, but also in deeds. The Year of Dance has in many ways been more important than perhaps expected, partly because of a better rapport between the modern dance groups and classical ballet, a process which has been supported actively by Dinna Bjørn. The National Company offered during the spring a triple-bill Tetley programme, all presented for the first time in Norway. The three works were: *Voluntaries*, *Sphinx*, and the *Rite of Spring*,

The Rite of Spring, choreographed by Glenn Tetley for The Norwegian National Ballet.
PHOTO: ERIK BERG

all well executed. The 1992/3 season concluded with *Don Quixote* in memory of Nureyev and with Nina Ananiashvilli as Kitri.

At the Black Box Theatre one had once again the chance to watch Japanese butoh dancers, as well as works by a number of Norwegian modern dance groups; among those, Collage's *Pinocchio* was popular with the children and more in the line of a mini-musical. There was also the première of *The View* by the unique but uneven choreographer, Jane Hveding. But as dance and ballet have played a highly visual part in the media during the rest of 1993 the epithet 'the Year of Dance' was well deserved.

Russia

Moscow

ELIZABETH SOURITZ

During the months this report attempts to cover (all of the 1992/3 season and the beginning of the next one) the ballet world in Moscow was busy, but the activity hardly involved the major companies.

The **Bolshoi** has not had any important premières. The *Don Quixote* revival promised by Grigorovich never materialized. The only two small new productions were in July 1993, a ballet by the ex-Bolshoi dancer Mikhail Lavrovsky, *Fantasia on the Casanova Theme*. Music was by Mozart, with dancers Alexander Vetrov, Alla Mikhalchenko, Galina Stepanenko, and others. In October came the Anton Dolin *Pas-de-quatre*.

The Bolshoi's repertory is very poor. What makes it even poorer is that many of the ballets it lists as being in the current repertory are shown just a couple of times during the season, sometimes only on foreign tours, or as suites and not entire productions. Since the Bolshoi tours a great deal (probably in the hope of making money, as all our theatres hope nowadays) one does not see much of the company in Moscow and very few of its ballets. A friend of mine visiting Moscow in October endured the ordeal of seeing *Giselle* three times, because not only was there nothing else to see, but even when a different programme was announced it was replaced by *Giselle*.

The Bolshoi building, which still has not undergone the serious repairs it is emphasized are needed, has been refurbished meanwhile to serve for all types of event—festivals, jubilees, competitions, performances of other companies, and so on. There were, for instance, two premières by the

Grigorovich Ballet, a company which most of the time travels abroad and seems to get much more attention from its director than does the Bolshoi, where he is still supposed to be choreographer-in-chief. One of the two premières was *Electra* in September 1992 with music from Richard Strauss's *Electra* and *Legend of Joseph*. These were choreographed by two young dancers, Sergei Bobrov and Andrei Melanin, under the supervision of Grigorovich and featuring Grigorovich's traditional dramatic and emphatic style. The other was in September 1993—*La Fille mal gardée*, revival and 'new stage version' (according to the programme) by Grigorovich.

Other events on the Bolshoi stage: in January 1993 a company assembled by Andris Liepa under the sponsorship of the Moscow Diaghilev Centre has shown (after a première in St Petersburg) three ballets by Michel Fokine little known in Russia—*Petrushka*, *The Firebird*, and *Schéhérazade*. Andris was Petrushka and the Prince Ivan, his sister Ilse Liepa—Zobeide, Julia Makhalina the Firebird, and Victor Yaremenko (from Kiev) the Golden Slave. It was a very lavish production, but one which lacked style. On the one hand the programme was announced under the title *The Return of the Firebird* which would suggest a restoration of the authentic choreography and sets. On the other hand Liepa spoke of a need to modernize. As a large group of dancers from the Moiseyev ensemble took part in the performance, the choreography of the crowd scenes had been reworked. They had more excitement in them, more drive, but the tricks, smacking of the Moiseyev programme, were not in tune with the original choreography. Costumes also were even more lavish than the ones by Bakst or Benois, but this lavishness was not always in the best taste.

The Bolshoi has also launched festivals to commemorate Marius Petipa (175 years since he was born) and Tchaikovsky (100 years since his death). What really happened was that the ballets of the current repertory which were initially staged by Petipa, *La Bayadère*, *Le Corsaire*, *Raymonda*, and the Tchaikovsky ballets, were all given in the space of a fortnight. The same happened for the Tchaikovsky memorial. Some jubilees were also celebrated on the Bolshoi stage. The **St Petersburg Ballet Academy** gave performances to honour Natalia Dudinskaya who was 80 in the autumn of 1992. On 30 May 1993, the 85 years of Marina Semenova were celebrated, and her student Galina Stepanenko danced *La Bayadère*, a ballet in which Semenova excelled. In October 1993, it was Maya Plisetskaya celebrating fifty years since she graduated from the ballet school. This time the heroine of the occasion danced herself—in Béjart's *Isadora* and in *La Folle de Chaillot*, with choreography by Gheorge Caciuleanu, and partly in *Carmen Suite*—partly, because it was arranged so that at certain moments her 'double' danced while she sat and watched in her characteristic haughty Carmen posture.

Also at the Bolshoi, starting on 19 September, the Seventh International Moscow Ballet Competition was held. The Moscow competition, held every four years since 1969, has always been quite an ambitious venture attracting young dancers from many traditionally balletic countries, except England for some reason unknown to me... and of course all the countries of the Socialist bloc. This year things were different. The exotic East and South had the upper hand: a large group from Egypt, Korea, Mongolia, an even larger one from Japan, dancers from various Latin-American countries. Among the women competing in *pas de deux* it was Yelena Kniazkova from the **Grigorovich Ballet** who received the gold medal. The French dancer Bernard Courte de Bouteiller, who won the gold medal, was considered to be the most interesting among the men. The fact that the attendance and the results of the competition were not as spectacular as in previous years has been mentioned by many critics. Some saw it as a sign of the decline of the Russian ballet. Of course the economic and political instability is also to blame, people being reluctant to come to our country—not without reason! During the last days of the competition the so-called White House was already in a state of siege. The last performance was on 2 October and the very next day the fighting started.

The Bolshoi Theatre can be considered as one of the casualties of this armed revolt. Not that it has been hit by bullets—the fighting was in another part of town—but all its plans for October were shattered. The Bolshoi was to have had a big international ball and preparations for it had been made months in advance. The idea was to have attracted people from all over the world to bring the sums of money that the theatre needed. Of course after the disturbances at the beginning of October, a large attendance at this ball was unlikely, so it had to be postponed.

The second most important Moscow ballet company, the **Stanislavsky Ballet**, also did not have any premières last season, only revivals. This season its choreographer-in-chief Dmitri Briantzev is rehearsing a new ballet, *Othello*, with music by Alexei Machavariani.

There are two more ballet companies in Moscow which can be considered of the first importance; the **Moscow Theatre of Ballet** (which used to be called Moscow Ensemble of Classical Ballet) with choreographers Natalia Kasatkina and Vladimir Vasiliev, and the **Ballet of the Palace of Congresses**, choreographer Andrei Petrov. Both give performances mostly on the stage at the Palace of Congresses and both have had premières—one each. Kasatkina and Vasiliev have produced a new version of *Cinderella* (under the title *The Glass Slipper*) and Andrei Petrov a new version of *The Nutcracker*. Neither is of any great interest as a work of choreography, but may help to fill the huge 6,000-seat Palace, especially during school holidays.

At the Palace of Congresses one can also see other dance events—festivals, recitals, performances by touring companies. This season the Vladimir Vasiliev Festival took place, partly on this stage partly in the concert-hall Rossiya, from 10 May to 23 May 1993. One was able to see four of his ballets, *Aniuta*, *Romeo and Juliet*, *Cinderella*, and *Macbeth*, also a concert programme and a master class by Vasiliev.

The situation of the big Moscow companies, still dependent on the state, is precarious, especially that of the Bolshoi, where it is due in great part to the policy of its choreographer-in-chief. Does that mean that life in Moscow ballet is being extinguished? Certainly not. To start with there is a great interest, especially among the young, for the newer trends in dance abroad and also for the kind of art that has not been practised recently in Russia—and there are people and institutions ready to provide for these needs. Various cultural centres, for instance the French Centre and the German Goethe Institute, the Theatre Union, private firms such as Ardani, and others, have organized festivals and seminars. Video and film showings have also helped foreign companies and teachers to come to Russia.

In September 1992 an American Dance Festival took place in Moscow. It consisted of performances by two companies, the **Dayton Dance Company** and the **Pilobulus**, and classes given by famous American modern dance teachers. The Dayton Company presented a programme which was a kind of anthology of black dance in the USA, with works by Donald McKayle, Talley Beatty, Alvin Ailey, Eleo Pomare, and others. This was quite a revelation for those interested in modern dance and its history. The Pilobulos performances were a delight to watch. In March 1993 we saw performances of another American group which arrived from Jacob's Pillow with the programme *Men Dancers*, *The Ted Shawn Legacy*. Twice during these months French dance films and videos could be watched during specially organized festivals. As to the **German Tanztheater**—in September 1993 several dancers and groups attached to the *Folkwang*—Pina Bausch, Susanne Linke, and Urs Dietrich, have shown their recent works.

One festival should be mentioned especially—it is the Isadora Duncan Retrospective which took place in January 1993. It included performances by various American groups, an international conference with the participation of specialists from the USA, Germany, Sweden, Russia etc., an exhibition of photos and drawings belonging to Ligoa Duncan, and a film show. One of the principal organizers of this festival was Carol Prattl who, along with Duncan dancer Barbara Kane, took part in a reconstruction of Isadora's *Orpheus* with some students of the Moscow Vera Belososrovich School Music and Plastique. This 'Retrospective' was combined with a Russian Duncan Festival under the title *Remembering Duncan*, where Moscow groups of so-called 'plastic' dance took part.

Duncan has had many followers in Russia long before she opened her school in 1921. Some groups were formed in the 1910s and worked through the 1920s, their style gradually changing, so that in many ways they became quite different from Duncan. Later in the 1930s and 1940s most of them disappeared as all types of 'free' dance were frowned upon by the authorities. Nevertheless, some exponents of this dance survived,

sometimes as teachers of callisthenics or working with kindergarten children. Now some of these groups are being revived and claim their affinity
to Duncan. The most interesting one and the most 'genuine', I believe, is a
group of pupils of Ludmilla Alexeyeva (1890–1964), who studied with Ellen
Rabenek (also known as Ellen Teis), one of the first Duncan dancers in
Russia. The Alexeyeva dancers and some other groups took part in the
festival.

All these festivals, seminars, conferences, and retrospectives point to an
acute interest among professionals and audiences for our past (Petipa,
Fokine, or Duncan studios) and for the hitherto unknown dance trends
coming from abroad. But what about our own young independent choreographers? Have they produced any experimental work?

One of the new ballet companies calls itself very ambitiously **Russian
Ballet of the XXI Century**. Its choreographer is Svetlana Voskresenskaya,
its first creation, *Salome*, performed in February 1993. The printed programme explains the idea behind the ballet: three forces that reign over the
world are struggling, but they are inseparable—Spirit, Sex, Power. This is
on paper, but all this philosophy seems to have little to do with what is happening on the stage. To start with, the spiritual never manifests itself
because all the relations between Salome and St John seem to be on the
same erotic level. At times it looks as if she is pursuing him, at times he
seems to be the active partner. Exactly the same happens when Salome is in
the presence of Herod; but as long as one has decided to overlook all this
philosophy and pay attention to the dancing, the ballet has a certain appeal.
Svetlana Voskresenskaya is not devoid of talent as a choreographer. Using
all types of dance—ballet, grotesque, free movements, acrobatics—and all
kinds of moods, from lyrical reverie in white robes to vulgar striptease, she
has displayed ingeniously devised solos, duets, and ensembles. And she has
managed to show at her best a very capable and versatile young dancer,
Galina Yakovleva.

A new company, the **Graphical Ballet**, has shown works by the late
Gennady Pesghanny, preserved by his pupils. The choreographer used
dancers' bodies along with props to create abstract forms and patterns.
This company worked in a tiny little theatre and attracted a certain amount
of people, mostly professionals. On the other hand the new **Russian
Chamber Ballet**, Moscow, choreographer Edwald Smirnov, was over-ambi-
tious. It chose for its première in November 1993, a beautiful building seating over 20,000, which now belongs to the Operetta but from the 1920s to
the 1950s had belonged to the Bolshoi as its second stage. The house was
nearly empty except for a group of critics invited to the opening. The two
ballets shown were *L'Arlésienne* after the Alphonse Daudet drama with
music by Bizet, and *Theatre at the Time of Nero and Seneca* after a play by
Eduard Radzinsky with music by Alfred Schnitke. Neither was very successful. In *L'Arlésienne*, the girl from Arles, whose image haunts Frederic

Galina Yakovleva of the Russian Ballet of the XXI Century in *Salome*, choreographed by Svetlana Voskresenskaya.

and drives him to suicide, appears to him alone at first, then she appears with a double, then in the company of several doubles, so that at the end all these identically dressed girls (some of them impersonated by extra-tall boys which makes them look even more forbidding) surround Frederic like menacing wilis. In the second ballet the story was quite impossible to understand; and all the inter-killings and rather unsavoury scenes of drunken revelry were not so much revolting as boring. Did the audience guess in advance that it was not worth braving the cold and darkness of the Moscow streets or is it that audiences are mostly attracted by names? In any case, names certainly have an appeal: one of the very popular drama performances in Moscow last season had to do with Nijinsky. It is a play by Alexei Burykin, 'W' (Nijinsky), which takes place in a mental clinic and the two actors—it is a two-man show—Oleg Menshikov and Alexander Feklistov, impersonate Nijinsky and various personages with whom he had come into contact.

Several new dance books deserve to be mentioned. A reprint of the Akim Volynsky *Book of Exultation* (1925) with an introduction and notes by Vadim Gayevsky, *Isadora: Her Tours in Russia*, a collection of articles by Russian authors written about Isadora Duncan at various times when she danced in Russia (that is to say from 1904 to 1922), and a book about Natalia Makarova, a collection of various articles and interviews. In St Petersburg a book about the dancer Nikolai Zubkovsky contains reminiscences and a description of the exercises he gave when teaching.

St Petersburg

ARKADY SOKOLOV-KAMINSKY

The ballet community of St Petersburg keeps on experimenting with new commercial ways of work and is gradually getting used to the newly acquired freedom of realizing artistic ideas—some of them quite pragmatic ideas—all of which is exciting and frightening. The community seems to be spellbound, not knowing what will happen next—it may be scaling new artistic mountain tops or falling into the abyss of petty interests and spontaneous desires.

However, on the surface daily life appears to be busy and intense. Events are numerous; there is also a lot of noisy publicity intended to lure the public to what is not really significant. All is vanity! It is vanity that is striving to camouflage smart pretensions and banal results. New small companies appear and they all claim to be original, for instance, the **Small Ballet**, choreographer Andrei Kusnetzov, the **All-men Ballet**, headed by Valery Mikhailovsky and **Fouetté**, choreographer Alexander Polubentzev. The number of ballet companies which now exist in St Petersburg approaches two dozen. All of them—the oldest well-known companies included—complain about general instability. Dancers, conductors, and choreographers make up for the low standards of living here in Russia by arranging contracts abroad, all of them trying to combine work here and there. Some are inclined to call this frantic activity 'A Feast during the Plague'. I do not think it is so. It is what ordinary theatrical life should be: it is like air, which gives life and strength to that delicate and tender plant called 'Art', and without which it would wither. And what about its new, strong and viable branches? I believe they will grow—in due course.

At the Maryinsky, priority is still given to the opera troupe headed by the chief conductor, Valery Gergiev; money and stage time are reserved above all mainly for the opera troupe. The privilege of the ballet troupe is mainly restricted to bringing in the currency earned during its tours abroad. Without this the position of both the troupes might be so much harder...

The first gala concert of the season was the benefit performance in honour of the legendary Natalia Dudinskaya. On 17 November 1992, the Maryinsky celebrated her eightieth birthday and sixty years of artistic activity, at which, for the first time, the Noble Knight of his Fair Lady was not present—Konstantin Sergeyev died that spring. So the celebration was slightly veiled in sadness; Natalia Dudinskaya could not help being sad when she spoke the words of gratitude at the end of the evening. The programme of the concert included Act II from *Cinderella*, staged by Konstantin Sergeyev, and his version of *The Fairy Doll* after the choreography of the brothers Sergei and Nikolai Legat, and *Paquita* rounded off the concert. Dudinskaya's former students danced in the concert, Irina Shaptchits, Irina Zhelonkina, Anastasia Dunets and others—all of them now dancers at the Maryinsky. Some graduates of the Academy, who are now students of the famous master, also took part in the concert. However, the only real heroine of the evening was Natalia Dudinskaya herself. And somehow one could not help recollecting her former benefit performances in which her colleagues at the theatre danced—Irina Kolpakova, Gabriella Komleva, Natalia Makarova, Alla Sizova, Kaleria Fedicheva—all brilliant ballerinas indeed.

This season, like the past season, demonstrated frightening gaps in the programme of the Maryinsky. For ten days on end there might not be a single performance for ordinary spectators. That meant that either new opera performances were being rehearsed or that some performance was being shot for TV or video, another way of earning money—of filling up the empty treasury of the theatre. Alas! one cannot but think that the theatre is creating a sort of wall between itself and the spectator, by regarding its inner troubles and problems as prior to anything else.

And what about premières? There were practically none. We may count as one *Anna Karenina*, an old production of the French choreographer André Prokovsky. That is another new trend in the work of the theatre. In former times there existed a minimum of premières for every theatre, which was to show the intensity of the company's artistic level, and the work was controlled from 'above'. Now the theatre has the freedom of choice: to stage new productions or not, and maybe to prefer only revivals. The most significant was the restaging of *The Nutcracker* by Vasily Vainonen on 20 November 1992. In the last few decades the performance of it has been the privilege of the Vaganova Academy of Russian Ballet, in which all the main parts and *corps de ballet* were danced by students. Now it has been done by the ballet dancers of the Maryinsky. By the way, at the 1934 pre-mière, Galina Ulanova and Konstantin Sergeyev also danced the main parts. But later we became used to watching this ballet danced by the students of the Academy: young children imbue the performance for children with unusual charm and spontaneity.

The 'grown-up' version of *The Nutcracker* was specially done for performing abroad; the traditional version will remain intact and will be shown 'at home' to the St Petersburg public. The scenery was a repeat of that by Suliko Virsaladze. Among all the dancers only one might well have passed muster—Victor Baranov (the Prince), whose image and elegant dancing were in harmony with the poetic role. As to Larisa Lezhnina (Masha, the Princess), her dance was somewhat primitively pronounced, with no regard for elaborate details and sometimes just out of tune with the orchestra. The children's trio showed clearly what was strange with and probably unsuitable for, the proposed version of the ballet. This nice simple number produces a charming effect when danced by small children who are only learning their first classical steps, so that they are usually hesitant but so touching. The trio done by professional dancers—Janna Ahupova, Irina Chistiakova, and Igor Beliaev—turned it into a parody, almost. The more the dancers tried to look like children, the more awkward and absurd the dance became, for the choreography has always taken into account the very limited possibilities of dancer-beginners.

The Maryinsky troupe has also revived again *The Legend of Love* by Yuri Grigorovich, which with *The Nutcracker* by V. Vainonen, have always been regarded as the two 'Soviet' classical ballets—there is not yet another word to describe that period of Russian history. *The Legend of Love* has been looked upon as a top achievement of the choreography of that period—now a new generation of dancers is performing it. Marina Chirkova, who danced the part of Mekhmene Banu in the third cast, was universally thought to be the brightest of all. The first performance was given on 15 January 1993 during the International Festival *The Diaghilev Seasons*.

The organizers of the Festival revived that legendary name in memory of those famous 'Seasons'. So the Festival programme included, besides ordinary repertory performances, 'A Night in Memory of Mikhail Fokine', which took place on 5 January 1993 at the Maryinsky. It showed three of his ballets—*Petrushka*, *Schéhérazade*, and *The Firebird*. The ballets were revived by the Moscow Diaghilev Centre with the actual help of Isabel Fokina, granddaughter of the choreographer. The much-advertised performance turned out to be a pretentious spectacle, done in a hurry so everything else in the performance was bound to stay in its shadow because of the gaudy luxury embracing everything. The accuracy of the reconstruction of the choreography left much to be questioned. Serge Diaghilev, whose name was not even mentioned in former, Soviet days, is being made much of now; sometimes his name is used to cover rather questionable experiments.

The spectacular and the superficial were supreme in *Anna Karenina*. Viacheslav Okunev, the designer, seemed to have tired of illusory scenery and he gave way to his dream of a stage full of concrete objects and details. The railway station with its porters and luggage; the tea-party in the garden with a samovar on the table; the making of a snowman. The routine of life seems to have swallowed up the psychological significance of the story. The scenes where the heroine reaches the peak of her emotional strain are no longer the centre of attention for the public—more sensational seem to them the episodes of luxurious balls in the palace halls, or the scenes at the Imperial Theatre, and it is in those scenes that the dance becomes really spectacular, and not so much due to the fact that a lot of dancers fill the stage. The choreographer, André Prokovsky, does not prevent us from enjoying Tchaikovsky's wonderful music, nor does he prevent us from admiring the picturesque scenes of town and country life. His choreography is full of reiterations and generalities, but remains all the time thoughtlessly pleasant. The showy Julia Makhalina (Anna) and the skilled Konstantin Zaklinsky (Vronsky) try to do their best to enrich weak choreography with the passion of modern cinema-thrillers. The second cast of Olga Likhovskaya (Anna), soft and feminine, and Andrei Yakovlev (Vronsky), outwardly dignified, seek for the psychological motivation that might explain the actions of their characters.

In the final dramatic scene of her death, it is not Anna who is the centre of attention, but the engine itself with clouds of steam, moving towards the spectators from the darkness, quite realistically and threateningly... The audience falls silent in admiration and then sighs, forgetting all about the miserable Anna. However, it was appropriate that the ballet should have appeared—just now. Its slick, flashy attractiveness, its primitive and daring emotional impact, the translation of a psychological drama into a banal love story—all these factors were readily appreciated by the modern spectator, since they distracted him from the numerous problems of everyday life, often unpleasant and too complicated. This kind of entertainment gives one an opportunity to relax—like all those endless and senseless Mexican serials that have engulfed our TV. They are there to distract one. . .

The ballet season at the Maryinsky was not brimming with new ideas, to put it mildly. They were ready to celebrate events of all sorts, though—jubilees, benefit performances, memorial dates. Like an elderly man is wont to dwell on his past, so the theatre felt inclined to recapture its own.

The 175th birthday anniversary of Marius Petipa—the great and beloved Petipa—was marked, seemed to be marked, by a conference at the Vaganova Academy of Russian Ballet, the programme of which was not up to the mark or adequate for the occasion. Also *La Bayadère* was performed

Olga Likhovskaya and Andrei Yakovlev of the Maryinsky Ballet in *Anna Karenina*, choreo-graphed by André Prokovsky.

at the Maryinsky on 11 March 1993. It is true, they promised that the main events would take place in the autumn, events worthy of the name of the great Petipa.

Another performance of *The Fairy Doll* and a concert given on 16 March 1993 in thankful memory of the late Konstantin Sergeyev—head of the Academy until a year ago—was quite different: warm and emotional. It seemed that well-known repertory pieces were done with unusual assiduity, affection, and warmth.

At the benefit performance of Svetlana Efremova, given on 19 December 1992, *La Sylphide* was presented. Her Sylphide bade farewell to life, rejecting her love for James, for her light-winged friends, for that charmed wood. The ballerina was also saying goodbye to the stage, on which twenty-six artistic years had flown so quickly by! Will she keep in her soul her love for that stage, for the theatre, for the troupe? Of late, the actors have been leaving the troupe extremely easily, if not willingly, preferring high salaries abroad to the prestige of the Maryinsky... Those who can and want to dance are enthusiastically invited by newly-built troupes abroad.

The **Maly Theatre of Opera and Ballet**, like the Maryinsky, is head over heels in love with foreign tours. No time left for premières. They are being prepared, though, and will appear only during the next season.

Angela Kondrashova and Vladimir Adzhamov in the Maly Ballet's production of *Slow Flows the Don*, choreographed by N. Boyarchikov.
PHOTO: V. I. VASILEVA

The most original appearance was made by a newly born St Petersburg group, the **All-Men Ballet** under Valery Mikhailovsky. Two programmes were shown, each consisting of two parts. One part presented modern choreographic pieces danced by men, the other part presented well-known classical masterpieces, in which women usually dance as well. Their roles were taken over by men, and they danced them on points. They caught, with evident delight, all the artistic clichés and tricks and all the manifestations of coquetry characteristic of women and displayed them sometimes with soft humour and sometimes with sharp sarcasm. In *The Dying Swan* and *The Vision of the Rose*, Mikhailovsky was quite successful in creating an original and very expressive masque of an elderly prima donna, who has long lost the perfection of dance, and who is desperately trying to substitute charm for old age and lack of technique. The comic situation was due to the fact that all the efforts of the prima donna to look charming and irresistible produced an opposite, if not a horrifying effect. The masque that the talented male dancer has created requires precise artistic approach. So far, it is true, the dancer has remained within the limits of good taste, without making it a vulgar comic piece.

South Africa

AMANDA BOTHA

The history of dance in South Africa shows that dance politics and dance power have to do with moral issues as well as with political, economic, organizational, and cultural issues. Dance politics has to be rooted in democratic theatre. That, in turn, should be translated into a concern for the socially relevant content of choreography, the importance of dance for a multiracial country with great cultural diversity, the significance of dance in education, access to dance for everyone, and finally a political strategy to guide a central national dance organization. It is clear that dance could be a powerful tool in the healing process of the nation. The power of choreography and dance can redirect the conscience and the fixed assumptions that people hold within our divided society towards new kinds of cultures of diverse nationhood. These will, many believe, characterize the next century.

Young grassroots companies and groups made a significant impact on the local dance scene. In Johannesburg, various platforms were created to give performing experience to young dancers and choreographers. The Johannesburg Dance Foundation presented programmes which premièred local choreography and original music by local composers. The University of Witwatersrand's School of Dramatic Art presented regular programmes show-casing new dance creations by young choreographers, and the Market Theatre Laboratory gave young dancers from townships, such as Diepkloof and Soweto, their first exposure to audiences. The **Pretoria Technikon** presented a programme of contemporary and African dance and an innovation, **Dance Factory**, situated in the Johannesburg City Hall complex, gave dancers, choreographers, and musicians an opportunity to explore the creative and performing aspects of dance. The local Royal Academy of Dancing co-ordinated a highly successful Ballet Outreach

Dance Movement programme for children of all ages which were conducted in public venues such as shopping centre malls and large open-air venues. In the other dance centres—Cape Town and Durban—similar activities at grassroots level were presented.

The Johannesburg Youth Ballet Dance '93 featured the work of three promising choreographers—Rulor Senekal, Susan Abraham, and Jackie Semela. This exciting event can be described as a vision of the future of the arts in South Africa which unfolds on stage. The programme, covering the cultural spectrum from traditional, contemporary, and classical dance, was a vibrant mosaic of colour, sound, and movement. It is an important educational role which is continuously being played by the many dance schools, ballet studios, and especially the University of Cape Town Ballet School under the directorship of Professor Elizabeth Trichardt, the Johannesburg Art, Ballet, Drama and Music School, the Pretoria Technikon Dance Department, and the newly formed dance school attached to the PACT Dance Company in Pretoria.

The Vita Life Dance Umbrella, which celebrated its fifth season, has become Southern Africa's most important platform for contemporary dance forms. The Dance Umbrella was held in venues all over Johannesburg. In 1993, ninety-two works representing some seventy choreographers were presented. The cultural diversity of the audience also reflected the cultural diversity of the performers and the performances. It is an important show-case for new choreography. Children and teenagers injected the fringe, and to an extent the main festival, with explosive energy in Afro-fusions and variations of township-jazz. The Laban Centre's Claire Baker attended as guest teacher. Her technique classes were very well attended. Before her return to the UK she gave classes in training schools outside Johannesburg, including Soweto.

The NedBank Arts Alive Dance Festival presented the PACT Dance Company and the Soweto Dance Theatre, featuring five new South African works, and the South African première of *Duo*, by American dancers/choreographers, Joannie Smith and Daniel Shapiro. The two companies are at the opposite ends of the funding and facilities spectrum—the one state-funded, the other community-based, originating from a break-dance troupe performing mainly in the streets.

The Pretoria Technikon hosted in 1993 the first Sanlam International Ballet Competition. It will be a biennial event and has already attracted the interest of young dancers from four countries. The three-day competition produced twenty semifinalists and ten finalists. Twenty-one-year-old Tracey Li from Hong Kong was the winner in the professional category and Rani Luther, aged 17, and a student at the Victoria College of Arts Secondary School in Melbourne, Australia, was the winner in the non-professional category. David Wall, former director of the Royal Academy of Dancing, chaired the adjudicating panel.

An exciting new company, although not yet fully professional, is the **Soweto Dance Project** under the leadership of choreographer Jackie Semela. The German-based **Transprojekte Köln** collaborated with this company in a venture called 'Movement Project' at the Wits Theatre, Johannesburg. Cologne's James Saunders directed an hour-long solo, *Transition*, performed by Afro-Brazilian dancer/choreographer Marcio Valeriano. Carly Dibahoane's work *On the Move* was also presented in a programme celebrating this co-operation.

The **Bop Dance Company** based in Mmabatho, Bophuthaswana, made their international début in Germany at the Stuttgart Cultural Festival with Sonje Mayo's work *Tears and Laughter*. The twelve-member company includes Soweto modern dance pioneer, Ellington Mazibuko, and former members of PACT and CAPAB companies. The company has an exciting indigenous repertory dealing primarily with the African experience. It was formed three years ago and David Krugel is the artistic director.

Two other local companies, Isabelle Doll's Soweto-based **Street Company** and Jayspri Moopen's **Tribanghi Dance Theatre** from Benoni also participated in the Stuttgart Cultural Festival.

Moving into Dance, a company founded by Sylvia Glasser, celebrated its fifteenth anniversary in Johannesburg. In 1992 this company danced at the World Expo in Seville and last year toured Australia, Holland, Namibia, and Zimbabwe. The company's star performer is 22-year-old Vincent Sekwati Mantsoe who has begun an international career.

The five professional companies—all state-subsidized—had generally a highly successful artistic year which saw a definite growth in attendance figures.

PACT Ballet experienced many highlights in the year under review. Two new full-length ballets were added to the repertory: *The Taming of the Shrew* and *The Merry Widow*. An overall attendance of 93,400 was recorded. Colin Peasley, Australian Ballet's Regisseur General, prepared the company for the performance of Robert Helpmann and Ronald Hynd's lavish three-act ballet *The Merry Widow*. Hynd staged the splendidly produced and performed production, which show-cases PACT's dance talent as the premier company in South Africa. Soloist Tanja Graafland received the Nederburg Award for her portrayal of Hanna Glawari.

Jane Bourne staged *The Taming of the Shrew*, the two-act ballet by John Cranko, an artistic and highly acclaimed performance. *Swan Lake* once again revealed the depth of talent in the company with outstanding performances by Leticia Müller as Odette/Odile and Christopher Montague as Prince Siegfried.

A triple bill, *Homage to Balanchine*, consisted of *Ballet Imperial*, *Agon*, and *Who Cares?* The Yugoslavian dancer Aleksandar Antonijević from the National Ballet of Canada was the guest artist. Leslie B. Dunner, principal conductor of the Dance Theatre of Harlem, New York, conducted the

Transvaal Philharmonic Orchestra in his first South African engagement. The other full-length productions were *Coppélia* and *Cinderella* in which Odette Millner, a former member of US Ballet West, gave her farewell performance.

The **PACT Dance Company** presents contemporary dance, featuring mainly South African choreography and dancers. It has a reputation for originality and excitement. The company has also been accepted as dynamic, controversial, and as being at the forefront of change. It can be described as a builder and educator of audiences in the new South Africa. A high standard is maintained and the repertory is versatile. The PDC gave about eighty performances and had an attendance figure of about 500,000. Many new works were performed—amongst them Robert North's *Death and the Maiden* which was described by critics as 'a sheer masterpiece'. Susan Abraham's performance of the maiden was hailed as 'one of the most poignant performances ever seen from the PDC'.

CAPAB Ballet, with its headquarters at the Nico Malan Opera House in Cape Town, presented thirteen productions and mounted two new full-length ballets by the company's director and resident choreographer, Veronica Paeper. Her production of *Hamlet* placed Paeper's creative

Dutch choreographer Rudi van Dantzig directs Candice Brathwaite and Sean Bovim while designer Toer van Schayk looks on, in CAPAB Ballet's *Four Last Songs*.   PHOTO: PETER STANFORD

innovations as a choreographer in world class. Critics were unanimous in their accolades for the new masterpiece danced to Peter Klatzow's original music. The production was also broadcast live on the TSS channel of the South African Broadcasting Corporation. Paeper won the Nederburg Award for her choreography and she and Klatzow won arts awards on South African TV for superior entertainment.

Paeper's second full-length ballet, *Sylvia in Hollywood* to music arrangements by Allan Stephenson, is a send-up of the classical work *Sylvia*. It is a joyous fun ballet, but apart from an excellent *pas de deux*, magnificently danced by Johan Jooste and Carol Kinsley, it is not choreographically satisfactory.

A young choreographer Mzonke Jama directed and staged his work *2 + 4 & 1* to live township music with the **Manyanani Dancers and Musicians** and the **Imvatba Yolwazi Dance Theatre**. British chef John Tovey presented a cooking demonstration, entitled *Entertaining on a Plate!* in the Nico Theatre. The proceeds of the season enabled the Nico for All Fund to invite 1,200 black children to a performance on the opera stage of *A Midsummer Night's Dream* where Mzonke Jama gave a Xhosa narration of the story.

In May 1992 **Jazzart** became **CAPAB's Contemporary Dance Company** and by March 1993 it had performed and run workshops and dance classes to more than 45,000 people. They also visited many schools in disadvantaged communities and gave productions in rural areas. A major work created by the company, entitled *Unclenching the Fist*, was staged by Jay Parker, initiated by studies at the Department of Forensic Medicine at the University of Cape Town. The work deals with interpersonal violence and was widely performed. It has been reworked three times, linked continuously to research with experts and people at risk. In addition, a total of eight seasons were presented, ranging from experimental to very accessible work. A community tour, organized by the Street Law Department of the University of the Western Cape, was also undertaken. The schools' programme had been performed at sixty-five schools, colleges, universities, and community centres.

The **NAPAC Dance Company** at the Playhouse Theatre in Durban experienced a year of changes and challenges to find a new direction in a changing South Africa; especially amongst a community who suffered greatly through political violence. Gary Trinder resigned as Artistic Director of the company and Lynn Maree, a South African dance administrator at the Southern Arts Board in Winchester, was appointed as his successor. She joined the company on 1 January 1994.

Seven productions were mounted. Trinder's association with the company was celebrated with a programme of four works, entitled *Intro* and *Allegro*. Three Balanchine works, all staged by Victoria Simon, former Balanchine dancer and now New York-based teacher, and Trinder's tribute to Nijinsky—created a decade ago for the Scottish Ballet—were also

Boyzie Cekwana and
Wendy Mason of the
NAPAC Dance Company
in *Derivations*.
PHOTO: BARRY DOWNARD

presented. The Balanchine works were *Concerto Barocco*, *Tarantella*, and *Pas de deux* to the music by Glazunov from *Raymonda*, 1989. Trinder's *Voices from God* is a starkly dramatic, experimental dance-theatre piece which incorporates spoken text. It explores the foundations of art, as an artist is confronted and challenged by his sexuality and artistic genius. Three of Nijinsky's most celebrated roles in *Petrushka*, *L'Après-midi d'un faune*, and *Le Spectre de la rose* are suggested in acrobatic solos. The text, inspired by Nijinsky diaries to music by Bach, echo his unfulfilled plan. This work was powerfully performed by Vietnam-born Anthony Huynh, Vincent Hantam, and Tracy Lee.

A production entitled *New Directions* by the NAPAC Company featured new works by South African choreographers: Head of Drama at Rhodes University, Professor Gary Gordon choreographed a piece entitled *Travellers*, Susan Abraham presented her acclaimed work *Bloodsport*, a new work, *The Moon in your Mouth*, was choreographed by Mark Hawkins, and Boyzie Cekwana, NAPAC's choreographer-in-residence, presented *Lonely, Won't Leave Me Alone*.

In conclusion a quote from Professor Njabulo Ndebele, Chairman of the National Arts Initiative:

I am one of those who has thought that the future of culture in our country lies in our ability to take full advantage of the untapped talents of individual South Africans, as well as the wealth of artistic tradition available to us. I was able to recognise in our dancers a committed attempt to take full advantage of those traditions. In this way we have been able to do, through dance, what our politicians have thus far found elusive. Our dancers have affirmed the unifying power of art.

South-East Asia

DARYL RIES

Inter-culturalism is the buzzword for the 1990s putting Asia at the forefront of a global awareness. The Japan Asia Dance Event '93, the Eighth International Dance Conference in Asia, spearheaded by the Hong Kong Academy for the Performing Arts, highlights the growing interest in Asia's performing arts development. The première of the Annual Asian Contemporary Dance Festival in July 1993 at New York's La Mama Theatre confirms there is an audience abroad for Asian contemporary dance and theatre. This is part of the phenomenon of inter-culturalism that has helped to revamp the Asian dance scene.

Hong Kong

International link-ups have contributed immeasurably to the development of local companies and audiences, making a global vision ever vital to an emerging arts policy in the territory. Add to that the galvanizing effect created by the movement for greater democracy in Hong Kong and the beginnings of real lobbying power and you can see why the arts are finally on the government agenda. Many people in the arts are pinning their hopes on the future Arts Council to devise a forward-looking policy that can ensure freedom of artistic expression in Hong Kong, especially in the post-1997 era. Most see the arts safeguarded by a continued focus on a clear Hong Kong identity inspired by global vision and scope. In addition, an arts-for-all mentality presides.

To this end the Hong Kong Arts Resource and Information Centre (ARIC) has published a bilingual Hong Kong Arts Directory providing practical information on the arts in Hong Kong, Macau, and eleven countries in the Asia-Pacific region, in addition to their broad agenda of inter-global conferences, most recently the Peal River Delta Arts Manager's Conference to initiate contacts in twelve South China cities.

The Asia Pacific Arts Directory, a project of UNESCO, is compiled in Hong Kong for 1994 publication, annually updated to be the most comprehensive guide to the cultural sector in the Asia-Pacific region.

Hong Kong is also the new Asia base for the Rockefeller Foundation's Asia Society, as well as the Asian Cultural Council, which confers grants to Asian artists for study in America. Grantees in 1993 included two dance students, one choreographer, and a dance composer selected from Hong Kong.

What is really new at the Hong Kong Ballet is a sense of refreshed mission, at the start of their fourteenth season. The company's première of top-ranking dancer Anthony Huynh's contemporary work, *The Voice*, is a star on the horizon for this thirteen-year-old home-grown troupe. Now, finally, they have their own choreographer, a fine talent nurtured in the sophisticated eclecticism of the company's repertory and an award-winner of international dance prizes. After eight years with the company, Vietnamese-born Huynh is at one with their Asian balletic talents, highlighted by his contemporary sensibility and his diverse dance vocabulary.

So Han Wah of the Hong Kong Ballet in *Who Cares?*

The Hong Kong Ballet with its world-class repertory performed Balanchine's *Who Cares?*, and Choo San Goh's *Unknown Territory* at the Governor's home for a ticket-only audience. Here again art mixed with the new open policy of the government.

Seven graduates from the Hong Kong Academy for the Performing Arts (APA) were hired by the Hong Kong Ballet—and several more by the City Contemporary Dance Company, which boasts a fine choreographic talent in Jacky Yu, an APA graduate. Pewan Chow, another graduate, followed in Yu's footsteps as recipient of an American Dance Festival study grant in

1993. Upon her appointment, Margaret Carlson, the Dean of Dance at the Academy and former Director of Music and Dance at the University of Akron said, 'Hong Kong has tremendous potential which can be seen through the high quality of performance and the wide range of activities presented. I hope the APA becomes a focus for all the talent available . . .'

The **City Contemporary Dance Company** has amalgamated in body and spirit with the **Guangdong Dance Company**, the first modern dance company in China, performing recently together in a large-scale production created in Hong Kong, *Tales from the Middle Kingdom*. The extravaganza, featuring the fifty professional dancers from Hong Kong and China, attempted a theatrical first for Asia with a fusion of traditional and contemporary music and choreography, dubbed 'The New China Experience'. With support from the local business sector and government, a viable commercial art-form akin to the American musical seems to be high on the local agenda.

However, the government still encourages traditional values as seen in the Regional Council's Silk Road Arts Festival with Chinese folk-dance troupes from Xinyiang, Shaanxi, and other cultural minority regions of China.

A new development, at this very late stage of Indian citizenry in Hong Kong, is Vrindaban—an Academy for Indian Classical Music and Dance. Their recent presentation of Classical Women in India concert featured the illustrious Meenakshi Seshadz in ancient ritual temple dances, for a predominantly Indian audience.

Taipei

Lin Ywai Min's *Nine Songs*, premièred in Taipei and Hong Kong in autumn 1993, confirms his position as South-east Asia's leading choreographer and dance innovator.

As founder of the Cloudgate Dance Theatre, twenty years ago, the twenty-four-member company is now considered the epitome of East–West fusion with its Graham base linked to Chinese Opera and martial-art forms.

Nine Songs, inspired by a series of ritual songs from ancient China, includes visual images and movement drawn from Bali to Tibet; the music is from Taiwanese aborigines and modern composers. In the words of Lin: 'I can't and don't intend to re-create what is lost. Instead *Nine Songs* serves as a springboard for my choreography, which is about China . . . and how a Chinese confronts his oriental, Middle Kingdom past—and the cruel reality of the present day.' Lin ends his *Nine Songs* with a stage lit with floating candles, a metaphor for his universal prayer for peace and homage to China's Tianamen victims.

Singapore

The National Arts Council envisages Singapore as Asia's 'vibrant global city for the arts' come 1999. But observers doubt that the arts can flourish in the highly restrictive and conservative climate of Singapore's government. A major obstacle is the Censorship Review Committee set up by the government 'to review and recommend changes . . . forward achieving a balance between . . . creating and maintaining a morally wholesome society'. However, to show that it means business in expanding the arts, the Island's Economic Development Board has teamed up with Australian Management Cameron Mackintosh International, to bring in hit musicals. *Les Miserables* was staged in Singapore for eleven weeks in early 1994, following on the heels of *Cats*.

Ellie Lai and Mohamed Noor Sarman of the Singapore Dance Theatre in *Momentum*, choreographed by Goh Choo San.

According to a leading Singaporean artist, 'Singapore, both in terms of artists and audience, is still immature. The people will need to be exposed to a broader spectrum of art.' Dick Lee, a famous local actor/singer, has attempted to give Asia its own musical with *Nagraland*—a mix of East–West ingredients—including updated Balinese choreography. Like most endeavours in South-east Asia today, it has done better economically than artistically—and commercialism is the name of the game.

South Korea

This year Seoul hosted the annual meeting of the Federation for Asian Cultural Promotion (FACP) now in its twelfth year. The corner-stone of the Federation is to promote the inherent culture of Asian countries in the Asian region and around the globe. A lot of ground has been covered in twelve years, with Asian performing artists crossing into the world arena of culture and the arts. Now a two-way cultural exchange between East and West has been effected, and the goal is to make such exchanges more frequent and rewarding.

Spain

LAURA CUMIN

The stellar events that brought Spain world-wide attention in 1992 gave way last year to less glamorous but more stable contexts. In the midst of a serious recession which has resulted in reduced funding for the arts, and in spite of the ongoing lack of infrastructure and support systems for local companies and choreographers, more dance is being programmed than ever.

It is perhaps classical ballet that faces the greatest difficulties at present. The transition of the **Ballet Lírico Nacional**, Spain's national ballet company, from classical to contemporary repertory is still controversial, although the ensemble is dancing beautifully and continues to grow in popularity. Director Nacho Duato underscored this new focus by changing the troupe's name to **Compañia Nacional de Danza** during their December 1992 season at Madrid's Teatro de la Zarzuela, where his *Duende* and William Forsythe's *In the Middle, Somewhat Elevated* were added to the repertory. Among other works taken on by the ensemble in 1993 were Duato's *Na Floresta*, the new *Cautiva*, and *Alone for a Second*, and Jiří Kylián's *Forgotten Land* and *Stepping Stones*.

As the national company consolidated its new identity, the country's outstanding private ensemble, the **Ballet de Victor Ullate**, astutely adjusted its repertory in January 1993 to include *Les Sylphides* and Balanchine's *Theme and Variations* and *Concerto Baroco*. Ullate also announced the group's new status as company in residence at the new Teatro de Madrid, with three seasons a year. The municipal theatre, which has hosted a series of successful dance events, will be under private management by January 1994, a controversial move prompted by the city's economic straits and peculiar cultural policies. It is uncertain whether Ullate's relationship with the theatre will continue. Company member Eduardo Lao is being groomed as a

Catherine Allard and Nacho Duato of the Compañia Nacional de Danza in *Cor Perdut*,
choreographed by Nacho Duato   PHOTO: MICHAEL SIOBODIAN

choreographer and has contributed two ballets to the repertory, in addition to Ullate's own *Arrayán Daraxa* and *De Triana a Sevilla*.

Other Spanish ballet companies have faced difficulties recently. Maria de Avila disbanded her young troupe in 1992. This outstanding pedagogue was honoured at a special gala event during last summer's Itálica Dance Festival as well as at 1993's International Dance Day Gala in Madrid. The **Ballet de Zaragoza**, in danger of folding because of financial problems, managed to survive and was the highlight of the Centro Cultural de la Villa's ballet season in Madrid last April. Rafael Martí's **Ballet de Euskadi**, a group of young dancers with potential but in need of choreographic and artistic guidance, also performed in the Spanish capital.

Alicia Alonso and the Ballet Nacional de Cuba made several visits to Spain, presenting successful seasons at Madrid's Teatro Albéniz in both 1992 and 1993, and returning to tour northern Spain in February 1993. Alonso made headlines once again when it was announced that she had been named Professor of Ballet at Madrid's Complutense University, where she will direct advanced level studies, the first time that dance has been included in the Spanish university curriculum.

Spain's 1992 Quincentennial Commission sponsored a series of dance performances which included a Grand Gala of Iberoamerican Dance, Cristina Hoyos's *Yerma* and *Lo Flamenco* from Spain, Julio Bocca and Eleanora Cassano with the **Ballet Contemporáneo del Teatro General San Martín** from Buenos Aires, Argentina, and the Cullberg Ballet from Sweden, all at Madrid's Teatro de la Zarzuela, with the latter company appearing in Barcelona as well.

The season also brought many changes to the world of Spanish dance and Flamenco. In December 1992, after a very successful Madrid season that included the revival of Antonio's *Fantasía Galaica*, director-choreographer José Antonio stepped down after six years at the head of the **Ballet Nacional de España**. He was replaced by a three-member team: Aurora Pons (recipient of a silver medal for achievement in the arts from the Ministry of Culture), Nana Lorca, and Victoria Eugenia. The company's first season under the new directorship, at the Teatro de Madrid, presented revivals of Antonio's *Allegro de Concierto* and José Granero's *Medea*, among others. Although budget cuts have necessitated a freeze on new productions the group spent last October touring in Japan and several performances in the USA are planned for 1994.

Mario Maya, winner of Spain's National Dance Award in 1992, brought his *Tres Moviementos Flamencos* to Madrid's Alcalá Palace Theatre in January 1993, returning to the capital in April to participate in the International Dance Day Gala. This same production was well received in New York in the autumn.

In June 1992 Producciones Maga presented the First International Spanish Dance and Flamenco Choreography Competition at Madrid's

Teatro Albéniz. The event drew participants from all over Spain and the Americas. The level of the dancing at the 1993 competition was, on the whole, much higher. First prize went to Florencio Campos while the second prize was shared by Elvira Andrés, and Montse Sánchez and Ramón Baeza. Miguel Angel Berna was chosen as an outstanding dancer.

Madrid's Centro Cultural de la Villa hosts a season of Spanish dance every autumn. In 1992 performances included Maria Rosa's *Ballet Español*, *Manolete*, and Luisillo's *Teatro de Danza Española*. The latter company, revenue-funded by the Comunidad de Madrid's Regional Cultural Council, is now in residence in Tres Cantos after establishing a municipal dance and theatre school in this growing Madrid suburb. The 1993 season presented Joaquín Ruiz and Maria Vivó's new company, among others, and a return engagement by Maria Rosa during which the famous veteran dancer and choreographer Antonio was presented with a medal from the City of Madrid for outstanding achievement in the arts. Antonio, whose contribution to Spanish dance has been extremely important, was hospitalized for several weeks in 1993 with a serious illness.

Madrid's 1992 Festival de Otoño (Autumn Festival) included a mixed programme of Kathak and Flamenco dance featuring the talented Indian dancer Durga Arya. A similar programme, organized by the same producer and presented as part of Madrid en Danza 1993 did not fare so well.

Arraigo, a spectacular gala of Spain's rich heritage of traditional dance and music, took place at the Teatro de la Zarzuela in December 1992, and has, happily, become an annual event.

In April 1993 Joaquín Cortés, accompanied by dancers Lola Greco and Joaquín Grilo, plus fourteen singers and musicians, presented *Cibayi*. Excellent performers, the trio demonstrated how other dance styles can enrich Flamenco. Cortés returned to the Zarzuela last November during the 1993 Festival de Otoño, this time with Grilo and Merche Esmeralda, and has become something of a cult figure in Spain.

Barcelona's Picasso Museum showed the artist's sets for *The Three-Cornered Hat* in February, while exhibits sponsored by the COM92 featured Elke Stolzenberg's Flamenco photographs and part of Juan María Bourio's copious Spanish dance archive. Bourio was the director of the famous dance studios on the Calle Amor de Díos where for the past thirty-five years many of the finest Flamenco and Spanish dance teachers in the country have taught. The owners of the building plan to create luxury apartments and offices and, after several months of uncertainty, protests, and demonstrations, Amor de Díos was relocated in December 1993 to Calle Fray Luis de León, 13.

Contemporary dance activity has also been intense. Madrid's 1992 Festival de Otoño programmed Trisha Brown's company as well as new works by Spaniards Teresa Nieto and Mal Pelo, and Portuguese artists Vera Mantero, Francisco Camacho, and Joana Providencia. The 1993 Festival included six commissioned works by local choreographers inspired by and performed in the Madrid underground. Barcelona's Mercat de les Flors and the Sala Olimpia's *Danza en Diciembre* series in Madrid also provide opportunities for contemporary choreographers, with many outstanding new works this season. The Cultural Affairs Department of the University of Salamanca has also initiated a series of residencies and performances for contemporary choreographers.

Moses Pendleton's company Momix spent the month of April at Madrid's Teatro Albéniz, and last May's VIII Madrid en Danza festival featured the Netherlands Dans Theater 3, Lar Lubovitch, and performances by ten local and national companies. *Espacios Insólitos*, originally conceived for Madrid Cultural Capital of Europe 1992, once again brought site-specific work to the city's streets, this time with pieces by Pedro Berdäyes, Teresa Nieto, Carmen Senra, and Felix Lozano. A similar event brought dancers and choreographers together in Barcelona's Güell Park last summer.

A new dance festival was created last May in Valladolid. Participating companies included NDT 3, the Cullberg Ballet, Ballet de Victor Ullate, and Carolyn Carlson, who also brought her *Commedia* to the Teatro de Madrid.

At the VII Certamen Coreográfico de Madrid in September 1992, Bebeto Cidra won first prize in this national competition for new work in contemporary dance and ballet. Awards also went to Carlos Alberto Ovares and to Susana Castro and Amalia Cabeza, while Eva Vilamitjana, Chevi Muraday, and Carmelo Fernández won scholarships to the Nikolais/Louis Dance Lab, Laban Centre, and American Dance Festival respectively. Iñaki Azpillaga, winner of first prize in 1992, presented a new full-length work as the Certamen's guest company this year. In Barcelona Francisco Lloberas won Catalonia's 1992 Ricard Moragas Choreography Prize.

Dance transitions in Spain this past year included Seville's summer international Itálica dance festival's move from its traditional outdoor venue to the city's new Teatro de la Maestranza, and the creation of a ten-member National Dance Advisory Council, a first for Spain. The Ministry of Culture's new National Theatre Network initiative, which began to function in 1992, could eventually prove beneficial for dance, although at present only the Ballet de Victor Ullate, Málaga Danza Teatro's dance history programme, and Carmen Cortés's *Love the Magician* have received substantial bookings. Dance professionals are concerned about restructuring in the Ministry of Culture, now under the direction of Carmen Alborch, which will affect the National Centre for New Theatrical Trends's Sala Olimpia. This 400-seat theatre is vital to Madrid's contemporary dance programming. Another important factor to be taken into consideration is the implementation of the new law regulating education, the LOGSE, which will have a profound influence on the teaching of dance in Spain.

Sweden

PETER BOHLIN

The task to find a successor to Mats Ek in the **Cullberg Ballet** was not an easy one. In the end Carolyn Carlson was appointed artistic director, with Bertrand d'At (ex-dancer and ballet-master in Ballet du XXe Siècle) as her assistant. During the 1992/3 season the Cullberg Ballet looked wonderful in the Swedish première of Ohad Naharin's *Arbos* and in Philip Taylor's creation *Breath Bandits*. Both choreographers have been invited to come back with more. Mats Ek's farewell ballet for his company was the poetic *Pointless Pastures*, created for the Hamburg Ballet. It was also in Hamburg, during the May Ballett-Tage, that the Cullberg Ballet gave its last performance under Mats Ek's guidance, and the event was hailed with ovations longer than ever before in the company's history.

So, where was Mats Ek going? In early autumn 1993, his new project for the Stockholm City Theatre was announced: a choreographic piece of theatre called *Dancing with One's Neighbour*. This, in my eyes, turned out to be the creation of the year in Sweden: a passionate, humorous, wild, and surprising mix of dance and theatre. Mats Ek's texts proved to be as poetic, acrobatic, and unconventional as his movement style, and to an extent that surpassed every expectation he made the four actors dance and the three dancers talk. A stunning climax was the actress Malin Ek's (Mats's sister, not a trained dancer) solo dance, which in a few minutes brought out the essence of a girl's life. Already from this creation it looks as if the Cullberg Ballet's loss will be the Swedish theatre's gain.

The period demonstrated several remarkable marriages of dance and text. At the Modern Dance Theatre in Stockholm, Margaretha Åsberg mingled Euripides and Heiner Müller into an intense *Medea Material*. At Sigurdteatern in Västerås Mia Törnqvist's play *In the Shadow of God*, Birgitta Egerbladh's movement direction, Helena Franzén's choreography, and Torbjörn Grass's music amalgamated into an amazing whole. With a charming array of events in *Wonderland*, the versatile free-lance Birgitta Egerbladh—choreographer, composer, performer—again gave a display of her humour and wit. At the City Theatre of Uppsala *Maria's Freedom*, a play by Theodor Kallifatides, was superbly mounted with Osnát Opatowsky's choreography, and in Visby Bruggeriteatern (the Brewery Theatre) there was a superb demonstration of choreographed theatre in *Dreamed Earth*, a selection of poetry by Gotland's own bard Gustaf Larsson. Indeed, the meeting of dance and text has proved to be a singularly fruitful, geographically well-spread trend on the current Swedish stage.

The Royal Swedish Ballet was truly splendid in the mounting of

Neumeier's *Peer Gynt*, which stretched the house's resources to the maximum. Tetley's *The Storm* also gave wonderful opportunities for young dancers to show their best. The company is full of talent with something extra special in Anna Valev (née Backman), created principal in autumn 1993 by the company's new artistic director Simon Mottram. The company's best new one-act ballet was Ulysses Dove's creation, *Dancing on the Front Porch of Heaven*. Simply breath-taking.

For the **Gothenburg Ballet**, the artistic director Robert North has created several full-length ballets, for example, *The Russian Story*, after the formula of three loosely connected one-act ballets. His best piece, however, has been one for children: *Prince Rama and the Demons*. The **Malmö Ballet** looked better than ever in Patrick King's long one-act ballet *Once Upon a Time*, and for the **Norrköping-Linköping Ballet** the new artistic director Micaela von Gegerfeldt managed to get a short piece by Mats Ek, *Dance etc*. For the same programme Cristina Caprioli created *Paragraphs of Disobedience*, with a contemporary, brutal look, in which the dancers were impressive.

Outside the main companies Patrick King's *Exit* proved that the once top dancer of the Cullberg Ballet has grown into an excellent choreographer. He also performed the solo *Glyft* (nonsensical also in Swedish) by Virpi Pahkinen who after a somewhat shaky start has developed a sculptural style quite her own. A bright innovation for 1993 was the Swedish Choreographers' Union's excellently organized seven-hour dance marathon *30 choreographers* in Stockholm in June, and for those who had not had enough that same day, Efva Lilja was offering a midnight première with the open-air version of *The Well*, performed from a huge scaffold, erected in the water of a summer pond.

Thinking really big, the Gothenburg group **Rubicon** offered, in August 1993, a matchless *Roof of the World*. From a set of tiers at the town's highest point the spectator could see acres and acres of roofs. On a selection of these, the choreographer Gun Lund had arranged an astounding sequence of events. Even a couple of giant yellow construction cranes took part! The creation demanded four years of preparations: it was well worth waiting for.

Switzerland

RICHARD MERZ

Even in Switzerland, a country so famous for its riches, money is getting short in every area of life, hence especially so in the realm of art. Even the opera-houses have to consider cutting their budgets and for them the easiest thing to do is to propose a reduction in the dance department or even to drop it.

The large and important companies are connected with these opera-houses. In this situation it is of great importance that such companies prove to the public the value and the importance of their existence and work. One way of doing this would be the proper cultivation of dance tradition, since only companies with ample means in every aspect are able to do so. For example, the ballets of Basle and Zurich benefit from companies and stages big enough to perform the important works of the dance tradition. But this has not been done. It is true that the titles of ballet classics such as *The Nutcracker*, *The Sleeping Beauty*, and even *Raymonda* did appear in the programmes of Zurich and Basle, even of Lucerne and Berne. However, what was performed under these titles had little or nothing to do with the original works.

The really odd thing is the use of these titles. It is understandable that the director of a company does not like traditional works or, what is more probable, does not know them properly. He is free not to deal with them, but in a stubborn way there is an insistence on using the titles and the scores even when doggedly determined to stage everything but the original work. Here choreography is not considered to be as important as the text of a play or the score of an opera. Both text and score need a staging for an actual performance—and so does choreography. Astonishingly, in the world of dance, choreography is considered often to be nothing but part of the staging. While conductors and singers do not usually alter the notes of the scores most ballet directors and dancers constantly change everything, using the traditional choreography not as a work to be respected and performed in its proper form and spirit but as a trampoline to get an easy launch for high-jumping self-realization.

There are different ways of using a well-known title as a cheap attraction for audiences whilst showing something else. In Basle Youri Vàmos prefers additional elements. His *Nutcracker*, for instance, is mixed up with the story of *A Christmas Carol* by Dickens while in his *Dornröschen—Die letzte Zarentochter (Sleeping Beauty)* the fairy-tale court of the original is replaced by the Imperial Russian court with the added story of the lady who claimed to be Anastasia, the surviving daughter of the last tsar. The dance style looks somehow classical, neither being the original nor a new achievement, but nice to look at. In Zurich, Bernd Roger Bienert is more radical in his approach to *The Nutcracker* and to *Raymonda*. For him a ballet classic first of all must not look like one, 'to be different' being the chief goal. And in that, indeed, he does succeed; if nothing else, those ballets are different. The original story is modernized in the same complicated and distorted way as is his astonishingly unmusical choreography in a foggy nowhere of style; just different.

The use of famous titles for ballet performances which then result in being other than those announced is a nuisance, even if the performance in itself, as an independent new ballet, is so highly vivid and enjoyable as was the case with *Dornröschen—Die schlafende Schönheit* by Thorsten Kreissig in Lucerne. But even in such a performance, it is arguable that the basic approach of this kind of use of the classics is wrong: whatever these choreographers have done, it does not—and could not—fit the music. Tchaikovsky's scores are meant for clearly defined situations. To use them for completely different stories and situations cannot work—*if* one listens to the music, which apparently neither choreographer did with any care.

Stadttheater Luzern's production of *Dornröschen—Die Schlafende Schönheit*, choreographed by Thorsten Kreissig.   PHOTO: PETER SCHNETZ

It is questionable whether this approach to the ballet classics is of any use to or for the art of dance. Without question it is dangerous in the actual situation. If the big companies and the big stages are used only for the personal experiments of their directors, those responsible for the public purse must ask the question, is so much money really needed for so little? Freelance people may ask themselves rightly why they get so little money for doing just the same thing, namely trying out their own possibilities and producing on stage their own personal dreams. Sometimes they do this more consistently and with more creative power than is found in the manipulated classics. For instance Beatrice Jaccard and Peter Schelling went a long and steady way in searching for *their* form of dancing. Starting with the smallest everyday movements they carefully observed, analysed, and developed them into a style which looks fluently natural and at the same time highly sophisticated. After years of exclusive partnership a third dancer, Massimo Bertinelli, joined them for a new piece, *Les deux corps du roi*, which is one of the few important achievements in the whole of the Swiss dance scene of last year.

United Kingdom

Subsidized companies

JANN PARRY

1993/4 was a year in which the effect of financial restrictions imposed on Britain's subsidized dance companies could no longer be disguised by clever programming. The Arts Council, which allocates government money for the arts, had been advised to expect a substantial reduction in its funds by the end of 1993. As a precaution, the Council put all its major clients on standstill grants and warned of likely cuts to come. In the event, government money for the arts was reduced by £3.2 million. The outgoing Arts Council Chairman, Lord Palumbo, spoke of a bleak and depressing period for the arts. As a consequence, artistic directors were obliged to play safe, their policies aimed at keeping box-office takings up and costs down. Those directors unable or unwilling to accept such limitations lost their jobs and companies running into deficit were threatened with closure.

The Royal Opera House Board of Management had to take drastic measures to reduce the £3.6 million deficit incurred by its three companies—the Royal Opera, **Royal Ballet**, and **Birmingham Royal Ballet**. Although the ROH receives the largest tranche of Arts Council funding—£18,952,000 for all three companies—its subsidy amounts to only 36 per cent of its income, far less than most European opera-houses. Because opera earns more at the box-office than ballet (opera tickets are more than twice the price of ballet tickets at Covent Garden), the number of Royal Ballet performances was reduced from 120 to 96, while those given by the Royal Opera were increased to 160.

Fewer ballets were given longer runs—nineteen performances of *Don Quixote* in 1993, for example, with another fourteen scheduled for 1994. Kenneth MacMillan's last three-act ballet, *Prince of the Pagodas*, was cancelled in favour of yet more performances of *The Sleeping Beauty*. A new

Sleeping Beauty production, by artistic director Anthony Dowell, had to be postponed until the next financial year and has now been given on tour in the United States in the summer of 1994.

The loss of Kenneth MacMillan, who died on 29 October 1992, was keenly felt. He had been scheduled to create a new work for the autumn of 1993—a slot that was filled instead by two young choreographers within the company, Matthew Hart and William Tuckett, both still in their early twenties. Although the Royal Ballet has always prided itself on developing its own in-house choreographers, the choice of two relative newcomers was seen as yet another cost-cutting device.

This was an unfair perception, since young choreographers deserve the chance to work with dancers of their own generation on the Opera House stage. Hart's *Fanfare*, to commissioned music by Brian Elias, and Tuckett's *If This is Still a Problem*, to Ravel's *Piano Concerto*, shared the season's opening programme with MacMillan's *Different Drummer* and Forsythe's *Herman Schmerman*. The evening was billed as 'Red Hot and Different', raising expectations that the two less-experienced choreographers could not fulfil: their ballets were well crafted but not mould-breaking.

It is encouraging, however, that the company has two such promising youngsters within its ranks, as well as Ashley Page, who spent much of the year choreographing in Turkey and the Netherlands. His next work for the company is scheduled for June 1994. Two Royal Ballet choreographers left the company to pursue free-lance careers: Jonathan Burrows and David Bintley. Bintley bade farewell in February with a new plotless ballet, *Tombeaux*, a fine monument to his ten years with the company. He returned, however, to work with the Birmingham Royal Ballet, of which he had been a member when it was still the Sadler's Wells Royal Ballet. Its artistic director, Peter Wright, who was knighted in 1993, had commissioned Bintley to mount his own three-act version of Delibes's *Sylvia*, to be premièred at the Birmingham Hippodrome in October. It proved more successful with regional audiences than with most London-based critics, who found its reworking of the libretto insufficiently radical and who compared Bintley's choreography unfavourably with Ashton's 1952 ballet to the same music. London ballet-goers will be able to make up their own minds when *Sylvia* is performed during BRB's annual season at Covent Garden in 1994.

BRB, now firmly established in Birmingham, is to be given a greater degree of management autonomy, although it will retain its strong links with the Royal Ballet in London. The start of 1994 saw its first tour abroad, to Turin, under its Birmingham title. It borrowed Irek Mukhamedov from the Royal Ballet to dance Colas in *La Fille mal gardée*, in return for having lent its Japanese ballerina, Miyako Yoshida, as guest artist in the Royal Ballet's *Don Quixote* and *The Nutcracker*.

BRB's great strength, in addition to Peter Wright's productions of the classics, is in its well-chosen programmes of one-act ballets. The emphasis in 1993/4 has been on works from the 1930s, to coincide with the Birmingham Symphony Orchestra's focus on that decade during its Millennium series. BRB has acquired Jooss's *The Green Table* (1932) and Massine's *Choreartium* (1933), as well as reviving de Valois's *Job* (1931). *Job* was performed in Birmingham and London to celebrate Dame Ninette de Valois's ninety-fifth birthday in June and given a special performance in Coventry Cathedral on 11 November 1993 to mark the cathedral's 950th anniversary.

The Birmingham Royal Ballet in *Street*, choreographed by Matthew Hart.
PHOTO: LESLIE E. SPATT

Encouragement was given to young conductors for ballet through a Conduct for Dance competition organized in conjunction with the Birmingham Conservatoire of Music. The four finalists showed what they could do in a programme of famous *pas de deux*, danced by members of both companies: the winner, Andrea Quinn, has been given further opportunities to work with BRB.

Ivan Nagy was replaced as artistic director of **English National Ballet** in March 1993 by Derek Deane. Deane, a former Royal Ballet principal dancer, had been deputy artistic director and resident choreographer at the

Teatro dell'Opera in Rome. He inherited a much-reduced deficit (now under £250,000) and a standstill Arts Council grant, which gave him little leeway to introduce new works to the repertory. However, fresh productions of *Swan Lake* by Raissa Struchkova and *The Sleeping Beauty* by Ronald Hynd had already been scheduled and proved very popular on tour.

Annual performances of *The Nutcracker*, now in Ben Stevenson's version, made a record £1.25 million over the 1992/3 Christmas period. A less predictable success was achieved by the company's London season at the newly-restored Savoy Theatre, for which Wayne Sleep created a Gilbert and Sullivan ballet, *Savoy Suite*. The other hit of the season was a modern dance work by Portuguese choreographer Olga Roriz, *The Seven Silences of Salome*—a sequence of seven spectacular male solos.

ENB's school, now numbering thirty-three pupils, has experienced a worrying shortage of male students, so the company's education unit has launched a special project, called *Striking a Balance*, to stimulate young men's interest in ballet—as audience members and potential dancers. The school, like most vocational schools in Britain, has had to battle against a drastic reduction in grants for students from local government authorities.

Grants for students attending dance and theatre schools are given at the discretion of local authorities, whose budgets have been restricted by the present government. Only Royal Ballet School students are eligible for mandatory grants. Other vocational schools either have to raise money for scholarships or accept only those students whose parents, or foreign governments, are able to pay tuition fees.

Northern Ballet Theatre, based in Halifax, has continued to win audiences and sponsors, thanks to policies introduced by its artistic director, Christopher Gable. By emphasizing drama and narrative in his productions—often at the expense of choreography—he has given the company a distinctive identity. In 1993/4, he added two full-length ballets to the repertory: *A Christmas Carol*, a singing-and-dancing account of Charles Dickens's festive fable, and *Cinderella*, based on the Grimm fairy-tale instead of the more sentimental version by Charles Perrault.

Both had specially written scores: *Cinderella*'s by Philip Feeney and *A Christmas Carol*'s by Carl Davis, with the addition of traditional carols. Massimo Moricone was commissioned to add choreography to what was essentially a Dickensian musical; Gable choreographed *Cinderella* himself, underlining the brutality of the story, except for a romantic *pas de deux* at the very end. In general, Gable's productions are enjoyed more by spectators new to ballet than by those who respond to dancing for its own sake.

He did, however, programme two new, plotless, one-act ballets—*D'Ensemble* by Graham Lustig and *Extenzion* by Derek Williams—in a triple bill with a revival of Gillian Lynne's *A Simple Man*, the popular work that helped save the company from extinction seven years ago.

London City Ballet nearly went under in the summer of 1993, faced

Jayne Regan and William
Walker of Northern Ballet
Theatre in *Romeo and
Juliet.*
PHOTO: ANTHONY CRICKMAY

with an imminent deficit and no prospect of Arts Council funding. The
Council, already responsible for five other ballet companies, has always
refused to accept LCB as a client. Final performances of its *Romeo and Juliet*
were announced in July—but the dancers returned from their holidays in
September to find that the company would be relaunched with a new, private sponsorship package.

Thanks to the reprieve, morale is now high. Few risks are being taken
with the repertory—*Coppélia, Les Sylphides, The Nutcracker Suite*—although
one of the triple bills in 1994 will include a commissioned work from
Vincent Redmon of the Birmingham Royal Ballet.

The Scottish Ballet, under the artistic directorship of Galina Samsova,
continued its links with the Kirov/St Petersburg Ballet by mounting the
same production of André Prokovsky's *Anna Karenina.* Two Kirov dancers,
Olga Likhovskaya and Andrei Yakovlev, joined the company as guests in
Glasgow and Edinburgh; their Russian interpretations were as different
from the home team's Noriko Ohara and Robert Hampton as vodka from
whisky.

Anna Karenina, first mounted for the Australian Ballet in 1979, with
Samsova as Anna, is predictable, old-fashioned fare. A more daring addition
to the repertory resulted from the commission of *A Midsummer Night's
Dream* from Robert Cohan—the first time this contemporary dance creator

had worked with a ballet company. The fusion of styles, which extended to the music by Mendelssohn and Barrington Pheloung, was fresh and invigorating, stretching dancers' and audiences' imaginations. The cross-over experiment will be followed in 1994 with a commission from Kim Brandstrup, who trained at the London Contemporary Dance School, before running his own Arc Dance Company.

Noriko Ohara and Lloyd Embleton of the Scottish Ballet in *A Midsummer Night's Dream*, choreographed by Robert Cohan.   PHOTO: BILL COOPER

London Contemporary Dance Theatre reached crisis point towards the end of 1993, when the Board of Management, unable to select a new artistic director, proposed closing down the company. LCDT has been without a long-term leader for almost five years, although Robert Cohan, its founder-director, came out of retirement in 1992 to take charge of the dancers and their repertory. Performance standards remained high and audience figures increased—but the Arts Council demanded a long-term artistic policy before it would renew the company's grant of almost £1 million by the end of 1993.

As the deadline approached, the Board first threatened to give up its struggle to meet Arts Council requirements and then, following a protest campaign by the dancers, came up with a scheme to preserve a smaller group of dancers, to be known as **The Place Company**: the name would identify them more closely with their headquarters at The Place in north-central London. This has its own studio theatre as well as housing the London Contemporary Dance School. The new plan would turn The Place into a National Choreographic Centre, integrating the Contemporary Dance Trust's many activities which include community education work and providing a flexible structure to support creators and performers.

This proposal, and the appointment of Richard Alston as artistic director of the Centre and The Place Company, has been met with Arts Council approval. Funding has been continued only until July 1994, when the new arrangements would come into effect. In any event, it seems as though LCDT's days as a large-scale contemporary dance repertory company are over; a reborn company would be 'artist-led', concentrating on works by its artistic director and a few other, mainly in-house choreographers. Whether this would affect the type of training given by the school—one of the most important modern dance schools in Europe—has yet to be decided.

Rambert Dance Company, Britain's other leading contemporary dance repertory company, has been suspended in a state of transition all year. Its Board sacked Richard Alston as artistic director in December 1992. Rambert had been losing money and audiences, even though it won many awards during Alston's seven years in charge. He was replaced by Christopher Bruce, the choreographer who had been a member of the company in its pre-Alston days.

Bruce's appointment came into effect in April 1994. In the mean time, the company of seventeen dancers has continued touring, without its usual London season. Its last London appearances, at the Royalty Theatre in June 1992, had been a financial disaster. Programmes contained existing works by Alston, *Strong Language*, and Siobhan Davies, *Embarque*, *Winnsboro' Cotton Mills Blues*, and new works by company members Paul Old, *Still Dance*, and Mark Baldwin, *Gone* and *Spirit*, who has since left to become a free-lance choreographer. Bruce introduced one of his own works, *Land*, first made for English National Ballet.

Bruce intends to enlarge the number of dancers to twenty-five and restore the company's orchestra, which had been disbanded to save money. He wants to remould Rambert along the lines of Nederlands Dans Theater, performing works by Jiří Kylián, Ohad Naharin, and Nacho Duato, as well as by himself—and possibly by Balanchine and Graham, if he can recruit appropriately trained dancers. He believes that audiences will respond with enthusiasm to a company combining ballet and modern dance techniques in a style that is relatively unfamiliar in this country.

The Arts Council has given qualified backing to his expansionist plans with a 35.5 per cent increase in funding, amounting to £1,200,000. Rambert looks set to become Britain's flagship company for contemporary dance, touring extensively and returning to the large theatres Alston had avoided when he turned the company into a chamber group. The future, however, is uncertain. Bruce may not get all the money he needs; a policy that works in Holland may not succeed in Britain; and Rambert will have to establish a different niche for itself in the ecology of British dance, competing with established ballet companies as well as up-and-coming contemporary groups.

Smaller British Companies

LESLEY-ANNE SAYERS

Britain's subsidized smaller dance companies currently provide a broad spectrum of work. They represent the diversity of Britain's contemporary culture in dance and provide the most challenging and innovative work.

But it has been another difficult year for the arts as a whole in Britain. The Arts Council faces a £3.2 million cut to its overall budget, and the reduced availability of local government funding is crippling regional theatre and drastically restricting the number of discretionary awards made to students gaining places on dance training courses. There is still a basic reluctance in Britain to acknowledge dance as a serious art-form, and its public subsidy is about half of that for drama or music. Britain lacks the infrastructure to encourage the development of business sponsorship. Funding policies appear to be following a stormy course, lurching between the equally debilitating forces of market economics and 'political correctness'. In an attitude of protectionism the English Arts Council has prioritized Contemporary Dance (which attracts the smallest number of theatre-going public in Britain), as a developing art-form. This should protect our existing smaller groups against any major cut-backs. But the need for regional theatres to 'play safe' means that avant-garde groups face reducing touring circuits. Therefore the availability of challenging new work to wider regional audiences is curtailed unless it transforms itself into television. Meanwhile, dance is, according to choreographer Lloyd Newson, 'a form in crisis'[1] and his latest work is a play. But whether 'crisis' is a significant term, just an over-used word this year, or a concept to be playfully, powerfully, explored through hurtling, frenzied, off-balance, perpetual motion, it has not detracted from the quality of work coming from our foremost groups.

Siobhan Davies has had another highly successful year and was the winner of a 1993 Olivier Award for outstanding achievement in dance. This is the first time this award has gone to an independent British choreographer. Having left **London Contemporary Dance Theatre** in 1987 she founded her own small company in 1988 and continues to be one of our most artistically mature and sophisticated artists. Her latest work, *Wanting to Tell Stories*, is set to the music of Kevin Volans and designed by David Buckland. Despite its title, this work is true to Davies's usual *métier* which resists the trend towards narrative as such. *Wanting to Tell Stories* exploits the suggestion of relationships between the dancers through, and interweaved with, Davies's lucid movement language and her formal complexity. Unlike many of today's choreographers, Davies is committed to exploring the ways in which dance communicates rather than in crossing over into dramatic theatre.

For others however, the need to explore issues and ideas often leads into a dependency upon spoken text. Ian Spink's group, **Second Stride**, went so far down this road that they lost their funding from the Arts Council's dance budget and have, for the past couple of years, been receiving combined arts funding instead. Their latest work, *Escape at Sea*, however, perhaps rather perversely, boasts no less than three choreographers; Ian Spink, Ashley Page, and Eyal Rubin. Joining the cast of some of Britain's most distinguished contemporary dancers is former Royal Ballet star, Lynn Seymour. For audience members who are not proficient in Russian and French, the text is little more than expressive sound, a deliberate obscuration of the dramatic means of communication. According to the programme notes *Escape at Sea* is a modernist fairy-tale, concerned with love and exile and has been inspired by *The Sleeping Beauty* and Chekhov's *The Seagull*. The general themes are clear to a certain extent but the audience is denied access to anything more personal than the idea of narrative as a theatrical device, and is left to appreciate the finer points of this group's dense exploration of the aesthetics of theatre. As sophisticated and intriguing as it is, this work ends up being little more than a victory celebration of style over content.

Exploring the nature and boundaries of the theatrical experience is also close to the heart of Lloyd Newson's work for **DV8**. *MSM* confronts audiences with a vision of male sex in public lavatories. I have called it a play, and Newson is perhaps now slightly ahead of current trends in drama as well as being a leading influence in dance, but this kind of performance art is closer to installation work in the visual arts than it is to the dramatic theatre of *Oleanna*, or *Aspects of War*, for example. It is the experience of the extraordinary nature of DV8's performance that is crucial to their success, not the argument or the dramatic resolution or intellectual challenge that any use of text helps them to provide.

Whether text is in Russian, or is taped from real-life interviews in English as it is in *MSM*, the general trend of dance theatre is to provide an intense theatrical experience rather than to tell a story as such. Any pretences it may have towards exploring 'issues', other than theatrical issues, are doubtful. It tends to lack any commitment to communicating an argument; text and meaning are played with as devices to be fractured from any dramatic or emotional coherence and displayed as ambiguous possibilities to evoke a reaction, and perhaps any reaction will do.

A particularly powerful manifestation of this preoccupation with 'theatrical experience' came this year from visiting Japanese artist, Saburo Teshigawara, whose work, *Bones in Pages*, was a highlight of Dance Umbrella 1993. Teshigawara's set consists of a wall made up of the pages of books, some of which he at one point frenziedly scatters across the space. There is also a corridor of shoes, evoking associations with holocausts like Hiroshima or Nazi concentration camps. It is a haunting piece that powerfully controls its own power over the audience. Aside from the intensely dramatic visual imagery, the work takes the audience on a sound journey through landslides and other apocalyptic moments and calmly meditative states. Our minds are invited to wander freely, like the black raven that flies around the set, until we are skilfully brought back to the vivid visual effects taking place in the confines of the stage space. The movement is frenetic, mechanistic; the work is a kind of contemporary *Modern Times* and Teshigawara is quite Chaplinesque in his poignant mixture of a stylized urban street language and the evocative, haunting techniques of mime theatre.

Amongst the British groups appearing at Dance Umbrella 1993 was Mark Murphy's company V-TOL (Vertical Take-Off and Landing) who have gained an increasing following over the last few years. Murphy's dance language is high energy, multi-directional, aggressive, and can be thrilling to watch. His latest work *'32 Feet Per Second Per Second* is a mixed-media piece concerned with sexual abuse and draws on the film imagery of Polanski, Scorcese, and Lynch. It has met with a degree of controversy because of the chauvinistic and violent central character, an anti-hero who beats up women. Murphy was seeking to explore a repulsive character and the breakdown of relationships between the sexes; the controversy points, however, to confusion over what is being 'said' by the choreographer, and to the difficulty of exploring something like this in the medium of dance. Murphy evidently has no intention of abandoning dance as his medium but plans to spend the coming year in film school.

Lea Anderson's group, **The Cholmondeleys**, are currently celebrating their tenth anniversary. Since graduating from the Laban Centre back in the early 1980s, Anderson has gone from strength to strength, running the all-male company **The Featherstonehaughs** as well as her all-female troupe, The Cholmondeleys. Her latest theatre work, *Precious*, brought the two companies together. Purporting to be concerned with 'a journey in alchemy', it is a magical work on the theme of transformation. Falling into four sections, entitled *Black, White, Red, Gold*, with appropriately coloured costumes by Sandy Powell, *Precious* has commissioned music by the Victims of Death. The first section is a frenetic tumbling act, male and female dancers thrown together in an exploration of off-balance. The movement combines high energy, stamina dance with movement drawn from awkward stumbling and groping. The witty and often touching *White* section consists of white-suited men dancing with giant black-and-white portraits of themselves. The women take over for the indolent but anguished *Red* section, dressed in slinky velvet and then, with all the imagistic power of a religious painting, they all come together for the golden finale. It is a curious piece and again is an example of dance theatre where meaning itself is a theatrical possibility, a game structure to be explored rather than a dramatic message to be communicated. As if in self-conscious reference to this aspect of the work, the final image is a dancer placing her finger to her lips as if hushing a persistent question. If these golden and meaningful-looking gestures were proclaiming a new order, it is the mystery of it all, the theatrical experience of it all, that matters.

Another highlight of the year was provided by Yolande Snaith's intriguing new work, *Diction*. On a chequer-board floor, designed by Robert Innes-Hopkins, with heaps of parchment pieces that are later scattered anarchically across the space, the players are given instructions in a variety of languages and gibberish by two speakers, who perch like umpires above the action. Magical and menacing by turns, a new world with its own mysterious but strict interior logic unfolds. At its best Snaith's work brings to mind the absurdist theatre of Ionesco and in this arbitrary, associative world she has found a channel for her eclectic ideas and distinctive movement language. Like Alice in Wonderland, on which she draws for this piece, Snaith has a love of riddles, game structures, and absurd logic. Her blend of visually exciting theatre with a distinctive and endlessly fascinating movement vocabulary makes her one of the most rewarding artists around.

Britain's smaller dance groups currently represent a wide variety of audiences and the need to do so is clearly evident in funding policies. While this is a welcome part of a widening of our cultural base and an increasing understanding of the diversity of dance forms, the downside is that in times of financial frugality 'interest groups' feel that they are competing with each other for access to the public purse. Overall, ballet still consumes a very high proportion of the dance budget through subsidy to major companies. The policy of prioritization of Contemporary Dance however, while not likely to alter that fact, is felt to mean a 'rationing' of project grants available to small-scale, classically-based companies. One small ballet group, however, that has managed to obtain project grants from the Arts Council is **VOLTaire Chamber Ballet**. This group is dedicated to new classically-based choreography for the small scale and have had a notable success this year with *Hunting and Gathering*, choreographed by their artistic director, Jennifer Jackson. Set to music by Kevin Volans, *Hunting and Gathering* is based on the rituals of the Shona tribe of Zimbabwe. The perceived need to make ballet 'relevant' to today's audiences and more accessible to wider audiences can be a debilitating pressure as well as a questionable ideal. *Hunting and Gathering*, however, has been hailed as a major work and a small-scale ballet company such as this, where new choreographers have the creative freedom to develop free of external pressures, is certainly much needed. VOLTaire demonstrates that new ballet on the intimate scale could have an artistic future in Britain given some investment.

Whilst we live in the era of the niche market when it comes to funding, many of our fringe groups are continuing to cross boundaries to a greater and greater extent. For example, **Shobana Jeyasingh** in her 1992 work, *The Making of Maps*, extended her distinctive dance territory in a rich exploration of her choreographic heritage in Bharatha Natyam in a Western context. The new work for 1993, *Romance with Footnotes*, continues to explore this rich terrain, linking the baroque music of Henry Purcell with the rhythms of Bharatha Natyam and looking at interactions of tradition with the new. *Romance with Footnotes* is a double bill combining a commissioned piece from Richard Alston, *Delicious Arbour*, with the title-work from Jeyasingh. In contrast to a lot of our smaller groups, Jeyasingh's work, like that of Siobhan Davies, looks like something for grown-ups; its maturity lies in the originality of its peculiar synthesis and the new dance language it has found that promises to be a rich source for many years to come. In times when audiences for Contemporary Dance groups are not as great as we would want, it is heartening to know the audience for this highly respected artist is growing markedly, up from 42 per cent capacity in 1991/2 to 72 per cent in spring 1993. Jeyasingh's film collaboration with Terry Braun, *Duets with Automobiles*, was broadcast on BBC2 in autumn 1993, which should help to introduce a wider audience to the work of this remarkable choreographer.

In terms of both audiences and critical acclaim, Matthew Bourne's amusing version of *The Nutcracker* made **Adventures in Motion Pictures** a great success at the 1993 Edinburgh Festival. As part of the Tchaikovsky centenary celebrations, it formed part of a double bill commissioned by Opera North and attracted large audiences. Bourne is a rare commodity in that he has gone from the 'fringe' in Contemporary Dance to choreographing for

Jeyaverni Jeganathan, Jasmine Simlahan, and Savita Shekhar of the Shobana Jeyasingh Dance Company. PHOTO: HUGO GLENDINNING

the West End stage and back again; he is capable of producing slick, accessible and very popular work and has a wit and charm in his choreography that has long made his future look full of possibilities. In collaborating with Opera North, he might at least have introduced a few opera-lovers to Contemporary Dance, for opera, although still a minority interest amongst British arts supporters, has recently enjoyed a huge surge in numbers of people attending, and currently attracts greater audiences in Britain than does ballet.

Another very distinctive British group currently enjoying a lot of success is **CandoCo Dance Company.** CandoCo, currently consisting of three dancers with physical disabilities and five able-bodied dancers, opened both the Dance 93 and Spring-Loaded festivals. The company have enjoyed a phenomenal success over the last couple of years bringing issues of dance and disability to a heightened consciousness as well as astounding audiences with the nature and quality of their work. Dispelling any notion that all integrated companies can hope for is applause for the efforts of the disabled, this company has succeeded in shifting attitudes towards the idea of 'disabled' dancers, stressing and stretching abilities, creatively exploring

Scott Ambler and Ally
Fitzpatrick of Adventures
in Motion Pictures in
Nutcracker.
PHOTO: HUGO GLENDINNING

'dysfunction' and proving that it is possible to be both a distinctive and successful dance company as well as an important force for changing attitudes.

What Britain's dance world has in terms of diversity it perhaps lacks in terms of a clear artistic identity. Nevertheless this diversity is currently the strength of dance in Britain because it is the site of struggle and the search for new meanings. Show-cases for emerging new talent such as The Place Theatre's annual 'Resolution' and 'Spring-Loaded' festivals in London, failed, however, to show much evidence of new talent or new ideas this year. Given shoe-string budgets and all the difficulties that independent dancers and choreographers face in Britain, this is not all that surprising.

Perhaps the most damaging aspect to the creative lives of Britain's choreographers is the continual pressure to produce new work without respite. As far as audiences and emerging young choreographers are concerned this denies them access to their cultural history; the dictatorship of 'the new' means that chances to reflect, see a revival, a new interpretation by a different dancer, belong to larger groups—to dance as a serious art-form perhaps, as opposed to youthful fringe challenge; there is a sense in which this model and lack of a clear future path diminishes artists working in our smaller companies. The model of dramatic theatre, where a successful avant-garde work from a subsidized group may transfer to the commercial theatre is not in place for dance. The importance of the small scale in development of dance needs greater recognition in Britain. Above all artists need space to think, be, and develop if their 'new' work is going to have anything much to offer the general public beyond another version of a previous success. Very few of our artists manage to obtain this form of investment in their future and it is desperately needed.

[1] *Dance Theatre Journal*, 10/4, Autumn 1993, 7.

USA

New York and East Coast

ROBERT GRESKOVIC

Dance in and around New York during the autumn of 1992 was meant to be a business-as-usual situation, but the aftermath of civil unrest in Los Angeles led to the cancellation of a November visit by **Houston Ballet** and the devastation caused by Hurricane Andrew in August left **Miami City Ballet** in a state of temporary crisis. An attempt to found a new ballet company at Jacob's Pillow (in Lee, Massachusetts)—**Ballet de Ville** under the direction of Peter Anastos—failed to take hold, due mostly to the artistic uncertainty of Anastos's initial programme of choreography. The Los Angeles 'riots' also affected the plans and shaky finances of the **Joffrey Ballet**, while the ever-delicate status of **American Ballet Theatre's** financial basis continued, leaving newly named director Kevin McKenzie to shepherd a company through a year with fewer and fewer weeks of guaranteed work.

The most newsworthy event of the year's end was a Christmas run of *The Hard Nut* by Mark Morris at the Brooklyn Academy of Music. This wildly idiosyncratic and intensely musical reworking of *The Nutcracker* by Tchaikovsky proved popular and of equal interest to those, like me, who love the nineteenth-century work and are amused to see it remade into a twentieth-century cartoon, as well as to those who long for the overexposed 'classic' to get its come-uppance. Morris's production, the last one he choreographed during his well-subsidized stay in Belgium, was most handsomely realized in scenic and costume-design terms.

New York City Ballet ended the year with the acquisition of two internationally acclaimed male dancers: Nikolaj Hübbe, from the **Royal Ballet of Denmark**, and Igor Zelensky from the **Kirov/Maryinsky Ballet**. During the winter season, Zelensky had the more successful entry into the company, where he seemed more suited to the cavalier and other roles he was given, such as the cavalier/partner in *Nutcracker* and in *Tchaikovsky Piano Concerto No. 2*. Hübbe's forays in the leading roles of *Donizetti Variations* were not nearly successful enough. The show-cases Peter Martins made for him in two new ballets, *Jazz* (to Wynton Marsaylis) and *Zakouski*, to four different Russian composers, were well danced but not especially meaningful as choreography.

NYCB's winter season remained a period of marking time for the company's ambitious 'Balanchine Celebration', which dominated the spring mightily. Here, in addition to a number of other by-products, Hübbe and Zelensky reversed success stories. The former had more roles and made much more of them, while the latter had fewer and made less impact. The seventy-three-ballet celebration was very well attended and mostly well received. The plan to show the works in mostly chronological order over the eight-week running time was the most inspired aspect of the company's Grand Plan. For all the dubious dating and the sometimes dubious performance of the dancing in these many ballets, the chance to see what now remains in the 'general store' at NYCB of the unprecedented canon of classicism created by Balanchine was much more rewarding than not. The programming laid out, as it probably never will again, Balanchine's cornucopia of ballet theatre. The luxury of seeing this array decade by decade, each of which was associated with its own ballerinas and leading male dancers, made a feast of evolutionary ballet dancing.

City Ballet's lead dancers are often sadly dull today in comparison to those who inspired Balanchine to make his richly varied works, but some shone as brightly as any could nowadays. Kyra Nichols took ballerina honours for glorious performances in roles originally created for Maria Tallchief, Tanaquil LeClercq, Violette Verdy, and Suzanne Farrell. Peter Boal, leading the male contingent, which in general today makes a stronger showing than the women dancers, stood out with new majesty. His début in *Harlequinade* was a special revelation.

Special reservations must be voiced about the number of leading roles Peter Martins gave to his son Nilas in this rich repertory. Nilas, who remains very limited technically and modest to the point of near invisibility, was awarded plum roles, such as the leads of *Apollo*, *Orpheus*, and central man in the Celebration's most unusual revival, the 1947 *Haieff Divertimento*. He brought glory to none.

American Ballet Theatre played a mere six-week season at the Metropolitan Opera House. Previously these seasons had been eight, or more, weeks. The repertory, which showed an almost pointed neglect of

Balanchine, was uneventful. A new company staging of MacMillan's *Manon* was well done, but even while ABT has an impressive array of male dancers, MacMillan's particular inventions based on the dancing of Anthony Dowell and David Wall ultimately eluded most of the men cast here. A rather weary and wan production of *Swan Lake*, left over from the era of Lucia Chase, whose directorship ended in 1980, re-entered repertory. This provided the season, however, with its most wondrous début: Julie Kent as Odette/Odile. This remarkably beautiful young woman allowed none of the old-fashioned nature of the staging to surface as she radiated a spiritual shimmer and a physical delicacy that made ballet dancing in 1993 look fresh and indelible.

After its world première in Iowa in January, 1993, the **Joffrey Ballet**'s *Billboards* finally played in New York in November. By this time the work had stirred up a good deal of pro and con response. Created by four different choreographers—Laura Dean, Charles Moulton, Margo Sappington, and Peter Pucci—to a selection of fourteen songs by Prince Rogers Nelson, aka rock star Prince, the evening-long suite was characterized either as 'a sign of the future and the way to get ballet in the consciousness of the contemporary public' or 'a cheap and slick trick, that will set the art-form back disastrously'. After seeing one performance, I would say the probable outcome of the event will lie somewhere in between these arguments. Consistently beaming sweetly from the centre of the large-scale visual and high-decibel sound aspects of the work was the shining simplicity of classical ballet dancing. Even the choreographers who made dogged grabs at 'innovation' in their dance-making could not fail to respond to the eternal niceties of classicism. Since the **Joffrey** has had a good deal of financial uncertainty of late, it has lost a goodly number of its veteran dancers. The largely young cast of performers who went through the paces of *Billboards* telescoped most endearingly the essential beauties of academic dancing. It is always folly to predict what is or is not taking place in the minds of unknown individuals, but I would be willing to surmise that many a neophyte really looking at the dancing of *Billboards* will be inspired to come back and see this ballet dancing thing some other time. Except for Sappington, whose billboard is called *Slide* and looks like no more than a poor man's William Forsythe—if that is not an oxymoron—all the other choreographers succumbed to some of ballet's most beguiling methods. Dean, whose post-modernist patterning and rigorous repetition gets a satisfying giddiness and expansiveness here, is responsible for the work's most rewarding segment.

Dance Theatre of Harlem played the New York State Theatre, home of City Ballet, for the first time during the spring of 1993. The repertory of this also financially-stressed organization was largely a familiar one, but the company's first performances of Alvin Ailey's *The River* were the highlight of the two well-attended weeks. Putting this Ailey piece to Duke Ellington

Virginia Johnson and Eddie J. Shellman of the Dance Theatre of Harlem in *Giselle*, choreographed by Frederic Franklin.   PHOTO: LESLIE E. SPATT

back on *pointe*, DTH brought it back to full life. Of late Ailey's own non-ballet company has performed it without employing *pointe* work where it had been used originally—in the production created for ABT.

Ailey's own troupe, now directed with consistent authority by Judith Jamison, has been enjoying a success as a second-generation organization like no other dance company around today. Jamison's strength is in the area of dancers. The troupe today is largely made up of dancers of her choosing and guidance. Both the men and women shine, but probably the men have the edge. Desmond Richardson and Aubrey Lynch are among the more notable dancers of Jamison's regime.

A mini-retrospective dominated the summer. **The Nikolais and Murray Louis Dance Company** gave a two-week, four-programme season showing the once so-called multimedia or avant-garde works of Alwin Nikolais, who had died in May. The season was planned before the choreographer/composer/costume-and-lighting-designer died. It was hardly comprehensive, but it gave a sense of the works that were once hailed for their innovation. Today's music videos and **Pilobolus Dance Theatre** et alia show where such explorations can lead. In the end they reduce their progenitor to something of a footnote in overall dance history.

After his first American season of *The Hard Nut* and before reviving it the following Christmastime, **Mark Morris** and company played a repertory season at the Brooklyn Academy of Music, in which Baryshnikov appeared, along with some of his **White Oak Dance Project** dancers. Baryshnikov

The Alvin Ailey American Dance Theatre in *The Winter in Lisbon*, choreographed by Billy Wilson.   PHOTO: JACK MITCHELL

and company were seen in *Mosaic* and *United*, a two-part work Morris showed here for the first time and which would then go into WODP repertory with Baryshnikov. This mysterious essay to the music of Henry Cowell (thus the title) was one of two especially intriguing new works. The other, *Home*, was set to some *nouveau* folk-songs and tunes by Michelle Shocked and Rob Wasserman. *Home*, in which Morris uncharacteristically appeared amid an ensemble of his dancers, contrasted buoyant clogging sections with darker, brooding moments enacted by the women dancers in the cast.

Merce Cunningham, whose long-time collaborator and fellow iconoclast John Cage died in July 1992, offered *Enter*, as one of his new works in 1993. This piece for sixteen dancers, which includes a part for the ever-fascinating 74-year-old Cunningham, takes mysterious shape beyond a scrim scrawled with some rocks, from a reproduction of a drawing by Cage.

Paul Taylor, who unveiled his none-too-well-received *Oz* in late 1992, came to New York in the autumn of 1993 with two marvellous works. The first, *Spindrift*, is somewhat over-designed by Santo Loquasto, but manages to present the very compelling Andrew Asnes as a kind of 'merman' amid a 'seascape with frieze of dancers'. The second, *A Field of Grass*, is a little masterwork in which some hippie-era songs get simultaneously illustrated and illuminated, thus making for a picture alternately pretty and penetrating. Unfortunately, the company is now unable to present its programmes with live music, so the older works associated with lush orchestral pieces must now, temporarily it is hoped, use 'canned' music.

Twyla Tharp, who started 1993 with a package of her high-priced tour alongside Mikhail Baryshnikov, came to New York in the autumn with a lecture/demonstration-like programme. With almost as much talking as dancing, this bill involved rehearsal-format performances of Tharp dances now in repertory, as well as a question-and-answer session surrounding the creation of a new dance phrase at each performance. Following Tharp and her dancers into the theatre was the Martha Graham Company, which offered a world première by Tharp, the first première ever by a choreographer not from Graham's 'fold'.

Tharp's *Demeter and Persephone*, a lively set of solo and ensemble dances worked to Eastern European Klezmer music, made the Graham company dancers look more vigorous than they have in a long time. Last autumn the company gave a so-called revival of the 1935 *Panorama*, Graham's first large group effort. The *Excerpts*, as they were called in the programme, were vividly rendered and remained intriguing as a fragment of Graham's early work. Like Taylor's company, Graham's is also forced to perform with taped music, but unlike Taylor's troupe this one, under the artistic direction of Ron Protas, is very worried about potentially negative press coverage. A so-called policy, which started last year and which was more firmly enforced this year, denies press seat allocations to certain writers, supposedly based on the 'nature' of their publication. The obvious delineation is really based on whether the company finds the individual 'supportive' of its efforts or not. The 'not's' don't have it and the company conducts a discriminatory policy that goes unremarked upon in major daily newspapers.

Miami and South Florida

LAURIE HORN

Miami has become a crossroads of the Americas. North American, Latin American, and Caribbean cultural traditions merge here in a simmering beanpot—and the dance world, not surprisingly, is one of the first to reflect the mix.

In Dade County—the official governmental agency embracing metropolitan Miami—more than half the population of two million speaks Spanish and roughly 600,000 are of Cuban origin. A significant percentage—somewhere between 60,000 and 100,000—are recent, often illegal, exiles from Haiti, many of whom went uncounted in the 1990 census. The area has absorbed the bulk of political exiles from Cuba, Nicaragua, and Haiti and also sizeable populations from Venezuela, Colombia, Costa Rica, Guatemala, El Salvador, Brazil, Argentina, Mexico ... even Spain.

Against this backdrop, Edward Villella and the eight-year-old **Miami City Ballet** have had to battle to develop his New York-driven Balanchine aesthetic. As rehearsed by Elyse Borne—former New York City Ballet soloist and now principal ballet-mistress in Miami—**Miami City Ballet**'s *corps de ballet* in the last two years has finally acquired the quality of good Balanchine. In the troupe's early years, emerging soloists caught the style and immediately took off for more prestigious venues. Now, as the company improves, Villella has been able to retain and attract better, more experienced, and taller dancers. Among the principals currently dancing, Iliana Lopez—a Venezuelan ballerina of Mozartean purity—and her husband Franklin Gamero have remained loyal since the company's second year; Cuban-born Marielena Mencia, trained in Miami at Ballet Concerto, and her husband, the Latvian/Venezuelan virtuoso Yanis Pikieris, rejoined the company in 1992 after Pikieris served briefly as interim director of France's **Ballet du Nord**. Too petite and too European in style to be a Balanchine 'type', Mencia nevertheless delivered a superbly nuanced performance in the Violette Verdy role in *Emeralds* in February 1993.

A new, home-grown generation of Balanchine interpreters is coming to the forefront in 26-year-old identical twins Maribel and Mabel Modrono, who received their early training from Susana Prieto in the blue-collar Miami suburb of Hialeah. Both, at the moment, are dancing diamond-hard

Balanchine ballerina roles; among their repertory are *Square Dance*, the troupe's jagged and brooding rendering of *The Four Temperaments*, *Concerto Barocco*, and the roles Dew Drop and Sugar Plum in the company's full-length staging of the Balanchine *Nutcracker*.

Hurricane Andrew's devastation of Miami's southern suburbs on 24 August 1992 severely cramped underwriting for the arts, and **Miami City Ballet** cut back on new productions in the 1992/3 season. The company's resident choreographer, Peruvian, Jimmy Gamonet de los Heros, pre-mièred a minor work titled *Pan Nuit Suite* in March 1993 to Gounod's *Walpurgisnacht*. Guest choreographer Peter Anastos's *The Lost World*, made to minimalist music by Peter Golub in the days immediately preceding and just after the hurricane, had an understandably disjointed quality to it. In addition, after two years of careful assembly, the troupe magnificently staged its first full-length ballet, *Jewels*. Unfortunately, the full ballet was given only twice: once in November 1992 in Fort Lauderdale and once in February 1993, in Miami.

Despite rough years for funding, the company seems to be holding its own economically. Its subscription base is 16,000 in three venues—Miami, Fort Lauderdale, and West Palm Beach. The troupe offers four repertory programmes a year plus *Nutcracker* at each site. When touring outside Florida is added to the equation, the company gave a total of 150 perfor-mances during the 1992/3 season.

Significant and progressive work in the Spanish dance world is being pro-duced in Miami by Rosita Segovia, who founded four years ago **Ballet Español Rosita Segovia** here. Barcelona-born Segovia, who was for eigh-teen years Antonio's partner during the 1950s and 1960s, has divided her time between Barcelona and Miami for two decades. During that period, she has trained new generations of Spanish dancers out of both cities. They are instantly recognizable for their flexible and precise upper bodies, their ability to dance equally well in hard shoes or the soft slippers of the *escuela bolera*, and for their clear, articulate castanets and heelwork. In recent years, chief among the dancers have been principals Rosa Mercedes, Cristina Masdueno, and Ana Diaz and soloists Ada Linares and Meria Jesus Vallve. Madrid-based virtuoso Paco Romero regularly joins the company as a quasi-permanent guest.

Segovia works in many styles of Spanish dance—*escuela bolera*, flamenco, and folkloric forms among them—but her most passionate interest is in Spanish neo-classicism: the blending of a straight, ballet-influenced line with assymetrical spacial patterns and assymetrical rhythms in both castanets and heelwork. The best examples of this genre currently in the company repertory are *Estudios*, a piece for three women who work counter-rhythms in castanets against the Rachmaninov *Rhapsody on a Theme of Paganini*; *Danzas Fantasticas*, a three-part group work to music by Spanish composer Joaquin Turina, and a new setting of the middle section of Joaquin Rodrigo's *Concierto de Aranjuez*. At the time of writing, Segovia was working on *Mediterraneo*, a new piece to music by John McLaughlin, and was preparing new choreography for *El Amor brujo* and *La Vida Breve* for the **Greater Miami Opera**.

The founding in the late 1980s of the New World School of the Arts, a public-supported high school and college, has meant an explosion of modern dance companies in Miami. Most interesting among them are **Houlihan & Dancers**, a troupe led by Gerri Houlihan, a former member of the Lar Lubovitch company, **Mary Street Dance Theater**, a strongly feminist troupe headed by Dale Andree; and **Leslie Neal Dance**. Out of Palm Beach county, choreographer Demetrius Klein is producing words and movement fusions soaked in raw physicality and religious questioning. Klein is in the midst of a struggle to resolve the dilemma of disparity between his own virtuoso physical ability and the often prosaic dancing of his troupe.

Many key intellectuals from Haiti either live in or move frequently through Miami's Haitian exile-community, and **Sosyete Koukouy**, an artistic society founded in Port au Prince in 1965 to promote Creole language and Haitian culture, is based here. Although its production of work is sporadic due to Haiti's current political and economic crisis, the society (translatable from the Creole as **Society of Firebirds**) finds it impossible to separate theatre, dance, music, religion, and politics. Last year's *Wake Up*— a dance-play using movement and imagery directly out of the *voudun* dance tradition intended as a propaganda tool to help the Haitian people resist dictatorship—was presented here during Katherine Dunham's much-publicized fast in support of President Jean-Baptiste Aristide.

Cuba's political fortunes also have produced new artistic trends in Miami. Until Villella's arrival, ballet tradition here was most influenced by Cuba, especially by the décor- and story-focused Ballet Russe/Original Ballet Russe/American Ballet Theatre aesthetic nurtured in pre-revolutionary Cuba by the same organizations which produced Alicia Fernando and Alberto Alonso. In the early 1960s, the first wave of exiles from Fidel Castro's regime founded rival schools and school-based companies in Miami. For thirty years they have given decent biennial productions of the nineteenth-century classics—usually with guest stars from **ABT**.

After the 1980 Mariel boatlift, a generation of exiled classical dancers trained in post-revolutionary Cuba brought with it an interest in Afro-Cuban forms. So far, no significant choreographer has emerged—despite an attempt in 1992 by newly exiled Victor Cuellar to re-establish his company here. In general, productions by this group of Cuban choreographers tend to tell African myths without effectively fusing African movement into balletic form. The experimentation continues in tiny companies which group and regroup with the latest wave of immigration.

San Francisco

PAUL PARISH

After eight years, Helgi Tomasson has made the **San Francisco Ballet** into a remarkable musical ensemble. He was brought in after the board turned on and repudiated their main choreographer, Michael Smuin, in an intriguing, baffling, unendingly disturbing revolution of public taste. It is as if they had thrown out D. H. Lawrence or Walt Whitman and voted in, say, T. S. Eliot—i.e. turned out an embarrassing but emotionally powerful bard and installed a fastidious Apollonian. Somewhere at the root of it is the massive psychic constriction which affected the whole country in the early 1980s. It kicked the loose sexual fantasizing, which in the 1970s had been accepted at all cultural levels, downstairs into the tabloids.

Even at their best, Smuin's ballets were always gesturally based; their rhythmic organization was subordinate to narrative point-making, and always with a sexual fantasy very near the surface. They had the strength of making direct use of the heart-breaking beauty of dancers' bodies: his *Romeo and Juliet*, *A Song for Dead Warriors*, *Shinju*, and *The Eternal Idol* were pictorial, unmistakable, larger than life, mythic—and they were very, very popular.

The case for change may have rested on the hidden premiss that Smuin's melodramas had succeeded too completely, that the pendulum had to swing. Certainly what we have now is a company who are increasingly and steadily moving forward, dancing from a musical rather than a narrative impulse.

Perhaps the strongest proof of this is the number of dancers who are not remarkable to look at until they start to move—and then they are so beautiful you cannot take your eyes off them. Furthermore they do not do anything that makes you want to look away. Elizabeth Loscavio, Kristen Long, Joanna Berman, Tina Leblanc are short, rounded women; none of them has the long-legged, small-torsoed ballerina build. Their proportions are no more idealized than Baryshnikov's—or Helgi Tomasson's, for that matter. All four of them are transfigured by the way they move—they turn out magnificently, and from their deepest impulses they enlarge, clarify, simplify, and open up the movement. In this way you can identify kinaesthetically, and be carried away, until in the end you can go home satisfied and happy.

The basic appeal of these dancers is in the way they move. Not that they do not have a sophisticated understanding of how to shade their lines, Loscavio most of all. However, even though one remembers her poses in *The Sleeping Beauty*, Act III, one still remembers her attitude in the Rose Adagio not as a position but as a breath. We saw her put her fate in God's hands, let go of her breath, then find she was still standing there, rising out of the ground effortlessly, like a fountain. Their eagerness and fearlessness, the love of discipline, and the energy—such a transfiguration can make you feel that you are looking into the heart of things. In short, we now have ballerinas. Only a few years ago, one complained that San Francisco Ballet lacked ballerinas—the *corps* was wonderful, but there was nobody to put in front of them who could bring the essence of a ballet to focus. Now we are starting to see them everywhere.

Kristen Long is a soloist who is rising fast but who has not often had full responsibility for a ballet. However she made a radiant case for Tomasson's *Haffner Symphony*. It changed the way one felt about the ballet which a year ago seemed like a coy reminiscence of Balanchine's *Divertimento No. 13*. The piece begins with a brilliant classical Allegro, which is purely formal. The Andante which follows however, suggests a story: it is an extended *pas* for the ballerina, who dances in duets, quartets, trios, with everyone else in the ballet (except the ballerino) behaving as though they were paying her calls on her birthday. There is nothing gestural in this, except in the spirit of their partnering; Long offers her foot in *pas de cheval*, to use the phrase Mary Ellen Moylan ascribed to Balanchine, 'as you would offer the hand if you were offering to shake hands'. Her demeanour seemed to me a very fine thing, of rare constancy, and it informed the ballet throughout, whether she was alone on the stage or at the heart of elaborate figurations.

I did not see Loscavio's *Swan Lake* nor her *Fille mal gardée*, both of which were highly praised. Her performance in the Marnee Morris role in *Who Cares*, *My One and Only*, and *Embraceable You* was the most astounding thing I saw all year. In her musicality she is like a physical force, or a god that takes possession of her and sweeps her round the room. Not that she looks like a zombie—she looks spontaneous, as if she were making this up. In *My One and Only*, she actually forgot the steps and shrugged her shoulders as if to say—I don't know what I'm going to do next—then cheerfully improvised some bright hops on *pointe* until she returned to the phrase darting off like a stone skipping over water. Superb technique, strength, and control are all there, but at the same time there is such a powerful musical imagination at play, it feels as though one is looking at the initial creation of a dance.

Joanna Berman has finally recovered from injuries that kept her, our most human dancer, mostly off-stage for two years. It was in Paul Taylor's *Company B*, to Second World War songs by the Andrews Sisters, that she made her come-back. As she danced *Rum and Coca-Cola*, she was a native goddess of the isles, wave-like, elusive, with a world of wit in her hips and a heap of boys at her feet.

Another performance that went over the top was Tina LeBlanc's Lise in Ashton's *Fille mal gardée*; a role she had performed famously with the Joffrey Ballet before moving here. In San Francisco Ballet's production she showed a steadily increasing warmth and sweetness in both mime and

San Francisco Ballet's production of *Swan Lake*, choreography by Tomasson/Petipa/ Ivanov.   PHOTO: LLOYD ENGLERT

dance. It was expertly paced, with maximum lightness in the punishingly fast *pas de chat/pas de bourrées* at the end, and before the light as air *pas de deux*. She had the extraordinary help of David Bintley, in town to rehearse his ballet *Job*, as Widow Simone.

Fille has been in the repertory since the days of Michael Smuin, and Widow Simone has always been performed as if it were Mother Ginger—as a pretext for mugging and flirting with the audience. Bintley is certainly hilarious, but he does treat the widow as if she had a mind with intentions in it, and who could remember what they were. I will never forget Bintley's profile (what a nose!) as the widow sits in her wagon on the way to the picnic, looking back at Alain, studying the face and person of her prospective son-in-law. Then the head turned, showed the other profile, studied Lise for a second, and broke off. Is this mime training, is it movement study, is it inspiration on just that day? Whatever it is, our dancers need more of it.

Job has gathered much more power this year; this year many in the audience were moved. The Grahamesque sincerity of Sabina Alleman as Job's wife gave a frontier strength to it, as did Yuri Zokov's coiled, wiry Satan, who strikes at Job's hopes like a snake. The whole work built, and was crowned by, the transcendent dancing of Eric Hoisington as the angelic youth who consoles Job. I found myself disturbed for days after by a sense of heart-break that came from that ballet.

Company B also had suggestions of heartache in it: the hectic celebrations, the fleeting emotions of young people thrown together in wartime. The ballet was a hit, and many went to see the **Paul Taylor Company** dance it when they passed through town. Briefly, San Francisco Ballet

Jan Erkert and Dancers in *Between Men*, choreographed by Jan Erkert.
PHOTO: BILL FREDERKING

danced it with more lightness, opening up the lacy rhythms, finding more fun in the girl singers' syncopations than the Taylor dancers did, but they did not make such gritty portraits as the Taylor Company.

The ballet starts with jumping numbers like 'The Pennsylvania Polka' and 'Oh Johnny'. Johnny is a brilliantly funny piece, featuring three girls throwing themselves at him, legs open like tentacles, attaching themselves in sequence like octopi on a post. Sad songs filter in, a line of men in silhouette move across the back of a duet to 'There Will Never Be Another You'. At a crucial turn in the music the boy fades to the back and joins the grey frieze marching off to war. The ballet closes with the group boogeying to 'Bei mir, bist du schön', but half-way through the finale, the dancers go into slow motion, and with poetic grace, they begin to fall, one by one.

Oakland Ballet had uninteresting seasons last year after a decade of extraordinary work—the first American revival of Nijinska's *Les Noces* in

Joseph Holmes Chicago Dance Theatre.

over a generation, the total reconstruction of her *Train bleu*, revival of *The Green Table*, Anna Sokolow's *Rooms*, ballets by Massine, and Loring. **San Jose/Cleveland Ballet**, on the other hand, not only presented a raw but exciting *Apollo* and made a good stab at Balanchine's *Square Dance* (complete with orchestra and caller on stage, and the original 'Western' costumes), they also made a triumphant vindication of their ballet, *The Overcoat*, which Flemming Flindt choreographed for Nureyev to music by Shostakovich. It was Nureyev's last American première in 1990. Though the audience gave him their puzzled applause, it was not a success when he danced it here. This year, the director of the company, Denis Nahat, came out of retirement and danced the part himself. He danced that night like a genius, with an exquisite ear for the music and a droll, preposterous line as if he had been drawn by Ronald Searle. In the dream sequence, when his overcoat came to dinner, Nahat's deftness, his courtesy to his chairs and to the table as he drew them into place, put me in mind of Charlie Chaplin— whose character, the little tramp, owed much to Gogol's Akaky Akakievich in the first place. Nahat's success was complete, the audience was enchanted with him as a performer. Beyond that he has vindicated the judgements he made in acquiring the ballet in the first place, in investing the huge sums that Beni Montresor's brilliant production required, in offering Nureyev an opportunity to advance his art and in defending the strengths of the ballet itself, which deserves to enter the international repertory. It is over-long, but it makes a world—with a great part for an interpretative dancer.

PART III

Education

Dance in Higher Education

PETER BRINSON

What effect does dance in higher education have on dance in theatres? What influence can it have on audiences as well as dancers and teachers? What is meant, anyway, by dance in higher education? Whatever the answers our gaze across the world shows dance entering higher education in many forms although comparatively new in some countries.

Dance in higher education *may* mean dance taught in universities gaining degree awards as in the UK and North America. It *may* mean advanced dance studies in special institutions where the courses lead not to a degree but to dance qualifications most certainly of postgraduate standard. Such institutions exist in Russia, China, and other countries. It *may* mean a combination of both as in Holland. Whatever dance education means at this level a network of advanced dance study exists across the world on which *World Ballet and Dance* will report in future. We begin with the UK.

During the last twenty years dance in British higher education has expanded from being taught and studied only as part of teacher training to a more comprehensive study embracing many career directions. Twenty years ago the idea of a Professor of Dance in a British university was laughable. Today there are four.

By comparison with the United States—or with Russia in other higher education forms—such development is microscopic. The first university dance course leading to a degree was instituted in the United States in 1927. The first British BA honours degree course in dance was validated only in 1977 at the Laban Centre for Movement and Dance in London. Since then many other dance degree courses have followed the Laban example in British higher education up to and including postgraduate doctorates.

All these courses are in contemporary, or modern, dance for which students can begin training within general school education. Classical ballet, which needs its own training and education from an early age, lies outside this development, except at the Royal Academy of Dancing. There a BA honours degree course in the Art and Teaching of Ballet will start in September 1994. This important initiative will be followed certainly by other British classical ballet institutions.

Dance in higher education therefore implies research and preparation for a range of other dance careers as well as a career performing or teaching. In the United States a university dance education often leads to a professional performing career. Robert Cohan, the distinguished American choreographer and co-founder of London Contemporary Dance Theatre in

London, explained how this came about. 'In American universities', he told the committee which produced an influential report *Dance Education and Training in Britain* in 1980,

nothing changed until the teachers changed, becoming either professional dancers or trained in a professional studio. As long as dance stayed theoretical nothing happened. It is generally accepted now that a student goes to university to major in dance in order to join a professional company. University dance students should have the same opportunity to become practising artists as have students of other arts.

Outside the United States and Canada this line of training for contemporary dance through higher education happens more rarely. It is beginning to happen in Australia and South Africa, occasionally in South America and Europe. In the UK the development of professional contemporary dance training alongside degree studies owes more to private institutions of dance like the Laban Centre and London Contemporary Dance School than it does to universities. Middlesex University has the only dance department at the moment openly moving to prepare dancers for the professional stage. The Laban Centre and London Contemporary Dance School, on the other hand, have been doing this for many years. Both have produced dancers and choreographers who have changed the face of British contemporary dance in the last two decades.

One result of the development of dance in British higher education has been to expand enormously the range of career options in dance. Dance administration, dance therapy, dance research, dance criticism, dance history, dance anthropology, dance sociology, dance politics, are all among career options available for study.

As dance careers have expanded, however, the Thatcher governments since 1979 have reduced funding for the arts, for higher education, and for local government through which student grants for training are administered. This has emphasized further a long-standing discrimination against vocational training for dance and drama.

In most subjects students who obtain appropriate qualifications at secondary level automatically receive funding to study at tertiary level. For dance and drama students and students of some other subjects this funding is not automatic. It is discretionary, meaning that a local authority may or may not award a grant for vocational training according to the funds it has available. This has always been unfair because students living in rich authorities might receive grants while more talented students in poorer authorities can receive nothing.

Since 1979 this illogical situation has grown worse. The government has reduced the money it gives to local authorities so that, in turn, local authorities have had to reduce what they can give in vocational training for drama and dance. Almost all vocational training in Britain is provided by private specialist institutions like the Laban Centre and London Contemporary Dance School. These institutions are not funded directly by government but by discretionary grants from local authorities or by the students themselves. The result has been to add to discrimination according to where you live a further discrimination according to who can pay. Students from poorer families, especially young black people, are unable to pursue the dance career of their choice. Britain loses much dance talent.

Such a government-induced muddle is part of a whole debate in the UK around further and vocational education. Our system is perceived to be far below other equally industrialized countries in terms of standards and ability to inspire students aged 16–17. Crazy as it seems the government does not give adequate priority to further education and vocational training as an investment for the future. Within this misjudgement it also misunderstands and undervalues the arts. Not only dance but also other subjects face crisis.

The good and positive news is, first, the success of dance in British higher education over the last twenty years in spite of all handicaps; secondly, the action which dancers and dance teachers themselves are taking to fight back. In the struggle to establish dance alongside other university subjects dance advocates have had to demonstrate to traditionalist opponents what dance would bring to universities. The benefits include an enrichment of the concept and nature of knowledge for which universities stand, especially knowledge non-verbally acquired or transmitted. It can enhance the study of other subjects such as history, physical education, physiology, anthropology, and sociology as well as other arts. It can enrich university life in general and attract students not otherwise attracted. It can broaden the perceptions and relevance of dance art itself. So it has turned out, raising immensely the status of dance and dance teaching in public estimation.

Equally effective in changing the public image of dance has been action taken by dancers and teachers to fight for dance against active government prejudice to cut back the arts. They have formed powerful national organizations such as Dance UK, a national forum for dance, and the Council for Dance Education and Training. These bring together in a united lobby many different dance organizations which used to see each other as rivals. In consequence there has grown up a politics of dance increasingly effective nationally and locally alongside a wider politics of the arts and of education.

Such developments are not special to the UK. They are happening in Australia, South Africa, the United States, Holland, and many other countries. The next step must be to bring these national bodies into international dialogue to gain further strength from shared experience. After all, dance in India, Africa, and Japan is organized differently and has different traditions from dance in Russia and Eastern Europe which is different again from dance in North America, Western Europe, and Australia. We have a lot to learn from each other at all levels of education and performance.

The international bodies to help this exchange of learning exist already but do not collaborate sufficiently nor embrace all countries. Like national organizations they too need to work more closely together. It will happen.

PART IV

Statistics

Australia

THE AUSTRALIAN BALLET

Australian Ballet Centre
2 Kavanagh Street
South Melbourne 3205
Tel: 61 3 684 8600
Fax: 61 3 686 7081

Artistic dir.: Maina Gielgud

Administrator: Ian McRae

Principal dancers: Vicki Attard, Lisa Bolte, Steven Heathcote, Greg Horsman, Adam Marchant, David McAllister, Lisa Pavane, Colin Peasley, Sian Stokes

No. of dancers: 30 male, 33 female

New works 93/4:

New Stanton Welch ballet

BANGARRA DANCE THEATRE

PO Box 218
Pyrmont
New South Wales 2009
Tel: 61 2 319 4560
Fax: 61 2 319 4569

Artistic dir.: Stephen Page

Choreographer: Stephen Page

No. of dancers: 18—traditional aboriginal dancers and contemporary trained dancers

New work 93/4:

Praying Mantis Dreaming, Ch.: Stephen Page

CHRISSIE PARROTT DANCE COM-PANY

PO Box 166
Mosman Park, WA 6012
Tel: 61 9 385 1252
Fax: 61 9 385 1259

Artistic dir.: Chrissie Parrott

General manager: Alix Rhodes

Principal dancers: Stefan Karlsson, Margrete Helgeby, Lisa Hearen, Jon Burtt, Claudia Alessi, Peter Sheedy, Tammy Meeuwissen

No. of dancers: 3 male, 4 female

New works 93/4:

Life, Love and Beauty

Sabotage—The Box

Satu Langit

See Ya Next Century

Wrath

DANCE NORTH

PO Box 1645
Townsville, QLD 4810
Tel: 61 77 722 549/722 828
Fax: 61 77 213 014

Artistic dir.: Cheryl Stock

General manager: Lorna Hempstead

No. of dancers: 3 male, 4 female

New works 93/4:

Andy's Arranging Flowers, Ch.: Leigh Warren

Broken Places, Ch.: Cheryl Stock

Please No More Palms, Ch.: Cheryl Stock
New works choreographed by Su Zheng, Xu and Csaba Buday

DANCEWORKS

PO Box 274
Albert Park
Victoria 3206
Tel: 61 3 696 1702
Fax: 61 3 696 1650

Artistic dir.: Helen Herbertson

Administrator: Paul Summers

No. of dancers: 3 male, 3 female

New works 93/4:

Breaking the Silence, Ch.: Helen Herbertson in collaboration with Dianne Reid, Ros Warby, Nicole Fletcher, Michael Collins

In the Company of Angels, Ch.: Helen Herbertson

Danceworks at the Gasworks, Ch.: Sandra Parker, Helen Herbertson, Dianne Reid

We're Big Boys and Girls Now, Ch.: Helen Herbertson

Image is Everything, Everything is Image: Helen Herbertson, Dianne Reid, Brett Daffy

Bamboo Bandits, Ch.: Helen Herbertson in collaboration with the dancers

**MERYL TANKARD AUSTRALIAN
DANCE THEATRE**

120 Gouger Street
Adelaide SA 5000
Tel: 61 8 212 2084
Fax: 61 8 231 1036

Artistic Dir.: Meryl Tankard

No. of dancers: 4 male, 3 female

New works 93/4:

Furioso, Ch.: Meryl Tankard

ONE EXTRA COMPANY

2/15 Broughton Street
Milson's Point NSW 2061
Tel: 61 2 957 4590
Fax: 61 2 957 4938

Artistic dir.: Graeme Watson

General manager: Rosemary Jones

New works 93/4:

Blossoms and Wrinkles, Ch.: Graeme Watson

Suburban Pirates, Ch.: Julie-Anne Long

Everything But . . ., Ch.: Graeme Watson

Drowning in a Sea of Dreams, Ch.: Graeme
Watson

Cannibal Race, Ch.: Julie-Anne Long

QUEENSLAND BALLET

The Thomas Dixon Centre
Corner Drake Street and Montague Road
West End QLD 4101
Tel: 61 7 846 5266
Fax: 61 7 846 1854

Artistic dir.: Harold Collins

General manager: Kay Francis

Choreographers: Pamela Buckman, Jacqui
Carroll, Rosetta Cook, Graeme Watson,
Natalie Weir

Principal dancers: Michelle Giammichele,
Graham Fletcher, Dale Johnston, Terri-Lee
Milne, Dione Ware, Shane Weatherby,
Peter St Clair

New Works 93/4:

The Tempest, ch.: Jacqui Carroll, *Mus.*: Carl
Vine

Bolero, Ch.: Jacqui Carroll, *Mus.*: Ravel

Propel, Ch.: Rosetta Cook, Martin Shaw,
Mus.: Phillip Boa and the Voodoo Club

Bamaga Diptych, Ch.: Harold Collins, *Mus.*:
Richard Mills

WEST AUSTRALIAN BALLET

2nd Floor, His Majesty's Theatre
825 Hay Street
Perth WA
Tel: 61 9 481 0707
Fax: 61 2 324 2402

Artistic dir.: Barry Moreland

General manager: Shane Colquhoun

Choreographers: Edmund Stripe, Elizabeth
Hill

Principal dancers: Ronnie van den Bergh,
Janet Tait, Lisa Miles, Marshall Rowles,
Elizabeth Hill, Catherine Phelan, Olivia
Moulton, Daryl Brandwood, Edmund
Stripe

No. of dancers: 8 male, 9 female

New works 93/4:

Hamlet, Ch.: Barry Moreland

Nexus, Ch.: Edmund Stripe

Medea, Ch.: Barry Moreland

Further information about Australian dance
companies from: Australian Dance Council
(Ausdance), PO Box 287, Jamison, ACT
2614, Australia. Tel: 61 6 248 8992, Fax: 61 6
247 4701

Austria

**BALLETT DES SALZBURGER LAND-
ESTHEATERS**

Schwarzstrasse 22
A-5020 Salzburg
Tel: 43 662 871512-0
Fax: 43 662 871512-13

Artistic dir.: Peter Breuer

Administrator: Freimuth Teufel

Choreographers: Erich Walter, Youri Vamos,

Robert Machherndl, Peter Breuer

Principal dancers: Andoni Aresti-Landa, Eric
Assandri, Alessandro Bizzi, Kenichi Soki,
Muriel Estanco, Maria Gruber, Katsue
Hirochi, Isabella Tomanec

No. of dancers: 12 male, 12 female

New work 93/4:

Romeo und Julia, Ch.: Glass, *Mus.*:
Tchaikovsky

Belgium

COMPAGNIE MICHELE ANNE DE MEY

Rue St Josse 49
B-1030 Brussels
Tel: 32 2 217 4127
Fax: 32 2 217 5167

Artistic dir.: Michele Anne de Mey

Administrator: Christine Tinlot

No. of dancers: 6 male, 4 female

New works 93/4:

Pulcinella

Sonatas 555

ROSAS

Van Volxemlaan 264
1190 Brussels
Tel: 32 2 347 0104
Fax: 32 2 343 5352

Artistic dir.: Anne Teresa de Keersmaeker

Administrator: Guy Gijpens

No. of dancers: 4 male, 7 female

New work 93/4:

Suite für Klavier Op. 25/Grosse Fuge

ROYAL BALLET OF FLANDERS

Kattendijkdok
Westkaai 16
B-2000 Antwerp
Tel: 32 3 234 3438
Fax: 32 3 233 5892

Artistic dir.: Robert Denvers

Administrator: Jan Vanderschoot

Choreographer: Danny Rosseel

Principal dancers: Lorena Feijoo, Lucinda Tallack-Garner, Aysem Sunal, Hiroko Sakakibara, Lenka Jarosikova, Hilde Van de Vloet, Chris Roelandt, Jan Vandeloo, Jean-François Boisnon, Rinat Imaëv, Tero Julku, Eric Frédéric

No. of dancers: 24 male, 27 female

New works 93/4:

Ostacoli, Ch.: John Wisman, *Mus.*: Anders Eliasson

Fatum, Ch.: Joseph Lazzini, *Mus.*: Tchaikovsky

Firebird, Ch.: Mauricio Wainrot, *Mus.*: Stravinsky

Brazil

BALÉ DE CIDADE DE SÃO PAULO

Rua João Passa Acqua 66
01326-020 Bela Vista
São Paolo
Tel: 55 11 239 3883, 239 1740
Fax: 55 11 223 5021

Artistic dir.: Ivonice Satie

Company dir.: Hugo Travers

Choreographers: Victor Navarro, Luis Arrieta, Suzana Yamauchi, Rodrigo Pederneiras, Oscar Araiz, Ivonice Satie

No. of dancers: 16 male, 20 female

New works 93/4:

Warm-Up, Ch.: Arrieta, *Mus.*: Bach

Le Sacré de printemps, Ch.: Arrieta, *Mus.*: Stravinsky

Curinga, Ch.: Yamauchi, *Mus.*: W. Russel

La Valse, Ch.: Arrieta, *Mus.*: Ravel

Nonette, Ch.: Costa, *Mus.*: Martinu

Cantares, Ch.: Araiz, *Mus.*: Ravel

Pavane, Ch.: Arrieta, *Mus.*: Ravel

Mozarteando, Ch.: Satie, *Mus.*: Mozart

New Production by Vasco Wellemkamp

New Production by Guillerme Botelho

Canada

DANNY GROSSMAN DANCE COMPANY

511 Bloor Street West
Toronto
Ontario M5S 1Y4
Tel: 1 416 531 8350
Fax: 1 416 531 1971

Artistic dir.: Danny Grossman

General manager: Jane Marsland

No. of dancers: 4 male, 5 female

DESROSIERS DANCE THEATRE

219 Broadview Avenue
Toronto
Ontario M4M 2G3
Tel: 1 416 463 5341
Fax: 1 416 463 4770

Artistic dir.: Robert Desrosiers

Administrator: Ursula Martin

Principal dancers: Jean-Aimé Lalonde, Robert Glumbek, Marie-Josée Dubois, Robin Wilds, Jennifer Lynn Dick

No. of dancers: 5 male, 5 female

New work 93/4:

Étude: The Interference

JUDITH MARCUSE DANCE COMPANY

106–206 East 6th Avenue
Vancouver, BC V5T 1J8
Tel: 1 604 872 4746
Fax: 1 604 872 7951

Artistic dir.: Judith Marcuse

Associate: Margery Lambert

Administrator: Laura MacMaster

No. of dancers: 4 male, 5 female

New work 93/4:

The States of Grace—a multi-faceted presentation involving film, dance, music, and theatre, commissioned for the XVth Commonwealth Games Arts and Culture Festival

LES GRANDS BALLETS CANADIENS

4816 Rue Rivard
Montréal
Québec H2J 2N6
Tel: 1 514 849 8681
Fax: 1 514 849 0098

Artistic dir.: Lawrence Rhodes

Director general: Wendy Reid

Choreographer emeritus: Fernand Nault

Principal dancers: Anik Bissonnette, Andrea Boardman, Daniela Buson, Min Tang, Marcello Angelini, Sylvain Lafortune, Kenneth Larson, Louis Robitaille, Min Hua Zhao

No. of dancers: 17 male, 18 female

New work 93/4:

Axioma 7, Ch.: Ohad Naharin

NATIONAL BALLET OF CANADA

157 King Street East
Toronto
Ontario M5C 1G9
Tel: 1 416 362 1041
Fax: 1 416 368 7443

Artistic dir.: Reid Anderson

Administrator: Robert Johnston

Principal dancers: Kimberly Glasco, Margaret Illmann, Karen Kain, Martine Lamy, Gizella Witkowsky, Rex Harrington, Serge Lavoie, Pierre Quinn, Jeremy Ransom, Raymond Smith

No. of dancers: 28 male, 35 female

New works 93/4:

The Actress, Ch.: James Kudelka

Herman Schmerman, Ch.: William Forsythe

New work choreographed by Glen Tetley

O VERTIGO DANSE

4455 de Rouen
Montreal
Quebec H1V 1H1
Tel: 1 514 251 9177
Fax: 1 514 251 7358

Artistic dir.: Ginette Laurin

Administrator: Mireille Martin

No. of dancers: 3 male, 7 female

New work 93/4:

Déluge (working title)—co-production of the National Arts Centre in Ottawa, Canada Dance Festival, and TNDI Châteauvallon (France)

ROYAL WINNIPEG BALLET

380 Graham Avenue
Winnipeg
Manitoba R3C 4K2
Tel: 1 204 956 0183
Fax: 1 204 943 1994

Artistic dir.: William Whitener

Administrator: Jeffrey J. Bentley

Choreographer: Mark Godden

Principal dancers: Evelyn Hart, Laura Graham, Elizabeth Olds, John Kaminski, Jorden Morris, Alexei Ratmanski, Zhang Wei-Qiang

No. of dancers: 12 male, 16 female

New work 93/4:

A new work, *Ch.*: Mark Godden

TORONTO DANCE THEATRE

80 Winchester Street
Toronto
Ontario M4X 1B2
Tel: 1 416 967 1365
Fax: 1 416 976 4379

Artistic dir.: David Earle

Administrator: Kenneth Peirson

Choreographers/founders: David Earle, Patricia Beatty, Peter Randazzo, Christopher House, James Kudelka

No. of dancers: 6 male, 7 female

New works 93/4:

Encarnado, Ch.: Christopher House

Four Towers, Ch.: Christopher House

New work, *Ch.*: David Earle

Chile

BALLET DE SANTIAGO

San Antonio 149
PO Box 18
Santiago
Tel: 56 2 638 1609
Fax: 56 2 633 2942

Artistic dir.: Marcia Haydée

Administrator: Andres Rodriguez

Choreographers: Hilda Riveros, Jaime Pinto

Principal dancers: Sara Nieto, Marcela Goicoechea, Jacqueline Cortes, Valentina Chepatcheva, Claudia Smiguel, Luis Ortigoza, Pablo Aharonian, Edgardo Hartley, Vladimir Guelbet, Berthica Prieto

No. of dancers: 30 male, 32 female

New works 93/4:

Coppelius the Magician, Ch.: Haydée, *Mus.*: Delibes

Carmen, Ch.: Hilda Riveros, *Mus.*: Bizet

Thousand and One Nights, Ch.: Haydée/Pinto, *Mus.*: Rimsky-Korsakov

Card Game, Ch.: Cranko, *Mus.*: Stravinsky

Petrushka, Ch.: Béjart, *Mus.*: Stravinsky

El Reto, Ch.: Hilda Riveros, *Mus.*: Vangelis

Pineapple Poll, Ch.: Cranko, *Mus.*: Sullivan

BALLET NACIONAL CHILENO

Universidad de Chile
Compañia 1264—Piso No. 8
Santiago
Tel: 56 2 696 7426
Fax: 56 2 222 5116

Artistic dir.: Maritza Parada Allende

Principal dancers: Cecilia Reyes, Berenice Perrin, Monica Valenzuela, Carola Alvear, Veronica Santibañez, Jorge Ruiz, Renato Peralta, Rodrigo Pasten

No. of dancers: 15 male, 15 female

New works 93/4:

Mesa Verde, Gran Ciudad, Pavana, Ch.: Kurt Jooss

Aryata, Canciones de un Vagabundo, Libertango, Ch.: Mauricio Wainrot

Deje un Laurel Sembrado, Ch.: Elena Gutierrez

Manantial de Piedra, Ch.: Gaby Concha

China

GUANGDONG MODERN DANCE COMPANY

13 Shui Yin Heng Lu
Sha He Ding
Guangzhou 510075
Tel: 86 20 7701212

Artistic dir.: Willy Tsao

Administrator: Yang Mei-gi

Choreographers: Shem Wei, Qiao Yang, Yan Ying, Su Ka

Principal dancers: Shen Wei, Qiao Yang, Yan Ying, Xing Liang

No. of dancers: 10 male, 8 female

New works 93/4:

Myths

Tales from the Middle Kingdom

Cuba

BALLET DE CAMAGÜEY

Carretera Central Este, No. 331
Esq A4
Camagüey
Tel: 53 96535–91909

Director: Jorge Vede

Choreographers: Lázaro Martínez, José Chávez, Osvaldo Beiro

Principal dancers: Bárbara García, Celia Rosales, Laura Urgelles, Rafaela Cento, Lídice del Río, Christine Ferrandó, Yicet Capallejas, Mónica Amaro, Guillermo Leiva, Orlando López, Victor Carnesoltas, Robero Machado

No. of dancers: 24 male, 44 female

New works 93/4:

Piezas Profanas, Ch.: Lázaro Martínez, *Mus.*: Raul Noriega

Genesis, Ch.: Iván Rolla, *Mus.*: Hector Villalobos

A Traves de Las Estrellas, Ch.: Iván Rolla, *Mus.*: Sergei Rachmaninov

La Aventura, Ch.: Osvaldo Beiro, *Mus.*: Michel Kama

Relaciones, Ch.: Lázaro Martínez, *Mus.*: Glass/Rossini/Shankar

Tchaikovsky, Ch.: after Balanchine, *Mus.*: Tchaikovsky

Paisaje, Ch.: Lázaro Martínez, *Mus.*: Kilar/Tielhemann

Tarantela, Ch.: George Balanchine, *Mus.*: Louis Gottschalk

Dulce Cisne de Avon, Ch.: Lázaro Martínez, *Mus.*: Banda Sonora

BALLET NACIONAL DE CUBA

Calzada No. 510 entre DyE
Vedado
C. Habana 10400
Tel: 52 32 7151/52 32 3551/52 32 2829
Fax: 537 33 3117

Artistic dir.: Alicia Alonso

Administrator: Augusto Gil Díaz

Choreographers: Alicia Alonso, Gustavo Herrera, Alberto Méndez, Iván Monreal, Iván Tenorio

Principal dancers: Loipa Araúja, Aurora Bosch, Amparo Brito, Rolando Candia, Lázaro Carreño, José Carreño, Lienz Chang, Marta García, María Elena Llorente, Josefina Méndez, Lourdes Novoa, Orlando Salgado, Rosario Suárez, Jorge Vega, José Zamorano

No. of dancers: 45 male, 65 female

New works 93/4:

Las Cuatro Estaciones, Ch.: Alicia Alonso/Alberto Méndez/Iván Tenorio/Gustavo Herrera/Iván Monreal, *Mus.*: Vivaldi

Lieder, Ch.: Iván Monreal, *Mus.*: Chopin

Juana, Razon y Amor, Ch.: Alicia Alonso, *Mus.*: J. Piñera

Romance, Ch.: Iván Monreal, *Mus.*: Dvořák

BALLET SANTIAGO DE CUBA

Teatro Heredia
Avenida de Las Américas y Avenida de los Desfiles
Santiago de Cuba C.P. 90400
Tel: 53 4 3226, 53 4 3834/4 3856/4 3878

Artistic dir. and principal choreographer: María Elena Martínez de la Torre

Choreographer: Lázaro Martínez

Principal dancers: Melba Cedeño, Idael Jerman, Wilmer de la Cruz, Rebeca Masó

No. of dancers: 9 male, 11 female

New work 93/4:

America Laberinto, Ch.: Marisol Ferrari (Venezuela)

COMPAÑÍA TEATRO DE LA DANZA DEL CARIBE

Santa Lucia 305, entre San Pedro y San Felix
Santiago de Cuba
Tel: 53 27626

Artistic dir.: Eduardo Rivero Walker

Administrator: Edison Reyes Cabeza

Choreographers: Eduardo Rivero, Arturo Castillo, Barbara Ramos, Arsenio Andrades

Principal dancers: Yamilla Prevals Fenerón, Lázaro Caballero Caminero, Arturo Alberto, Castillo Fidalgo, Abeldo Gonzáles Fonseca, Arsenio Rafael, Andrades Calderón

No. of dancers: 10 male, 8 female

New works 93/4:

Ceremonial de la Danza, Ch.: Rivero

Coligacíon, Ch.: Arturo Castillo

DANZA ABIERTA

Calzada 456 e/E y F
Vedado
Cuidad de la Habana
Tel: 53 7 328685/35238
Fax: 53 7 333117/39025/333461

Artistic dir.: Marianela Boán

Administrator: Alejandro Aguilar

Choreographers: Marianela Boán, Victor Varela, José Angel Hevía, Xenia Cruz

No. of dancers: 1 male, 6 female

New works 93/4:

Juan Salvador Gaviota, Ch.: Marianela Boán, *Mus.:* George Winston

Fast Food, Ch.: Marianela Boán, *Mus.:* Beethoven

Desprendimiento, Ch.: Marianela Boán

Vaiven, Ch.: Xenia Cruz, *Mus.:* Meredith Monk

Lol, Ch.: Xenia Cruz, *Mus.:* Meredith Monk

DANZA LIBRE

Calle Maximo Gomez No. 1607
Entre Varona y Marmol
Guantánamo
Tel: 53 3 5153

Artistic dir.: Elfrida Mahler

Administrator: Angel Coello

Choreographers: Ramiro Guerra, Isaías Rojas, Alfredo Velázquez, Tomás Guilarte, Elfrida Mahler

No. of dancers: 8 male, 8 female

New works 93/4:

Suite Yoruba, Ch.: Ramiro Guerra

Tiempo De Quimeras, Ch.: Guerra

Dos Bandos, Ch.: Isaías Rojas

Festin De Baltazar, Ch.: Elfrida Mahler

El Eterno Retorno, Ch.: Tomás Guilarte

Triptico Oriental, Ch.: Ramiro Guerra

Wimelera

DANZA-TEATRO DE CUBA 'RETAZOS'

Calle 6 No. 364 e/37 y 39
Vedado
Cuidad Habana 6
Tel: 53 81 2437, 53 98 5043
Fax: 537 333 143

Artistic dir.: Isabel Bustos

Administrator: Guillermo Márquez

Choreographer: Isabel Bustos

No. of dancers: 3 male, 4 female

New works 93/4:

Ah que tu escapes

Collage Musical de Ireno Garcia

La Casa de María

Boleros

Marat Sade

Denmark

NEW DANISH DANCE THEATRE

8D, IV, Meinungsgade
DK-2200 Copenhagen N
Tel: 45 3139 87 87
Fax: 45 3537 49 98

Artistic dirs.: Anette Abildgaard, Warren Spears

Administrator: Poul Richard Pedersen

No. of dancers: 4 male, 4 female

New works 93/4:

Wunderbaum, Ch.: Anette Abildgaard

Stravinsky, Ch.: Warren Spears

Tanne, Ch.: Warren Spears

ROYAL DANISH BALLET

Royal Theatre
PO Box 2185
1017 Copenhagen K
Tel: 45 33 32 20 20
Fax: 45 33 15 03 60

Artistic dir.: Peter Schaufuss

Associates: Lise la Cour, Johnny Eliason

Administrator: Michael Christiansen

Principal dancers: Kirsten Simone, Sorella Englund, Eva Kloberg, Mette-Ida Kirk, Heidi Ryom, Lis Jeppesen, Rose Gad, Silja Schandorff, Christina Olsson, Niels Kehlet, Flemming Ryberg, Tommy Frishøi, Poul-Erik Hesselkilde, Arne Villumsen, Yuri Possokhov, Peter Bo Bendixen, Alexander Kølpin, Kenneth Greve, Lloyd Riggins

No. of dancers: 40 male, 47 female

New works 93/4:

The Sleeping Beauty, Ch.: Helgi Tomasson after Petipa, *Mus.*: Tchaikovsky

New ballet by Anna Lærkesen, *Ch.*: Anna Lærkesen

New ballet by Laura Dean, *Ch.*: Laura Dean, *Mus.*: Richard Kosinski and John Zeretzke

Des Knaben Wunderhorn, Ch.: John Neumeier, *Mus.*: Gustav Mahler

Mahler's Fifth Symphony, Ch.: John Neumeier, *Mus.*: Gustav Mahler

TEATER TANGO

Vesterbrogade 62 D
DK Copenhagen V
Tel: 45 3124 98 33
Fax: 45 3124 98 33

Artistic dir.: Rhea Leman

Administrator: Mucki Nordgren

No. of dancers: 3 male, 3 female

New works 93/4:

Broken Table

De Nøgne Blik

UPPERCUT DANSETEATER

Rathsacksvej 32
1862 Frederiksberg C
Tel: 45 3131 48 41
Fax: 45 3124 02 91

Artistic dirs.: Sheila de Val and Cher Geurtze

Administrator: Lone Nyhuus

No. of dancers: 2 male, 2 female

New works 93/4:

Birds and Stones

Outsider, Ch.: Craig MaGuire

Estonia

DANCE THEATRE FINE 5

Heina 9–2
EE0006 Tallinn
Tel: 372 2 47 19 94
Fax: 372 2 60 16 12

Administrator: Tiina Ollesk

Choreographer: Rene Nõmmik

No. of dancers: 3 male, 2 female

New works 93/4:

Die Nacht, Ch.: R. Nõmmik

Ammaduabuu, Ch.: R. Nõmmik

DANCE THETRE NORDSTAR

c/o Estonia Thetre
Estonia pst. 4
EE0001 Tallinn
Tel: 372 2 53 51 63
Fax: 372 2 44 35 84

Artistic dir.: Saima Kranig

Principal dancers: Larissa Sintsova, Saima Kranig

No. of dancers: 3 male, 4 female

New work 93/4:

Presence of Memory, Ch.: K. Oberly, *Mus.*: Dvořák

ESTONIA THEATRE BALLET COMPANY

Estonia pst. 4
EE0001 Tallin
Tel: 372 2 44 30 31
Fax: 372 2 31 30 80

Artistic dir.: Viesturs Jansons

General manager: Jaak Viller

Choreographer: Mai Murdmaa

Principal dancers: Kaie Kõrb, Kati Ivaste, Inna Sõrmus, Tatjana Kilgas, Tatjana Voronina, Ingrid Iter, Tiiu Vilks, Toomas Rätsepp, Mikhail Netshejev, Viktor Kuzmin, Juri Mihhejev

No. of dancers: 20 male, 35 female

New works 93/4:

Carmina Burana, Ch.: Mai Murdmaa, *Mus.*: Carl Orff

Catulli Carmina, Ch.: Mai Murdmaa, *Mus.*: Carl Orff

Fairytale in Pictures, Ch.: Bournonville, *Mus.*: W. Holm.

VANEMUINE THEATRE BALLET COMPANY

6 Vanemuise Street
EE 2400 Tartu
Tel: 372 34 73761
Fax: 372 34 31513

Artistic dir.: Ülo Vilimaa

Choreographer: Mare Tommingas

Principal dancers: Jelena Karpova, Dagmar Rang, Aivar Kallaste, Oleg Titov

No. of dancers: 10 male, 16 female

New works 93/4:

Joseph and His Brothers

The Wonderful Mandarin

The Nutcracker

The Goblin

The Centre for Dance Information in Estonia—c/o EPKA, Suur Karja 23, EE0001 Tallinn, Tel: 372 2 44 92 55

Finland

DANCE THEATRE ERI

SF-Yliopistonkatu 7
20110 Turku
Tel: 358 21 501032
Fax: 358 21 501041

Artistic dir.: Tiina Lindfors, Lassi Sairela, Eeva Soini

Choreographers: Tiina Lindfors, Lassi Sairela, Eeva Soini

No. of dancers: 2 male, 3 female

New works 93/4:

Harlequinos of the Night, Ch.: Tiina Lindfors

Tango is a Serious Matter, Ch.: Lassi Sairela, Eeva Soini, Tiina Lindfors

Sancta Barbara, Ch.: Tiina Lindfors

Three new pieces, *Ch.*: Lassi Sairela, Fred Negendanck, Jarck Benschop

New piece, *Ch.*: Kai Lehikoinen

Little Prince, Ch.: Tiina Lindfors

DANCE THEATRE RAATIKKO

Viertolankuja 4
01300 Vantaa
Tel: 358 0 873 2306
Fax: 358 0 873 3294

Artistic dir.: Marja Korhola

Administrator: Ulla Jarla

Choreographer: Marja Korhola

No. of dancers: 2 male, 4 female

New works 93/4:

Dance of the Angels, Ch.: Marja Korhola

The Fan, Ch.: Marja Korhola

FINNISH NATIONAL BALLET

Helsinginkatu 58
00250 Helsinki
Tel: 358 0 403 021
Fax: 358 0 403 02305

Artistic dir.: Jorma Uotinen

Choreographers: Marjo Kuusela, Tommi Kitti, Carolyn Carlson, Rudi van Dantzig, Heinz Spoerli, John Neumeier, Oscar Araiz

No. of dancers: 33 male, 33 female

New work 93/4:

A new creation, *Ch.*: Jorma Uotinen

France

CENTRE CHORÉGRAPHIQUE NATIONAL DE NANTES

Studio Jacques Garnier
23 rue Noire
44000 Nantes
Tel: 33 40 93 30 97
Fax: 33 40 93 30 11

Artistic dir.: Claude Brumachon

Administrator: Agnes Izrine

Principal dancers: Benjamin Lamarche, Valerie Soulard, Veronique Redoux, Hervé Maigret, Christian Bakalov, Fernando Carillo

No. of dancers: 7 male, 7 female

New works 93/4:

Nina ou la voleuse d'esprits

Émigrants
Bohème
Les Avalanches

LYON OPÉRA BALLET

1 Place de la Comeaie
69001 Lyon
Tel: 33 72 00 45 81
Fax: 33 72 00 45 85

Artistic dir.: Yorgos Loukos

Administrator: Philippe Durand

Choreographer: Bill T. Jones

No. of dancers: 18 male, 18 female

Germany

BALLETT DER DEUTSCHEN OPER BERLIN

Richard Wagner Strasse 10
10585 Berlin
Tel: 49 30 3438 1
Fax: 49 30 3438 232

Administrator: Steven Scott

Choreographers: Karole Armitage, Michael Clark, Molissa Fenley, Bill T. Jones, Stephen Petronio, Peter Schaufuss, Meg Stuart

Principal dancers: Arantxa Argüelles, Katalene Borsboom, Christine Camillo, Lisa Cullum, Zara Deakin, Marie-Pierre Flechais, Katarzyna Gdaniec, Theresa Jarvis, Maryvonne Robino, Silke Sense, Bart de Block, Yannick Boquin, Iouri Borodine, Alexandre de la Caffinière, Vladimir Damianov, Xavier Ferla, Stefano Giannetti, Maximiliano Guerra, Martin James, Tomas Karlborg, Jean-Lucien Massot, Göran Svalberg

No. of dancers: 25 male, 36 female

New works 93/4:

Schwanensee, Ch.: Peter Schaufuss

Next Wave, Ch.: Meg Stuart, Molissa Fenley, Karole Armitage

BALLETT FRANKFURT

Untermainanlage 11
60311 Frankfurt
Tel: 49 69 212 37 319
Fax: 49 69 212 37 565

Artistic dir.: William Forsythe

Administrator: Dr Martin Steinhoff

No. of dancers: 17 male, 19 female

New works 93/4:

Quintett, Ch.: William Forsythe

As a Garden in this Setting, Ch.: William Forsythe

The Hermit and the Navigator, Ch.: Amanda Miller

BALLETT SCHINDOWSKI

Musiktheater im Revier
Kennedyplatz
D-45881 Gelsenkirchen
Tel: 49 209 40 97 138
Fax: 49 209 40 97 250

Artistic dir. and principal choreographer:
Bernd Schindowski

General manager: Gianni Malfer

Choreographers: Rose-Marie Guiraud,
Rubens Reis, Henning Paar, Bennie
Voorhaar

Principal dancers: Carmen Balochini, Rita
Barretto, Emma-Louise Jordan, Victoria
Keepax, Eunice Oliveira, Scheyla Silva,
Eduardo Laranjeira, Henning Paar, Rubens
Reis, Cassio Vitaliano

No. of dancers: 13 male, 12 female

New works 93/4:

Firebird, Ch.: Bernd Schindowski

Stabat Mater, Ch.: Bernd Schindowski

Wenn die Instrumente tanzen... (production
for children), *Ch.:* Bernd Schindowski

Ein deutsches Requiem, Ch.: Bernd
Schindowski

BALLETTENSEMBLE DER SÄCHSISCHEN STAATSOPER DRESDEN

Theaterplatz 2
01067 Dresden
Tel: 37 51 4842469
Fax: 37 51 4842669

Artistic dir.: Vladimir Derevianko

Choreographer: Stephan Thoss

No. of dancers: 23 male, 34 female

New work 93/4:

Romeo und Julia

BALLETT DER STAATSOPER UNTER DEN LINDEN

Unter den Linden 7
10117 Berlin
Tel: 49 30 20354469
Fax: 49 30 20354637

Artistic dir.: Michael Denard

Administrator: Dr Christiane Theobald

Choreographers: Maurice Béjart, Roland
Petit, Jorma Uotinen, Maryse Delente,
Helge Musial

Principal dancers: Steffi Scherzer, Oliver
Matz, Victoria Lahiguera, Bettina Thiel,
Torsten Händler, Jörg Lucas, Mario
Perricone, Raimondo Rebeck, Beatrice
Knop, Tatjana Marinowa, Brit Rodemund,
Helga Schiele, Barbara Schroeder, Nicole
Siepert, Korina Stolz-Franke, Jana
Timptner, Ekkehard Axmann, W.
Ginkulow, Dietmar Jacob, Marek Rozycki,
Josef-Hanus Sklenar, Ralf Stengel, Pedro
Hebenstreit

No. of dancers: 35 male, 46 female

New works 93/4:

Dix—oder Eros und Tod

Wozzeck—Reflexe

HAMBURG BALLET

Ballettzentrum Hamburg
Caspar-Voght-Strasse 54
D-20535 Hamburg
Tel: 49 40 21 11 88-0
Fax: 49 40 21 11 88-88

Artistic dir.: John Neumeier

Administrator: Ulrike Schmidt

Principal dancers: Stefanie Arndt, Gamal
Gouda, Bettina Beckman, Jean Laban, Anna
Grabka, Ivan Liška, Gigi Hyatt, Janusz
Mazoń, Chantal Lefèvre, Anders Nordström

No. of dancers: 25 male, 32 female

New works 93/4:

Undine, Ch.: John Neumeier, *Mus.:* Hans
Werner Henze

Trilogie M.R., Ch.: John Neumeier, *Mus.:*
Ravel

HEIDELBERG BALLET

Friedrichstrasse 5
D-69117 Heidelberg
Tel: 49 6221 58 35 10
Fax: 49 6221 58 35 99

Artistic dir.: Liz King

Administrator: Manfred Biskup

No. of dancers: 7 male, 7 female

New work 93/4:

Fools, Ch.: Liz King

TANZTHEATER DER KOMISCHEN OPER BERLIN

Komische Oper
Behrenstrasse 55–57
D-10117 Berlin
Tel: 49 30 22 02 761
Fax: 49 30 22 99 029

Artistic dir.: Doris Laine

Administrator: Werner Rackwitz (from 1 Jan. 1994 Albert Kost)

Choreographers: Tom Schilling, Arila Siegert, Birgit Scherzer, Jan Linkens, Robert North, Flemming Flindt, Marc Bogaerts, Dietmar Seyffert, Emöke Pöstenyi

Principal dancers: Hannelore Bey, Jutta Deutschland, Alma Munteanu, Angela Reinhardt, Katrin Dix, Heike Keller, Uta Opitz, Angela Philipp, Katherine Panter, Cristina Palade, Flora Savrasova, Beate Vollack, Dieter Hülse, Jürgen Hohmann, Gregor Seyffert, Thomas Vollmer, Pietro Ferlito, Uwe Küssner, Mario Nötzel, Javier Serrano, Werner Mente, Jens-Peter Urbich, Mugur Valsami

No. of dancers: 32 male, 23 female

New works 93/4:

Circe und Odysseus, *Ch.*: Arila Siegert, *Mus.*: Gerald Humel

Coppélia, *Ch.*: Jochen Ulrich, *Mus.*: Leo Delibes

Hong Kong

CITY CONTEMPORARY DANCE COMPANY

Ground Floor
110 Shatin Pass Road
Wong Tai Sin
Kowloon
Tel: 852 326 8597
Fax: 852 351 4199

Artistic dir.: Willy Tsao

Administrator: Chow Yung Ping

Choreographer: Helen Lai

Principal dancers: Abby Chan, Cristina L. Fargas, Yvette Huang, Ritchie Law, Lam Lee, Antoinette Mak, Wang Ling Ling, Wong Man Chui, Mandy Yim, Steven Bremner, Deng Yu, Mikey Lee, Goh Boon Ann, Ong Yong Lock, Andy Wong, Yap Poo Meng

No. of dancers: 7 male, 9 female

New works 93/4:

Open Party

Nine Songs

The Pink

Dancing in the Sun

CCDC 15th Anniversary Celebration

Quartet to the End of Time

Journey to the West

HONG KONG ACADEMY FOR PERFORMING ARTS DANCE ENSEMBLE

The Hong Kong Academy for Performing Arts
School of Dance
1 Gloucester Road
Wanchai
Tel: 852 584 1539
Fax: 852 802 3856

Artistic dir.: Margaret Carlson

Administrator: Loretta Tang

Choreographers: Amanda Olivier, Tom Brown, Liu You-Lan, Sheng Pei-qi, Mohamed Drissi, Betsy Fisher, Ko Chun-kwai, Zhang Da-yong, Aaron Wan, Pewan Chow, Cheung Yuen-chiu

Principal dancers: students from the Advanced Diploma and Professional Diploma classes

No. of dancers: 15 male, 85 female

New works 93/4:

Carnival of the Animals

Le Bœuf sur le Toit

An Hui Flower Drum Lantern Dances

Romance under the Moon

Feline Party

Paquita

All Item is Wonder Zap

Games, Rainbow Round My Shoulder, *Ch.*: Donald MacKayle

Hungary

ARTUS

1113 Budapest
Kökörcsin u.9
Tel: 36 1 1667505
Fax: 36 1 1667505

Artistic dir.: Gábor Goda

Administrator: Beatrice Rossi

Choreographers: Gábor Goda, Ildikó Mándy

Principal dancers: Ildikó Mándy, Eva Regenart, Csaba Méhes, Ferenc Kalman, Gábor Goda, Ernst Suss, Istvan Horvath

No. of dancers: 5 male, 2 female

New works 93/4:

Song of the Pearl

Blue Monday

Human Garden

HUNGARIAN NATIONAL BALLET

State Opera House
1061 Budapest
Andrássy út 22
Tel: 36 1 1320 923
Fax: 36 1 1319 817

Artistic dir.: György Szakály

Administrator: Zsolt Galántai

Choreographers: László Seregi, Antal Fodor

Principal dancers: Ildikó Pongor, Zoltán Nagy jr, Katalin Volf, Zoltán Solymosi, Katalin Hágai, György Szakály, Krisztina Végh, Tibor Kováts, Edit Szabadi, Sándor Jezerniczky, Regina Balaton, Tibor Eichner

No. of dancers: 55 male, 70 female

New works 93/4:

The Wooden Prince, Ch.: Antal Fodor

The Miraculous Mandarin, Ch.: Antal Fodor

The Moor of Venice, Ch.: Lilla Pártay

The Taming of the Shrew, Ch.: László Seregi

Israel

BAT-DOR DANCE COMPANY

30 Ibn Gvirol Street
Tel Aviv 64078
Tel: 972 3 6963175
Fax: 972 3 6955587

Artistic dir.: Jeannette Ordman

Company manager: Kenneth Mason

Choreographer: Domy Reiter-Soffer

Principal dancers: Alexander Alexander, Vladislav Manayenkov, Amir Levy, Patricia Aharoni, Eleanor Vlodavsky, Helen Pavova, Yael Levitin

No. of dancers: 10 male, 10 female

ISRAEL BALLET

Hey Beiyar 2
Tel Aviv 62093
Tel: 972 3 6966610
Fax: 972 3 6957081

Artistic dir.: Berta Yampolsky

Administrator: Hillel Markman

Choreographer: Berta Yampolsky

Principal dancers: Wendy Lucking, Naama Yadlin, Nina Gershman, Maya Pevsner, Bruno Verzino, Iqbal Khawaja, Orna Kugel, Sarkisov Vyacheslav, Kevin Cunningham

No. of dancers: 10 male, 20 female

New works 93/4:

Mephisto Waltz, Ch.: Berta Yampolsky

Les Biches, Ch.: Krzysztof Pastor

KIBBUTZ CONTEMPORARY DANCE COMPANY

10 Dubnov Street
PO Box 40014
Tel Aviv 61400
Tel: 972 3 5452688
Fax: 972 3 5452689

Artistic dir.: Yehudit Arnon

General manager: Dan Rudolf

Choreographer: Rami Be'er

No. of dancers: 7 male, 11 female

New works 93/4:

Naked City, Ch.: Rami Be'er

Slow Me Up/Speed Me Down, *Ch.*: Gideon Obarzanek

The Silver Grapefruit, *Ch.*: Ziv Frenkel

Façade, *Ch.*: Martha Inbar

Connections, *Ch.*: Hedda Oren

Gentlemen's Agreement, *Ch.*: Jasmin Vardimon

As It Sounds, *Ch.*: Shelli Gonen

Stardust, *Ch.*: Amir Kolben

OSHRA ELKAYAM MOVEMENT THEATRE

119 Bar Kohva Street
46440 Hertzliya
Tel: 972 9 544039

Artistic dir.: Oshra Elkayam

Administrator: Jacob Edelist

No. of dancers: 2 male, 2 female

New work 93/4:

Sparkls

YARON MARGOLIN DANCE COMPANY

106/15 Derech Biet Lechem
Jerusalem 93630
Tel: 972 2 438624/716197
Fax: 972 2 513040

Artistic dir.: Yaron Margolin

Administrator: Edna Stroz

Choreographers: Yael Haramati, Yaron Margolin, Naftali Ironi

Principal dancers: Yaron Margolin, Yael Haramati, Gal Chen

No. of dancers: 3 male, 2 female

New works 93/4:

Consolation, *Ch.*: Margolin/Ironi, *Mus.*: Liszt

Ishlame, *Ch.*: Margolin/Ironi, *Mus.*: Balakirov

The Seeds of the Water, *Ch.*: Margolin/Ironi, *Mus.*: Liszt

Italy

BALLET OF TEATRO ALLA SCALA

Via Filodrammatici 2 20121
Milan 1
Tel: 39 02 88791
Fax: 39 02 8879441

Artistic dir.: Elisabetta Terabust

Administrator: Carlo Fontana

Principal dancers: Elisabetta Armiato, Ornella Costalonga, Oriella Dorella (*étoile*), Annamaria Grossi, Vera Karpenko,

Maurizia Luceri, Anita Magyari, Loredana Mapelli, Bruna Radice, Adraiana Scameroni, Isabel Seabra, Vittorio D'Amato, Paolo Podini, Francisco Sedeno, Biago Tambone, Maurizio Vanadia, Bruno Vescovo, Michele Villanova

No. of dancers: 36 male, 52 female

New works 93/4:

Contemporary Project by Massimo Moricone, Virgilio Sieni, Enzo Cosimi

Japan

MATSUYAMA BALLET COMPANY

3-10-16 Minami-Aoyama
Minato-ku
Tokyo 00107
Tel: 81 3 3408 6640
Fax: 81 3 3498 7986

Artistic dir.: Mikiko Matsuyama

Administrator: Masao Shimizu

Choreographer: Tetsutaro Shimizu

Principal dancers: Yoko Morishita, Tetsutaro Shimizu, Hiroko Kurata, Akiko Yamakawa, Kumi Hiramoto, Akemi Sato

No. of dancers: 20 male, 40 female

New work 93/4:

Swan Lake (new version)

TOKYO BALLET

5-1-20 Yakumo
Meguro-ku
Tokyo 152
Tel: 81 3 3725 8000
Fax: 81 3 3718 0858

Artistic dir.: Shiro Mizoshita

Choreographer: Hiroko Tomoda

Principal dancers: Naoki Takagishi,
Munetaka Iida, Kazuo Kimura, Yasuyuki
Shuto, Haruo Goto, Yukari Saito, Mayumi
Katsumata, Shiori Sano, Mika Yoshioka,
Miki Aizu, Yukie Iwaki, Sayuri Iwamoto

No. of dancers: 30 male, 60 female

New works 93/4:

M, Ch.: Maurice Béjart

New Creation, *Ch.*: Jiří Kilyán

Korea

CHANG MU DANCE COMPANY

5–92 Chang Jeon Dong
Mapo
Seoul 121–190
Tel: 82 2 337 5961
Fax: 82 2 335 0484

Artistic dir.: Kim Maeja

Administrator: Kim Yoon Tae

Choreographer: Kang Mee Ree

No. of dancers: 22 male, 40 female

Principal dancers: Kang Mee Ree, Kim Sun
Mee, Ma Bok II, Kim Eun Hee, Choi Mee
Ae, Choi Jee Yeon, Choi Kyung Ran, Lee
Myung Jin, Kim Young Duck, Park Duck
Sang, Koo Eun Hee, Kim Kyung Soon, Kim
Hee Jung, Shin Eun Jin, Cheon Hae Jung,
Han So Young, Kim Sung Ok, Kim Eun
Jeong, Son So Young, Lee Jin Sook, Chang
Hae Soo, Kim Hyo Jin, Choi Jun Myung,
Kim Hyang, Son Mee Jeong, Eun Hae Jin,
Han Young Shin, Cheon Mee Ra, Kim
Hyeon Jung, Kang Jee Hee

No. of dancers: 11 male, 66 female

UNIVERSAL BALLET COMPANY

25 Neung Dong
Sungdong-ku
Seoul 133–180
Tel: 82 2 452 1392
Fax: 82 2 456 3271

Artistic dir.: Roy Tobias

Choreographers: Roy Tobias, Adrienne
Dellas

Principal dancers: Julia Moon, Sun-Hee Park,
Ji-Hyan Yuh, Min-Hwa Choi, Jae-Hong
Park, Kyu-Dong Kwak

No. of dancers: 22 male, 40 female

New works 93/4:

Invocation, Ch.: Roy Tobias, *Mus.*: Mozart

Straight to the Heart, Ch.: Roy Tobias, *Mus.*:
Kreisler

Toy Shop, Ch.: Jae-Hong Park, *Mus.*: Bizet

Wedding Party, Ch.: Roy Tobias, *Mus.*: Joplin

Numina, Ch.: Roy Tobias, *Mus.*: Mozart

The Sleeping Beauty, Ch.: Petipa/Oleg
Vinogradov, *Mus.*: Tchaikovsky

Theme and Variations, Ch.: Balanchine

The Netherlands

DUTCH NATIONAL BALLET

PO Box 16486
1001 RN Amsterdam
Waterlooplain 22
1011 PG Amsterdam
Tel: 31 20 5518225
Fax: 31 20 5518070

Artistic dir.: Wayne Eagling

Administrator: Dick Hendricks

Choreographers: Rudi van Dantzig, Toer van
Schayk

Principal dancers: Nathalie Caris, Coleen
Davis, Caroline Sayo Iura, Jane Lord, Karin
Schnabel, Valerie Valentine, Jeanette
Vondersaar, Fred Berlips, Wim Broeckx,
Clint Farha, Alan Land

No. of dancers: 36 male, 48 female

New works 93/4:

New work by Wayne Eagling (April/May
1994)

New work by Rudi van Dantzig (June 1994)

New work by Toar van Schayk (June 1994)

INTRODANS
Vijfzinnenstraat 80–82
6811 LN Arnhem
Tel: 31 85 512111
Fax: 31 85 515647

Artistic dir.: Ton Wiggers

Administrator: Hans Focking

Choreographers: Mark Bruce, Mirjam Diedrich, Graham Lustig, Jean-Christophe Maillot, Gian Franco Paoluzi, Heinz Spoerli, Philip Taylor, John Wisman

No. of dancers: 9 male, 9 female

New works 93/4:

Transit, Ch.: Graham Lustig

Tauwww, Ch.: Mirjam Diedrich

Maximiliana or The Illegal Practice of Astronomy, Ch.: Gian Franco Paoluzi

Sacred Space, Ch.: Philip Taylor

Mater, Ch.: Tony Wiggers

New ballet by Tony Wiggers

New ballet by Jean-Christophe Maillot

INTRODANS EDUCATIEF
Vijfzinnenstraat 80–82
6811 LN Arnhem
Tel: 31 85 5152111
Fax: 31 85 515647

Director: Roel Voorintholt

Associate choreographers: Philip Taylor, Conny Janssen, Tony Wiggers

No. of dancers: 4 male, 4 female

New works 93/4:

Donder op, Ch.: Conny Janssen, Philip Taylor, Roel Voorintholt for young audiences from age 7

NEDERLANDS DANS THEATER 1
Postbus 333
2501 CH Den Haag
Tel: 31 70 3609931
Fax: 31 70 3617156

Artistic dir.: Jiří Kylián

General dir.: Michael de Roo

Choreographers: Jiří Kylián, Hans van Manen

No. of dancers: 16 male, 17 female

New works 93/4:

Alone, for a Second, Ch.: Nacho Duato, *Mus.*: collage Erik Satie

World premières choreographed by William Forsythe, Jiří Kylián, Hans van Manen

NEDERLANDS DANS THEATER 2
Postbus 333
2501 CH Den Haag
Tel: 31 70 3609931
Fax: 31 70 3617156

Artistic dir.: Jiří Kylián

General director: Michael de Roo

Choreographers: Jiří Kylián, Hans van Manen

No. of dancers: 7 male, 7 female

New works 93/4:

Concertante, Ch.: Hans van Manen, *Mus.*: Frank Martin

Petrol-Head Lover, Ch.: Gideon Obarzanek

World premières choreographed by Lionel Hoche, Paul Lightfoot

NEDERLANDS DANS THEATER 3
Postbus 333
2501 CH Den Haag
Tel: 31 70 3609931
Fax: 31 70 3617156

Artistic dir.: Jiří Kylián

General director: Michael de Roo

Choreographers: Jiří Kylián, Hans van Manen

No. of dancers: 2 male, 2 female

New works 93/4:

Them, Ch.: Carolyn Carlson

Different Partners, Ch.: Hans van Manen, *Mus.*: Stravinsky

World premières choreographed by Jiří Kylián, Paul Lightfoot, Susanne Linke, Maurice Béjart

REFLEX DANCE COMPANY
Akkerstraat 97
NL-9717 KZ Groningen
Tel: 31 50 719888
Fax: 31 50 714561

Artistic dir.: Patrizia Tuerlings

Administrator: Charles Rijsbosch

No. of dancers: 4 male, 6 female

New works 93/4:

New works choreographed by Patrizia Tuerlings and Hans Tuerlings

Co-production with Raz (Tilburg/Netherl.)
New works by Marc Vanrunxt, Jappe Claes, and Patrizia Tuerlings

New Zealand

DOUGLAS WRIGHT DANCE COMPANY

PO Box 6833
Newton
Auckland
Tel: 64 9 849 3100

Artistic dir.: Douglas Wright

Manager: Fenn Gordon

New work 93/4:

Forever, Ch.: Douglas Wright

FOOTNOTE DANCE COMPANY

PO Box 3387
Wellington
Tel: 64 4 384 9285
Fax: 64 4 801 5010

Artistic dir.: Deidre Tarrant

Manager: Carolyn McKeefry

New works 93/4:

New works choreographed by Shona McCullagh, Ann Dewey, Merenia Gray

JENDEN AND SOLINO

21 Medway Street
Island Bay
Wellington
Tel: 64 4 383 7801

Artistic dir.: Paul Jenden

New work 93/4:

The Gay Fandango, Ch.: Paul Jenden

JORDAN AND PRESENT COMPANY

PO Box 9653
Wellington
Tel: 64 4 382 9112

Artistic dir.: Susan Jordan

No. of dancers: 5 female

New work 93/4:

Bone of Contention

JUMP GIANTS

29 Summer Street
Ponsonby
Auckland
Tel: 64 9 378 6677

Artistic dir.: Brian Carbee

Manager: Evan Blackman

New work 93/4:

Bedrock, Ch.: Brian Carbee

MICHAEL PARMENTER'S COMMOTION COMPANY

PO Box 9296
Te Aro
Wellington
Tel: 64 4 385 7185
Fax: 64 4 385 7585

Artistic dir.: Michael Parmenter

Manager: Simon Ellis

Principal dancers: Helen Winchester, Michael Parmenter, Helen Keeley, Taane Meta, Lisa Densem

No. of dancers: 4 male, 5 female

New work 93/4:

The Dark Forest

ROYAL NEW ZEALAND BALLET COMPANY

29 Brandon Street
Telecom Dance Centre
Wellington
Tel: 64 4 499 1107
Fax: 64 4 499 0773

Artistic dir.: Ashley Killar

Administrator: John Page

Choreographers: Grey Veredon, Douglas Wright, Michael Parmenter, Eric Langvet, Ashley Killar

Principal dancers: Kerry Anne Gilberd, Anne Anderson, Karin Wakefield, Eric Langvet, Killian O'Callaghan, Ou Lu

No. of dancers: 13 male, 13 female

New works 93/4:

World News, *Ch.*: Eric Langvet

Sarabande, *Ch.*: Ashley Killar

Tantra, *Ch.*: Michael Parmenter

Dark Waves, *Ch.*: Ashley Killar

Giselle, *Ch.*: Ashley Killar

Petrushka, *Ch.*: Russell Kerr

TAIAO DANCE THEATRE

PO Box 5857
Wellesley Street
Auckland
Tel: 64 9 376 5792

Artistic dir.: Stephen Bradshaw

Manager: Gail Richards

Norway

COLLAGE DANCE COMPANY

Drammensveien 130
N-0277 Oslo
Tel: 47 22 44 34 50
Fax: 47 22 44 32 40

Artistic dir.: Lise Nordal

General manager: Fredrik Chr. Bolin

No. of dancers: 2 male, 4 female

New work 93/4:

Ibsen Dances/Création '94 autour d'Ibsen, *Ch.*: Karine Saporta, *Mus.*: Asmund Feidje, co-production for 20th anniversary jubilee

JANE HVEDING DANCE COMPANY

Kirkevn 50
0368 Oslo
Tel: 22 46 37 28

Artistic dir.: Jane Hveding

Choreographer: Jane Hveding

No. of dancers: 3 male, 6 female

New works 93/4:

Utsikten

Grieg på kroken

Pssst!

Et lite narrespill

Die Kunst der Fuge

Russia

BOLSHOI BALLET

Theatre Square 2
Moscow
Tel: 7 095 292 99 86/292 21 20

Principal Choreographer: Yuri Grigorovich

Principal dancers: Nina Ananiashvili, Yelena Andrienko, Natalia Arkhipova, Natalia Bessmertnova, Yelena Bobrova, Maria Bylova, Elvira Drozdova, Marina Filippova, Nadezhda Gracheva, Yulia Levina, Erica Luzina, Natalia Malindina, Yulia Malkhasianz, Alla Mikhalchenko, Irina Nesterova, Larisa Okhotnikhova, Nadezhda Pavlova, Elina Palshina, Inna Petrova, Irina Piatkina, Tatiana Rastorguyeva, Nina Semizirova, Olesia Shulzhitskaya, Svetlana Slavnaya, Nina Speranskaya, Olga Starikova, Galina Stepanenko, Yulia Volodina, Irina Zibrova, Oxana Zvetnitskaya. Sergei Bobrov, Andrei Buravtzev, Nikolai Dorokhov, Alexei Fadeyechev, Sergei Filin, Sergei Gromov, Yuri Klevtsov, Andrei Melanin, Vladimir Moiseyev, Vladimir Niporozhny, Andrei Nikonov, Leonid Nikonov, Mark Peretokin, Alexander Petukhov, Alexei Popovchenko, Ruslan Pronin, Andrei Shakhin, Mikhail Sharkov, Gediminas Taranda, Andrei Uvarov, Yuri Vasluchenko, Alexander Vetrov, Yuri Vetrov, Viacheslav Yelagin, Igor Zakharkin

New works 93/4:

Fantasia on the Casanova Theme, *Ch.*: Mikhail Lavrosky, *Mus.*: Mozart

Pas-de-quatre, *Ch.*: Anton Dolin, *Mus.*: Cesare Pugni

MALY BALLET

Ploshchad Iskusstva
191011 St Petersburg
Tel: 812 219 1943, 219 1986, 219 1110
Fax: 812 314 3653

Choreographer: Nikolai Boyarchikov

Principal dancers: Irina Kirsanova, Natalia Kirichek, Regina Kuzmicheva, Anjella Kondrasheva, Anna Linnik, Natalia Chapurskaya, Tatiana Eremicheva, Ludmila Polonskaya, Elvira Habibulina, Vladimir Adjamov, Andrey Batalov, Viacheslav Ilyin, Kiril Miasnikov, Konstantin Novoselov, Yuri Petukhov, Pavel Romaniuk, Gennadi Sudakov

No. of dancers: 44 male, 58 female

MARYINSKY BALLET

State Academic Maryinsky Theatre
Theatre Square 1
190000 St Petersburg
Tel: 812 144 44 41
Fax: 812 144 45 50 Kirov SU

Choreographer: Oleg Vinogradov

Principal dancers: Altynai Asylmuratova, Janna Ahupova, Tatiana Bereznaya (Terehova), Annelina Kashirina, Margarita Kullik, Olga Likhovskaya, Julia Makhalina, Natalia Pavlova, Irina Sitnikova, Olga Chenchikova, Irina Chistiakova, Irina Shapchits (Zavialova), Elena Sherstneva, Veronica Ivanova, Larisa Lezhnina, Galina Zakrutkina, Viktor Baranov, Ravil Bagautdinov, Mahar Vaziev, Sergei Viharev, Andrei Garbuz, Alexander Gulyaev, Marat Daukaev, Konstantin Zaklinsky, Nikolai Kovmir, Vladimir Kolesnikov, Alexander Kurkov, Evgeny Neff, Vitali Tsvetkov, Farukh Ruzimatov, Mihail Zavyalov, Igor Zelensky, Vladimir Kim, Andrei Yakovlev, Dmitri Korneev

No. of dancers: 66 male, 84 female

New work 93/4:

Anna Karenina, Ch.: André Prokovsky, *Mus.*: Tchaikovsky

Singapore

SINGAPORE DANCE THEATRE

Fort Canning Centre, 2nd Storey
Cox Terrace
Singapore 0617
Tel: 65 3380611
Fax: 65 3389748

Founder dirs.: Goh Soo Khim, Anthony Then

General manager: Ng Siew Eng

No. of dancers: 10 male, 10 female

New works 93/4:

Appassionato, Ch.: Graham Lustig

The Butterfly Lovers, Ch.: Liu Ying

Four new works choreographed by Eric Languet, Yuri Ng, Fan Dong Kai, Edmund Stripe

South Africa

NAPAC DANCE COMPANY

PO Box 5353
Durban 4000
Tel: 27 31 304 3631
Fax: 27 31 306 2166

Artistic dir.: Mark Hawkins

Director: Lynne Maree

Choreographer: Boyzie Cekwana

Principal dancers: Vincent Hantam, Llewelyn Malan, Mark Hawkins, Boyzie Cekwana, Ayako Yoshikawa, Tracy Li, Mary-ann De Wet, Selva Hannam, Lesley-Ann Mitchell

No. of dancers: 10 male, 15 female

New works 93/4:

Travellers, Ch.: Gary Gordon, *Mus.*: Kevin Volans

The Moon in your Mouth, Ch.: Mark Hawkins, *Mus.*: René Veldsman

Lonely Won't Leave Me Alone, Ch.: Boyzie Cekwana, *Mus.*: André Abrehamse

I've Got No . . . but I want, Ch.: Mark Hawkins

Neither Fish Nor Flesh, Ch.: Boyzie Cekwana, *Mus.*: T. Trent D'Arby

Kenshin, Ch.: Mark Hawkins, *Mus.*: David Smith

Mute Art, Remaining Open to Feelings, Ch.: Garry Trinder

New works choreographed by Neville Campbell, Boyzie Cekwana, Robyn Orlin, Mark Hawkins, Janet Smith

PACT BALLET

PO Box 566
Pretoria 0001
SA
Tel: 27 12 3221665
Fax: 27 322 3913

Artistic dir.: Dawn Weller-Raistrick

Administrator: Martin Raistrick

Principal dancers: Jeremy Coles, Johnny Bouang, Christopher Montague, Nigel Hannah, Tanja Graafland, Leticia Müller, Nadine Sacker

No. of dancers: 25 male, 41 female

New works 93/4:

The Merry Widow, Ch.: Ronald Hynd

Still Life At The Penguin Café, Ch.: David Bintley

Spain

BALLET DE ZARAGOZA
Centro Cultural Palafox
Calle Domingo Miral
50 009 Zaragoza
Tel: 34 76 566411
Fax: 34 76 569077

Artistic dir.: Mauro Galindo

Administrator: Víctor Fernández

Principal dancers: Elisabet Ros, Marta Crecente, Federico Bosch, Amador Castilla

No. of dancers: 10 male, 14 female

New works 93/4:

The Nutcracker, Ch.: Galindo, *Mus.*: Tchaikovsky

Destemplanza, Ch.: Graziano, *Mus.*: Walters

La Chunga, Ch.: Siveroni

New work choreographed by Kirsten Debrock

COMPAÑIA ANTONIA ANDREU
Marques Viudo de Pontejos 1
28012 Madrid
Tel: 34 91 521 91 83
Fax: 34 91 521 91 83

Artistic dir.: Antonia Andreu

Administrator: Sonia Suarez

Choreographer: Antonia Andreu

No. of dancers: 2 male, 5 female

New works 93/4:

Monsieur B

Danza en el Metro

COMPAÑIA METROS S.C.P.
La Granja 13 No. 1
08024 Barcelona
Tel: 34 3 217 5664
Fax: 34 3 777 6817

Artistic dir.: Ramon Oller

Administrator: Montse Prat

No. of dancers: 3 male, 5 female

New works 93/4:

Estem Divinament

Rentides de Debó

Corre, Corre, Diva

GELABERT-AZZOPARDI COMPAÑIA DE DANSA
Torrent de L'Olla, 146 ent 3a
08012 Barcelona
Tel: 34 3 416 0068
Fax: 34 3 237 1243

Artistic dir.: Cesc Gelabert, Lydia Azzopardi

Administrator: Montse Garcia Otzet

No. of dancers: 4 male, 4 female

New works 93/4:

El Jardiner

Solos

DANAT DANZA

Apdo Correos 9388
08080 Barcelona
Tel: 34 3 442 1757
Fax: 34 3 443 2556

Artistic dirs.: Sabine Dahrendorf, Alfonso Ordóñez

Administrators: Pilar Galvez, Vicenta Hellin

No. of dancers: 4 male, 4 female

New work 93/4:

Ottepel

LA RIBOT DANZA

Nicolás Usera 64
28026 Madrid
Tel: 34 1 475 4922
Fax: 34 1 475 4922

Artistic dir.: María José Ribot

No. of dancers: 1 male, 1 female

New works 93/4:

Piezas Distinguidas

Los Trancos del Avestruz

El Triste que Nunca os Vido

Sweden

CULLBERG BALLET

S-145 83 Norsborg
Tel: 46 8 531 99 377/8
Fax: 46 8 531 99 159

Artistic dir.: Carolyn Carlson

Administrator: Marian Laurell

No. of dancers: 10 male, 10 female

New works 93/4:

X-Dream, Ch.: Per Jonsson

Haunted Passages, Ch.: Philip Taylor

Tabula Rasa and excerpts from *Kyr, Ch.*: Ohad Naharin

EFVA LILJA DANSPRODUKTION

Festsalen
S-16104 Bromma
Tel: 46 8 87 87 20
Fax: 46 8 87 87 20

Artistic dir.: Efva Lilja

Administrator: Barbro Gramén

No. of dancers: 4 male, 3 female

New works 93/4:

Homestead, Ch.: Efva Lilja, *Mus.*: Tommy Zwedberg

Entre nos Espaces, Ch.: Efva Lilja, *Mus.*: Tommy Zwedberg

Blicken, Ch.: Efva Lilja, *Mus.*: Tommy Zwedberg

GOTHENBURG BALLET

Stora Teatern
Box 53116
S-400 15 Gothenburg

Tel: 46 31 17 47 45
Fax: 46 31 13 71 57

Artistic dir.: Robert North

Principal dancers: Liselott Berg, Sheri Cook, Helle Fritz-Petersen, Eva Wallgren, Åse Werner, Ersin Aycan, Trinidad Bermudez, Vaclav Havlik, Ivor Howard, Owe Jonzon, Julian Moss, István Nagy

No. of dancers: 17 male, 21 female

New works 93/4:

The Russian Story, Ch.: Robert North, *Mus.*: Tchaikovsky, Shostakovich

The Snowman, Ch.: Robert North, *Mus.*: Howard Blake

ROYAL SWEDISH BALLET

PO Box 16094
S-103 22 Stockholm
Tel: 46 8 791 43 00
Fax: 46 8 10 79 45

Artistic dir.: Simon Mottram

Administrator: Dag Simonsen

Principal dancers: Anneli Alhanko, Johanna Björnson, Weit Carlsson, Pär Isberg, Marie Lindqvist, Hans Nilsson, Madeleine Onne, Per Arthur Segerström, Göran Svalberg, Mats Wegmann, Jan-Erik Wikström

No. of dancers: 36 male, 48 female

New work 93/4:

The Elephant Child, Ch.: Ann-Cathrine Byström, *Mus.*: André Chini

Switzerland

BALLETT DES STADTTHEATERS BERN

Nägeligasse 1
CH-3000 Bern 7
Tel: 41 31 312 17 11
Fax: 41 31 311 39 47

Artistic dir.: François Klaus

Administrator: Ernst Gosteli

General manager: Eike Gramss

Principal dancer: Augustus Damian

No. of dancers: 10 male, 10 female

New works 93/4:

Vier Letzte Lieder

Othello

Peer Gynt

Die Liebenden von Verona

BASLER BALLETT

Theater Basel
CH-4010 Basel
Tel: 41 61 295 14 48
Fax: 41 61 295 15 95

Artistic dir.: Youri Vàmos

Administrator: Peter Marschel

Principal dancers: Joyce Cuoco, Paul Boyd

No. of dancers: 18 male, 19 female

COMPAGNIE PHILIPPE SAIRE

CP 422
1110 Morges
Tel: 41 21 803 08 50
Fax: 41 21 803 06 62

Artistic dir.: Philippe Saire

Administrator: Thierry Luisier

Choreographer: Jean-Marie Bosshard

No. of dancers: 6 male, 4 female

New work 93/4:

La Nébuleuse du Crabe

LUZERNER BALLETT

Stadttheater Luzern
Theaterstrasse 2
CH-6002 Luzern
Tel: 41 23 33 63
Fax: 41 23 33 67

Artistic dir.: Thorsten Kreissig

Choreographer: Thorsten Kreissig

No. of dancers: 7 male, 8 female

ZÜRICH BALLET

Opera House Zürich
Falkenstrasse 1
CH-8008 Zürich
Tel: 41 1 251 69 20
Fax: 41 1 251 58 96

Artistic dir.: Bernd R. Bienert

Administrator: Günter J. Ingmanns

General manager: Alexander Pereira

Guest choreographers: Bertrand d'At, Jorma Uotinen, Mats Ek, Hans van Manen, Lionel Hoche, Amanda Miller

No. of dancers: 18 male, 19 female

United Kingdom

ADVENTURES IN MOTION PICTURES

Sadler's Wells
Rosebery Avenue
London EC1R 4TN
Tel: 071 278 6563
Fax: 071 713 6040

Artistic dir.: Matthew Bourne

Administrator: Simon Lacey

Choreographer: Matthew Bourne

No. of dancers: 4 male, 4 female

New work 93/4:

Highland Fling (première)

BIRMINGHAM ROYAL BALLET

Birmingham Hippodrome
Thorp Street
Birmingham B5 4AU
Tel: 021 622 2555
Fax: 021 622 5038

Artistic dir.: Sir Peter Wright

Administrator: Derek Purnell

General manager: Jay Jolley

Principal dancers: Sherilyn Kennedy, Sandra Madgwick, Marion Tait, Ravenna Tucker, Miyako Yoshida, Joseph Cipolla, Kevin O'Hare, Michael O'Hare

No. of dancers: 26 male, 33 female

New works 93/4:

Sylvia, *Ch.*: Bintley, *Mus.*: Delibes

New ballet, *Ch.*: Oliver Hindle

THE CHOLMONDELEYS AND THE FEATHERSTONEHAUGHS

The Place
17 Dukes Road
London WC1H 9AB
Tel: 071 383 3231
Fax: 071 383 4851

Artistic dir.: Lea Anderson

Administrator: Ian James

New works 93/4:

Precious

Le Spectre de la rose

Joan

Space

Metalcholica

ENGLISH NATIONAL BALLET

Markova House
39 Jay Mews
London SW7 2ES
Tel: 071 581 1245
Fax: 071 225 0827

Artistic dir.: Derek Deane

Administrator: Carole McPhee

Principal dancers: Tim Almaas, Agnes Oakes, Paul Chalmer, Yat Sen Chang, Evelyne Desutter, Thomas Edur, Susan Jaffe (guest artist), Josephine Jewkes, Cecilia Kerche, Cyril Pierre

No. of dancers: 28 male, 37 female

New works 93/4:

Giselle, *Ch.*: Derek Deane

Taglioni pas de quatre, restaged by Lyn Wallis

Square Dance, restaged by Nanette Glushak

New work by Bigonzetti

LONDON CITY BALLET

London Studio Centre
42–50 York Way
London N1 9AB
Tel: 071 837 3133
Fax: 071 713 6072

Artistic dir.: Harold King

Administrator: Melanie Morrison

Principal dancers: Marius Els, Beverly Jane Fry, Kim Miller, Tracey Newham Alvey, Jane Sanig, Roger van Fleteren, Jack Wyngaard

No. of dancers: 13 male, 19 female

New work 93/4:

New work, *Ch.*: Vincent Redmon

NORTHERN BALLET THEATRE

Spring Hall
Huddersfield Road
Halifax HX3 0AQ
Tel: 0422 380420
Fax: 0422 380531

Artistic dir.: Christopher Gable

Business dir.: Catherine Robins

Principal dancers: Graciela Kaplan, Jeremy Kerridge, Peter Parker, Jayne Regan, Lorena Vidal, William Walker, Victoria Westall

No. of dancers: 16 male, 18 female

New works 93/4:

Cinderella, *Ch.*: Christopher Gable, *Mus.*: Philip Feeney

Romeo and Juliet, *Ch.*: Massimo Moricone, *Mus.*: Prokofiev

Swan Lake (new version)

PHOENIX DANCE COMPANY

Yorkshire Dance Centre
3 St Peter's Buildings
St Peter's Square
Leeds LS9 8AH
Tel: 0532 423486
Fax: 0532 444736

Artistic dir.: Margaret Morris

Administrative dir.: Maryanne McNamara

Principal dancers: Stephen Derrick, Booker T. Louis, Chantal Donaldson, Dawn Donaldson, Pamela Johnson, Seline Thomas, Ricky Holgate

No. of dancers: 5 male, 5 female

New works 93/4:

Heart of Chaos, *Ch.*: Darshan Singh Bhuller

Face our own Face, *Ch.*: Pamela L. Johnson

Fatal Strategy, *Ch.*: Donald Byrd

Windrush, *Ch.*: Emilyn Claid

RICOCHET DANCE COMPANY

84 Englefield Road
London N1 3LG
Tel: 071 226 7433
Fax: 081 881 2819

Artistic dirs.: Kate Gowar/Karin Potisk

Administrator: Carolyn Naish

Choreographers: Russell Maliphant, Yolande Snaith

No. of dancers: 2 male, 3 female

New works 93/4:

Working title, *Ch.*: Gill Clarke

Corpus Antagonus, *Ch.*: Russell Maliphant

Five Lives. *Ch.*: Yolande Snaith

SCOTTISH BALLET

261 West Princes Street
Glasgow G4 9EE
Tel: 041 331 2931
Fax: 041 331 2629

Artistic dir.: Galina Samsova

Chief executive: Peter Kyle

Principal dancers: Noriko Ohara, Robert Hampton, Linda Packer, Daria Klimentova

No. of dancers: 17 male, 23 female

New works 93/4:

The Sleeping Beauty

New work, *Ch.*: Kim Brandstrup

SECOND STRIDE

Sadler's Wells
Rosebery Avenue
London EC1R 4TN
Tel: 071 278 2917/6589
Fax: 071 278 5927

Artistic dir.: Ian Spink

General manager: Lucy Mason

Principal dancers: Lucy Burge, Lauren Potter, Philippe Giraudeau, Catherine Malore, Julien Joly, James Demaria, Desirée Cherrington, Rosemary Allen, Matthew Hawkins

New work 93/4:

Escape at Sea

SHOBANA JEYASINGH DANCE COMPANY

The Place Theatre
17 Dukes Road
London WC1H 9AB
Tel: 071 383 3252
Fax: 071 383 4851

Artistic dir.: Shobana Jeyasingh

General manager: Penny Andrews

No. of dancers: 5 female

New works 93/4:

Romance. . . with Footnotes, *Ch.*: Shobana Jeyasingh, *Mus.*: Glyn Perrin

Delicious Arbour, *Ch.*: Richard Alston, *Mus.*: Henry Purcell

USA

AMERICAN BALLET THEATRE

890 Broadway
New York, NY 10003
Tel: 1 212 477 3030
Fax: 1 212 245 5938

Artistic dir.: Kevin McKenzie

Executive dir.: Gary Dunning

Principal dancers: Victor Barbee, Gil Boggs, Jeremy Collins, Christine Dunham, Guillaume Graffin, Cynthia Harvey, Robert Hill, Susan Jaffe, Julie Kent, Amanda McKerrow, Kathleen Moore, Michael Owen, Johan Renvall, Marianna Tcherkassky, Cheryl Yeager

No. of dancers: 31 male, 40 female

New works 93/4:

The Nutcracker, *Ch.*: Kevin McKenzie

A Brahms Symphony, *Ch.*: Lar Lubovitch

New work, *Ch.*: James Kudelka

BALLET CHICAGO

222 S. Riverside No. 865
Chicago, IL 60606
Tel: 1 312 993 7575
Fax: 1 312 993 1974

Artistic dir.: Daniel Duell

Administrator: Colleen Lober

Choreographer: Gordon Peirce Schmidt

Principal dancers: Meridith Benson, Heidi Vierthaler, William Baierbach, Jason Paul Frautschi

No. of dancers: 9 male, 12 female

New works 93/4:

The Gift of the Magi

Hansel and Gretel

GARTH FAGAN DANCE

50 Chestnut Street
Rochester, NY 14604
Tel: 1 716 454 3260
Fax: 1 716 454 6191

Artistic dir.: Garth Fagan

Administrator: Matilda Hohensee

Principal dancers: Steve Humphrey, Norwood Pennewell, Bit Knighton, Valentina Alexander, Natalie Rogers, Chris Morrison, Sharon Skepple

No. of dancers: 8 male, 8 female

New works 93/4:

Drafts of Shadows, Ch.: Garth Fagan

Jukebox for Alvin, Ch.: Garth Fagan

JAN ERKERT & DANCERS

2121 W. Webster Avenue
Chicago, IL 60647
Tel: 1 312 252 6557

Artistic dir.: Jan Erkert

Administrator: Bernt Lewy

Choreographer: Jan Erkert

No. of dancers: 2 male, 5 female

JOSEPH HOLMES CHICAGO DANCE THEATRE

1935 South Halsted 4th Floor
Chicago, IL 60608
Tel: 1 312 942 0065
Fax: 1 312 942 0815

Company co-ordinator: Robyn Davis

Managing dir.: Mary Webster

No. of dancers: 5 male, 5 female

New works 93/4:

Crossing the Line, Ch.: James Kelly

Sweet in the Morning, Ch.: Leni Wylliams

MERCE CUNNINGHAM DANCE COMPANY

55 Bethune Street
New York, NY 10014
Tel: 1 212 255 8240
Fax: 1 212 633 2453

Artistic dir.: Merce Cunningham

Executive dir.: Art Becofsky

No. of dancers: 8 male, 8 female

New works 93/4:

Doubletoss, Ch.: Merce Cunningham, *Mus.*: Takehisa Kosugi

CRWDSPCR, Ch.: Merce Cunningham, *Mus.*: John King

Breakers, Ch.: Merce Cunningham, *Mus.*: John Driscoll

Ocean, Ch.: Merce Cunningham

MIAMI CITY BALLET

905 Lincoln Road
Miami Beach, FL 33139
Tel: 1 305 532 4880
Fax: 1 305 532 2726/4855

Artistic dir.: Edward Villella

Administrator/General manager: Pamela Miller/Barbara Singer

Choreographer: Jimmy Gamonet De Los Heros

Principal dancers: Marin Boieru, Liana Lopez, Franklin Gamero, Yanis Pikieris

No. of dancers: 20 male, 17 female

New works 93/4:

The Four Temperaments, Ch.: George Balanchine

Divertimento Espanol, Ch.: Jimmy Gamonet De Los Heros

D Symphonies, Ch.: Jimmy Gamonet De Los Heros

MORDINE AND COMPANY DANCE THEATER

4730 North Sheridan Road
Chicago, IL 60640
Tel: 1 312 271 7804

Fax: 1 312 271 7046

Artistic dir.: Shirley Mordine

Managing dir.: Stefanie Rothman

Choreographer: Shirley Mordine

No. of dancers: 2 male, 4 female

New work 93/4:

Edge Mode

NEW YORK CITY BALLET

New York State Theater
20 Lincoln Center
New York, NY 10023
Tel: 1 212 870 5500
Fax: 1 212 870 4244

Artistic dir.: Peter Martins

Administrator: Gary MacDougal

Principal dancers: Helen Alexopoulos, Merrill Ashley, Maria Calegari, Judith Fugate, Nichol Hlinka, Darci Kistler, Valentina Kozlova, Lourdes Lopez, Kyra Nichols, Melinda Roy, Margaret Tracey, Heather Watts, Wendy Whelan, Peter Boal, Lindsay Fischer, Gen Horiuchi, Nikolaj Hübbe, Leonid Kozlov, Robert LaFosse, Adam Luders, Nilas Martins, Philip Neal, Jock Soto, Damian Woetzel, Igor Zelensky

No. of dancers: 45 male, 60 female

OAKLAND BALLET

Alice Arts Center
1428 Alice Street
Oakland, CA 94612
Tel: 1 510 452 9288
Fax: 1 510 452 9557

Artistic dir.: Ronn Guidi

Administrator: Ron Thiele

Choreographers: Eugene Loring, Willam Christensen, Leonide Massine, Frederic Franklin

Principal dancers: Mario Alonzo, Ben Barnhart, Cynthia Chin, Natalia Eremin, Joannene Fogel, Sean France, Joy Gim, Anton Labuschagne, Lara Deans Lowe, Michael Lowe, Jenna McClintock, Wal Moraes, Stephanie Powell, Abra Rudisill, Joral Schmalle, Omar Shabazz, Carlo Sierras, Ron Thiele

No. of dancers: 17 male, 19 female

New work 93/4:

Romeo and Juliet

SAN FRANCISCO BALLET

455 Franklin Street
San Francisco, CA 94102
Tel: 1 415 861 5600
Fax: 1 415 861 2684

Artistic dir.: Helgi Tomasson

Executive dir.: Arthur Jacobus

General manager: Glenn McCoy

Principal dancers: Sabina Allemann, Joanna Berman, Antonio Castilla, Evelyn Cisneros, Jeremy Collins, Rex Harrington, Tina LeBlanc, Stephen Legate, Shannon Lilly, Elizabeth Loscavio, Muriel Maffre, Mikko Nissinen, Anthony Randazzo, Christopher Stowell, Wendy Van Dyck, Ashley Wheater, Yuri Zhukov

No. of dancers: 31 male, 34 female

New works 93/4:

Romeo and Juliet, Ch.: Tomasson, *Mus.:* Prokofiev

New work, *Ch.:* Mark Morris

New work, *Ch.:* Anna Lærkesen

SARASOTA BALLET OF FLORIDA

PO Box 49094
Sarasota, FL 34230-6094
Tel: 1 813 954 7171
Fax: 1 813 951 0042

Artistic dir.: Robert de Waren

Executive dir.: Donald Creason

Choreographers: Vassili Sulich, André Prokovsky, Dieter Ammann, Christopher Fleming

Principal dancers: Diane Partington, Alexei Dovgopolyi, Rey Dizon, Stephanie Murrish, Daniil Gaifullin

No. of dancers: 8 male, 10 female

TRISHA BROWN COMPANY

225 Lafayette Street
Suite 807
New York, NY 10012
Tel: 1 212 334 9374
Fax: 1 212 334 9438

Artistic dir.: Trisha Brown

Executive dir.: Susan Fait-Meyers

No. of dancers: 6 male, 7 female

TULSA BALLET THEATRE
4512 S. Peoria
Tulsa, OK 74105
Tel: 1 918 749 6030
Fax: 1 918 749 0532

Artistic dir.: Roman L. Jasinski
General manager: Connie Cronley
Principal dancer: Aleksandr Lunev
No. of dancers: 11 male, 15 female

Editor's note: We regret some major omissions. However, this is a statistics section, not a complete directory, and we have only been able to publish those companies who completed and returned our request form for up-to-date information.

PART V

Looking Forward

Looking Forward...

Always it has been difficult in the dance world to look forward. For financial and other reasons, dance companies rarely can plan more than one year ahead. *World Ballet and Dance* has a problem, therefore, in bringing news of what is planned beyond the year of each annual issue. At the time this fifth issue, for example, was being prepared—at the very beginning of 1994, even established festivals, in some cases, had not finalized their dates for 1995, still less their programmes. The same is true for academic conferences. We hope to solve this problem for future issues through special arrangements now under discussion. These discussions have already begun to produce results and we are able to present below some of the events planned already for 1995.

Festivals, Conferences, Competitions

Australia

Green Mill Dance Project, Melbourne, 9–27 January 1995. Founded in 1993, the Green Mill Dance Project is Melbourne's annual festival of choreography and dance. Becoming the most significant annual choreographic gathering in the southern hemisphere, it assembles choreographers and dancers not only from all the professional dance companies of Australia—an important creative influence in a country whose distances hinder choreographic exchange—but from dance companies and dance styles throughout the Pacific region. Attending the first two festivals were choreographers from Indonesia, New Zealand, the Philippines, India, Taiwan, Malaysia, Vietnam, China, and Japan as well as Australia. The two-week programme includes lectures, discussions, and study sessions alongside professional dance classes, choreographic creation, and choreographic presentations. The theme for the 1995 festival is: Is Technology the Future for Dance? Proposals of not more than one typed page in length stating title, technological requirements, and with a brief biography of the proposer, should be sent to:
The Administrator
Green Mill Dance Project
Level 6
2, Kavanagh Street
South Melbourne
Victoria 3205
Tel: 61 3 684 8749
Fax: 61 3 686 6186

Cuba

International Dance Festival, May 1995.
The National Council for Scenic Art in co-ordination with the Council of Camagüey are organizing the festival which, it is hoped, will involve Cuban dance groups with visiting overseas companies. It is planned to hold workshops and conferences related to all aspects of dance today.
For information contact:
The International Festival Organizer
Ballet de Camagüey
Carretera Central Este, No. 331, Esq A4
Camagüey
Tel: 53 7 322 9 6535

International Folklore Laboratories.
For two weeks in January and July of each year, the IFL hold events for all those interested in Afro-Cuban and Hispanic Cuban Folkdance.
For information contact:
Lili Benet
Folk Cuban Dept.
Calle Folklorica
Havana
Tel: 53 7 3 4560/3 4395
or:
Artex
Fax: 53 7 33 1560

Finland

ITI International Ballet Competition, Helsinki, 9–21 June 1995.
For dancers in two divisions: Senior, age 19–26 and Junior, age 15–18, as well as choreographers.
For information contact:
The Finnish Centre of the International Theatre Institute
Teatterikulma
Meritullinkatu 33
00170 Helsinki
Tel: 358 0 135 7887
Fax: 358 0 135 5522

France

Rencontres Chorégraphiques Internationales de Bagnolet.
One of the most important European choreographic festivals held every

two years in June in a different French city. The next festival will be in June 1996 with enrolments in September 1995. For information contact:
The Recontres Chorégraphiques Internationales de Bagnolet
45 Rue Benoit Hure
93170 Bagnolet

Holland

The Holland Festival, 1–30 June 1995.
This festival takes place annually throughout June and always includes dance. For information contact:
Holland Festival
Kl Gartmanplantsoen 21
1017 Pk Amsterdam
Tel: 31 20 6276 566

United Kingdom

The Edinburgh International Festival, 13 August–2 September.
The largest annual International Arts Festival, which usually includes a substantial dance programme. Details not yet available but for further information contact:
Administration, Edinburgh International Festival
21 Market Street
Edinburgh EH 1BW
Tel: 031 226 4001
Fax: 031 226 7669

Bonnie Bird New Choreography Awards 1995.
Three awards of £1,250 each are available from the Bonnie Bird Choreography Fund for the choreographic development of dance artists who have some experience already in making and showing work. Intended to assist emerging choreographers, the money can be put towards the making of a work, or research and development. Deadline for applications: 31 March 1995. Write for application form to:
BBCF
The Laban Centre
Laurie Grove
New Cross
London SE14 6NH
Tel: 081 692 4070
Fax: 081 694 8749

United States

Annual Conference of the Congress on Research for Dance, 3–6 November 1995, to be held at Texas Women's University, Denton, Texas. Although the deadline for submission of proposals and papers will be passed by the time this issue of *World Ballet and Dance* appears, it will not be too late for those who wish to attend. For further information:
Kim Grover-Haskin, CORD
Conference Co-Chair
Texas Women's University's Programme in Dance
PO Box 23747
Denton
Texas 76204
Tel: 1 817 2085

Index